Philosophy: Key Texts

Philosophy: Key Texts

Second edition

Julian Baggini

and

Gareth Southwell

palgrave
macmillan

First edition published 2002
Second revised edition published 2012 by
PALGRAVE MACMILLAN

Palgrave Macmillan in the UK is an imprint of Macmillan Publishers Limited, registered in England, company number 785998, of Houndmills, Basingstoke, Hampshire RG21 6XS.

Palgrave Macmillan in the US is a division of St Martin's Press LLC, 175 Fifth Avenue, New York, NY 10010.

Palgrave Macmillan is the global academic imprint of the above companies and has companies and representatives throughout the world.

Palgrave® and Macmillan® are registered trademarks in the United States, the United Kingdom, Europe and other countries.

ISBN 978–0–230–29661–9 hardback
ISBN 978–0–230–29662–6 paperback

This book is printed on paper suitable for recycling and made from fully managed and sustained forest sources. Logging, pulping and manufacturing processes are expected to conform to the environmental regulations of the country of origin.

A catalogue record for this book is available from the British Library.

A catalog record for this book is available from the Library of Congress.

10   9   8   7   6   5   4   3   2   1
21 20 19 18 17 16 15 14 13 12

Printed and bound in Great Britain by
CPI Antony Rowe, Chippenham and Eastbourne

Contents

Preface to the Second Edition   viii

Acknowledgements   ix

Introduction   1
  Styles of reading   2
  Arguments   3
  Assessing premises   5
  Inferences   6
  The archaeology of arguments   8
  Arguments within arguments   9
  Back to style   10
  The principle of charity   10
  Six key texts   11

1 Plato: *Republic* (*c.*375 BC)   13
  Background   13
  The text   14
  Preliminary discussion: What is justice?   16
  The basis of society   19
  Education   20
  Rulers and auxiliaries   23
  Society and the individual   25
  Women, marriage and family   27
  The philosopher rulers   29
  The good   30
  The education of the philosopher   36
  Unjust societies   38
  Art revisited   42
  Afterlife   43
  Conclusion   44

2 René Descartes: *Meditations on First Philosophy* (1641)   49
  Background   49
  The text   50
  First meditation   51
  Second meditation   56

The piece of wax 59
Third meditation 60
The existence of God 61
Fourth meditation 64
Fifth meditation 67
Sixth meditation 71
Conclusion 74

3 **David Hume: *An Enquiry concerning Human***
***Understanding* (1748)** 77
Background 77
The text 78
    I Of the Different Species of Philosophy 78
    II Of the Origin of Ideas 80
    III Of the Association of Ideas 83
    IV Sceptical Doubts Concerning the Operations of the
        Understanding 83
    V Sceptical Solution of these Doubts 86
    VI Of Probability 88
    VII Of the Idea of Necessary Connexion 88
    VIII Of Liberty and Necessity 91
    IX Of the Reason of Animals 93
    X Of Miracles 94
    XI Of a Particular Providence and of a Future State 96
    XII Of the Academical or Sceptical Philosophy 98

4 **John Stuart Mill: *On Liberty* (1859)** 104
Background 104
The text 105
    I Introductory 106
    II On the Liberty of Thought and Discussion 111
    III Of Individuality, as One of the Elements of Well-Being 118
    IV Of the Limits to the Authority of Society over the
        Individual 125
    V Applications 132
Conclusion 137

5 **Friedrich Nietzsche: *Beyond Good and Evil* (1886)** 142
Background 142
The text 143
Preface 144
Part One: On the Prejudices of Philosophers 145

Part Two: The Free Spirit   148
Part Three: The Religious Nature   154
Part Four: Maxims and Interludes   161
Part Five: On the Natural History of Morals   162
Part Six: We Scholars   164
Part Seven: Our Virtues   166
Part Eight: Peoples and Fatherlands   169
Part Nine: What is Noble?   171
From High Mountains: *Epode*   172
Conclusion   173

6 **Jean-Paul Sartre: *Existentialism and Humanism* (1947)**   177
   Background   177
   The text   178
   The attack on existentialism   179
   Humanism   180
   Existentialism   180
   Subjectivity   182
   Anguish   183
   Abandonment   185
   Despair   188
   The *cogito*   189
   The human condition   191
   Does it matter what you do?   192
   Can you judge others?   192
   A case of give and take   194
   Humanism again   194
   Conclusion   195

Glossary   198

Further Reading   199

Index   200

Preface to the Second Edition

This book is designed to help the reader approach six key works of Western philosophy. It is not a substitute for reading the books themselves, but it will act as a guide for those thinking about or preparing to read or study the books for the first time.

The introduction contains some advice on how to read and make sense of original philosophical texts. Reading philosophy is not like reading a novel and the advice given here should make your encounters with such texts more rewarding.

Each chapter comprises an introduction which sets out the context of the book and its background, a systematic commentary on the text, a summary, a glossary of key terms and suggestions for further reading.

The commentaries combine two main features. First, they summarise and explain the main arguments of each text, clarifying and distilling their core. Second, the commentaries also contain critical points, questioning the validity or soundness of arguments, or bringing out unclarity or ambiguity in the text. The main purpose of this is not to provide an exhaustive catalogue of criticisms which could be made of the text, but to highlight potential weaknesses and to encourage the reader to question the claims being made in the texts for themselves.

There is also a glossary of key philosophical words at the end of the book, along with suggestions for further reading in philosophy.

Although the book was written with the input of both authors, the chapters on Plato's *Republic*, Mill's *On Liberty* and Nietzsche's *Beyond Good and Evil* are mostly the work of Gareth, while those on Descartes's *Meditations*, Hume's *Enquiry* and Sartre's *Existentialism and Humanism* are mainly Julian's fault.

Acknowledgements

Terka Acton, Priyanka Gibbons, Penny Simmons and the anonymous readers at the publishers who helped make this book possible and then better than it otherwise would have been.

Julian also thanks his former students whose feedback on the teaching materials that formed the bases of the first edition of this book encouraged him to develop them further.

Gareth thanks Julian, for his generosity and support; Dad and Dor, for the sumptuous shed, wherein most of this was written; Mam and Mike, for their frequent and timely help; Phill and Carol, for the kind loan of their laptop, on which most of this was written; the Royal Literary Fund and the Society of Authors, for their literary alms; and Jo, for her only very occasionally daunted optimism (I loves you, babes).

Introduction

Western philosophy has a wonderful literature. The great books of philosophy surely merit inclusion among any collection of the greatest books of humankind. Plato's *Republic* or Descartes's *Meditations* are as important a part of humanity's literature as Shakespeare's *Hamlet* or Chaucer's *Canterbury Tales*.

However, whereas most experiences of education in the English-speaking world would involve exposure to the great poets, playwrights and dramatists, they often do not include any study at all of the great works of philosophy.

This is a double loss. First, it means that we typically end our educations in ignorance of one of the most interesting and important strands in our intellectual history. Second, having never picked up a philosophy text in our lives, we find ourselves ill-equipped to make up for this deficiency in the future. If we do pluck up the courage to delve into an original work of philosophy, we often find ourselves baffled, confused and unable to navigate the strange kind of writing we find there.

What exactly is a philosophy text after all? It is usually not instructional. It isn't fiction. It certainly isn't science. Nor is it history. It's not religion either – we are not presented with a complete world-view which is handed down from above. It's something else, something distinctive and often strange.

The main aim of this book is to provide a set of keys which will enable you to pick up, read and make sense of six major texts in the Western philosophical tradition. As well as providing routes into these particular texts, the book should also familiarise you with some of the more general features of philosophical writing, so that many more texts should become approachable and comprehensible. The book is not a substitute for reading the texts themselves (although whether you go on to read any or all of them is entirely your choice, of course). In that sense it is both a menu and a map. As a menu, it allows you to see what the texts have to offer, to taste them first before deciding whether to consume them in their entirety. As a map, it provides guidance on how to navigate through the texts without getting lost.

The main purpose of this introduction is to provide some general advice on how to make your reading of a philosophical text fruitful. We will also say a little about the particular texts chosen.

Styles of reading

In the Western world, although there are still too many people without basic literacy skills, the ability to read is presumed to be something fairly simple, like riding a bike or swimming, that anyone without certain specific disabilities can do. It does not require any special ability or training. It is properly democratic – anyone can do it and though someone may be able to read faster or have a larger vocabulary, the idea that one can read better, worse or just differently than someone else strikes one as a little odd.

But, in fact, different types of writing do demand different styles of reading. For example, one of us (Julian) finds it quite hard to read poetry. He is aware that to read poetry properly, one needs to attend to features of the writing that one often glosses over, such as the rhythms and sounds of the words. This is very different to when one is reading for information, when one is concerned with what the words mean or what they are telling you to do. Because he doesn't often read poetry, this style of reading does not come easily to him and as a result he is sure that much of what is good in poetry passes him by.

Reading philosophy also has its particular (though not necessarily unique) style and if one is not used to it, it can be difficult to do. We would identify three characteristic features of an effective reading style for philosophy: it should generally be slow, critical and analytic.

When we say you need to read philosophy slowly, we do not mean that one should generally lengthen the time one takes over each word or the pauses between them. Rather, we mean that reading philosophy often requires one to pause or reread sentences or whole paragraphs. It is not always obvious what the significance or meaning of a particular passage is at first glance. Sometimes, one needs to go back over a passage several times to really grasp what it is getting at. On other occasions one needs to stop and ponder what has just been said, to try and make sense of it in one's own mind. In short, to an unusually high degree, one needs to be thinking carefully about what one is reading to make sure it is being understood. And this means one needs to include a lot of thinking time in one's reading which is in addition to the time it takes to actually read the words on the page.

This is very different to reading a novel, for example, where part of the pleasure can be the narrative pace which pushes one forward to the next page. It is also different to reading something like history, where one may need to reread in order to learn or memorise the content, but not usually because it was hard to understand the first time.

The second characteristic of an effective reading style for philosophy is that one reads critically. By 'critically' we do not mean that one should always be looking to disagree with what is said. Rather, one should be constantly questioning the text, asking whether its assertions are justified, its arguments well-supported or its conclusions credible. Philosophy texts present arguments and we need to decide whether these arguments work, not just whether we agree with the conclusions or whether the author has been persuasive (see the section on arguments below). To do this we should always be testing and questioning what is presented to us.

Finally, one needs to read philosophy analytically. What we mean by this should become clearer when we look at the importance of arguments in philosophical writing. What this essentially means is that as one reads one should be trying to see how the various parts of the text fit together, how conclusions are derived from premises and how one part of the text supports or disagrees with other parts. What one is analysing here is the way in which the various claims and arguments of the book fit together. Only by doing this can we make sense of the whole of the text. If we cannot do this, we will see in the text only a series of unrelated, unsupported claims.

We have already talked at several points about the role of argument in philosophy texts. We need now to examine this feature of philosophical writing more closely.

Arguments

An argument in philosophy is not a row or dispute, but simply an attempt to establish a conclusion on a rational basis. The simplest forms of argument are three-line inferences known as syllogisms, an example of which is:

1. No dogs have wings.
2. Rufus has wings.
3. Therefore, Rufus is not a dog.

Syllogisms are examples of *deductive* arguments. They have two premises (lines 1 and 2 above), from which a conclusion (line 3) is derived. In a *valid* deductive argument, the truth of the conclusion follows as a matter of necessity from the truth of the premises. Put another way, if the premises are true, the conclusion then *must* be true.

In the example above, we can see that this is a valid deductive argument. If it is true that no dogs have wings and it is true that Rufus has wings, then it must be true that Rufus is not a dog. The vital thing to note here is that we are saying the conclusion must be true *if* the premises are true. One can never tell if the conclusion of a deductive argument *is* actually true unless one knows that the premises are true *and* that the argument is valid. If both these conditions obtain, we say the argument is *sound*.

How do we know if the premises are true? There is no simple answer to this. Some premises will have been established by other arguments. But eventually, we have to end up with premises that are not themselves conclusions of other arguments. Sometimes, this will be because there is evidence from experience that the premises are true. For instance, experience does seem to suggest that no dogs have wings. On other occasions, it may be because the premise is what we might call self-evidently true. Do we really need any proof, for example, that $1 + 1 = 2$? Isn't that obviously true? On other occasions a premise may be true by definition. 'A widow is a woman whose husband has died' is true just because of what those words all mean.

This touches on major issues in philosophy and in the texts discussed in this book, we will see several attempts to pinpoint the types of premises which can function as fundamental truths, which do not need to be proved themselves. We need not consider this further here, but should simply note that arguments have to start from somewhere.

Deductive arguments are the most rigorous form of argument and there are basically two ways of finding fault with them. The first is to find that they are not valid: in other words, that the conclusion does not necessarily follow from the premises. For example:

1. Jack studies the Qur'an.
2. Muslims study the Qur'an.
3. Therefore, Jack is a Muslim.

This is invalid because the premises (lines 1 and 2) might both be true, but the conclusion (line 3) could still be false. For example, Jack may be Jewish and reading the Qur'an because he is a student of comparative religion. This means the truth of the premises does not guarantee the truth of the conclusion, so the argument is not valid.

There is a second way in which arguments can be found wanting. Consider this example:

1. Jack studies the Qur'an.
2. Only Muslims study the Qur'an.
3. Therefore, Jack is a Muslim.

In this case, the argument is valid. If it is true that Jack is studying the Qur'an and if it is true that only Muslims study the Qur'an, then Jack must be a Muslim. But, of course, it is not true that only Muslims study the Qur'an. This means that although the argument is valid, it is not sound since one of its premises is false.

Note that in an unsound or an invalid argument the conclusion can be true. It might be the case that Jack is a Muslim. But both arguments are still inadequate because they do not *establish* that he is a Muslim. In other words, the 'therefore' that precedes the conclusion is not justified: it is not because of what has been said in the premises that the conclusion is true.

When you come to read actual philosophical texts, you will rarely see arguments set out in the form above. What we have done so far is looked at schematised, idealised, stripped-down versions of arguments. In actual philosophical texts, things are not so straightforward. However, understanding the basic principles which govern simple deductive arguments like the ones above will help you to make sense of and assess arguments in actual philosophical works. This is because all works of philosophy essentially put forward arguments. So how do you apply what we have said about arguments to these texts?

Assessing premises

First of all, in any philosophical text there are some beliefs, sentences or propositions which function as the premises. You need to look for these if you are to understand how the argument works and whether it is valid or sound. When looking for premises, you are looking for the beliefs which form the bases of the arguments.

For example, in Sartre's *Existentialism and Humanism*, you will find that many of his arguments are based on the premise that human beings have free will. In Descartes's *Meditations*, you will find that one basic premise is that a thing's essence is that which it cannot be conceived without. In Hume's *Enquiry concerning Human Understanding*, you will find that one premise is that all we are directly aware of are the contents of our own minds.

Having identified these premises, you then need to consider on what grounds they stand. In Hume's case, for example, the premise is based on experience. To see if the premise is true, one therefore has to decide if what Hume says corresponds to experience. In Descartes's case, it seems that his basic premise about essences is not based on experience, but is somehow taken to be self-evidently true. In this case, one needs to decide if it really is self-evident or whether such a premise should in fact be based in experience. In Sartre's case, we need to consider on what grounds we can say we are in fact free. It is not clear why Sartre thinks this is so basic as to not require any proof or demonstration, but as readers we can consider for ourselves whether his premise is admissible.

As these examples show, once we are attuned to the idea that a philosophical text will be offering us arguments and that arguments rest on premises, we can begin to look for these premises in the text, consider the adequacy of the support they are given in the text, and also assess them independently of the text, bringing our own doubts or considerations to bear on them. We can also distinguish between what the argument rests on and what the argument aims to show, which is its conclusion.

Inferences

Having distinguished the premises and the conclusions, we can then try to examine the argumentative link between them. Has the philosopher in question demonstrated that the conclusion does necessarily follow from the premises? If they have not, is this because of a small error that we can rectify or are the flaws more fundamental? In order to make such a judgement we must understand what a valid deduction looks like.

However, there are more ways of moving from premises to conclusion than just deduction. One such method is induction. This is where we use the evidence of the past or present to reach conclusions about things we are not able to observe, in the past, present or future.

Such arguments often look like deductive arguments. For example:

1. Mary claimed to have run 100 metres in eight seconds.
2. No woman has ever run 100 metres in less than ten seconds.
3. Therefore, Mary is lying.

Superficially, this looks like a deductive argument. But as a deductive argument, it fails. The fact that no one has ever done what Mary claims to have done (or even come close) does not guarantee that Mary is lying. A deductive argument is only valid if the truth of the premises *guarantees* the truth of the conclusion and this is not what happens here. Does this mean the argument fails?

Not necessarily. This argument should be read as an inductive argument, not as a deductive one. Here, the evidence of experience (that no woman has run 100 metres in under ten seconds) is being used to support a conclusion (Mary is lying) which we cannot verify by any direct observation or application of pure logic. In such an argument the movement from premises to conclusion has logical gaps. But there are many times when this kind of reasoning is all we can go on. It is this kind of reasoning, for example, that enables us to predict that if we let go of a ball, it will drop rather than float away. Unless we can use our general experience as a guide to what we have not experienced, we are unable to function in the world.

So when evaluating an argument, one might find that it is deductively unsound. But then you need to consider whether it is the type of argument where inductive justifications are more appropriate. If it is, you need to use more judgement in your assessment of the argument, because the rules for the correct use of an inductive argument are not as clear-cut as those for deduction. You need to ask whether experience provides enough evidence to support the conclusion and there is no generally accepted formula for deciding what is enough.

One other way of justifying the inference from premises to conclusion is by a method known as abduction, or 'argument to best explanation'. This is pretty much self-explanatory and a simple example will help make it clear. Consider, as Bertrand Russell does in *The Problems of Philosophy*, the question of whether or not our perceptions of things are caused by objects independent of us or whether they are just figments of our imaginations. It is no good appealing to experience to solve this one, since what is being countenanced is the possibility that experience is itself misleading. One cannot appeal to what is in dispute to settle the dispute. So how do we resolve this issue?

Russell employs abduction to solve the conundrum. If things do exist independently of us, then this explains why there is so much regularity in our experiences, why things are generally where we left them and so on. It also explains why we are not in total control of our environment; rather, our environment constrains us in many ways. If, on the other hand, we were dreaming all this, why would our experiences be so regular and orderly? Why wouldn't things happen spontaneously, without cause, as they do in dreams? Why are we unable to control things just by our own powers of thought?

When we compare the two possibilities, therefore, we see that one just offers a better explanation than another. In that situation, I am justified in concluding that the better explanation is probably the true one. As with induction, there are no hard and fast rules for determining what a better explanation is like. Some judgement is required.

Deduction, induction and abduction are three different forms of reasoning. But all have in common a pattern of movement from premises to conclusions based on an appropriate and acceptable method of inference. When reading a philosophical text, you don't just need to be able to identify the premises and conclusions – you also need to be able to identify and assess the way in which the writer argues to the conclusions from their premises.

The archaeology of arguments

Assessing arguments in the way described is not always easy. Sometimes, the structure and form of an argument are very clear. But on other occasions it takes some concentrated thought to tease out the premises, the conclusions and their relations. Conclusions are easier to spot, because they tend to be preceded by words and phrases such as 'therefore', 'it follows that', 'thus' or 'hence'. Premises, however, can be very elusive.

Indeed, sometimes premises can go entirely unstated. This tends to be the case when an argument rests upon an assumption that perhaps even the author herself does not realise she is making. For example, Descartes's *Meditations* seems to be premised on the assumption that something that cannot be doubted must be true. Descartes never directly justifies this assumption, but it does seem to underlie a lot of his arguments.

Having dug up a premise like this, we can then scrutinise it to see if it stands up. In this case, we might conclude it does not. After all, whether we can doubt something or not surely only tells us about our own capacity for credulity. Isn't it more than possible that we can doubt things that are true as easily as we can find it impossible to doubt what is in fact false?

Often, it is when one engages in this kind of archaeology that one ends up making the most telling criticisms. The weakest premises are often those which the writer herself has failed to realise require justification. This is because such premises are often mere assumptions, and it is always dangerous in philosophy to assume anything.

Arguments within arguments

An argument is like a little mechanism which produces conclusions from premises. The great works of philosophy often contain many such small mechanisms, all working together as part of a larger, single mechanism. In order to properly understand such a text, one therefore needs not only to be able to see how each individual argument works, but how they all fit together into the bigger picture.

One of the greatest examples of this is Descartes's *Meditations*. Zoom out and you can see how the book fits together as one, single argument. It moves from a systematic doubt of all assumed knowledge, through to the establishment of a secure foundation for knowledge, and then carefully builds on these foundations until an entire edifice of knowledge is completed. It is a remarkable text and one can see how each meditation advances the argument forward to its next stage.

But if one stays with this overview, one misses the many crucial details. In order to properly assess the overarching argument of the *Meditations*, one needs to zoom in to look at the various smaller arguments contained in each meditation. The momentum which moves the whole book forward is ultimately created by these small arguments.

Further, these arguments often depend upon each other. Often the conclusion of one argument becomes a premise for another, moving through the book like something on a factory assembly line. In isolation, an argument may appear baseless. But when one looks at what has come before, one can sometimes find its proper foundation. In isolation, an argument can also look trivial or uninteresting. Only when you can see why the conclusion it generates is needed elsewhere can you properly understand its significance.

One can see, then, that in order to be able to read a philosophy text properly, one must be able to zoom in and out in this way. One needs to be able to look at each individual argument and see how it works, but one also needs to see how each argument fits into the whole.

Back to style

Returning to our earlier comments about styles of reading, we can now see more clearly why it needs to be slow, critical and analytic. If one is to identify and uncover premises, identify and assess the mode of inference which leads to the conclusions, and see how everything fits together into the bigger picture, there is a lot one needs to actually be doing other than merely taking in the words on the page. For this reason, reading philosophy is best understood as a special kind of activity, unlike much other reading.

This activity cannot be performed properly if the reading is done too quickly. It is only possible to pick out and identify all the relevant parts and relations of the arguments if they are read analytically. And one is not going to be able to make fair assessments if one is not reading critically.

The principle of charity

Many people find that part of the fun of reading philosophy is learning to spot bad arguments. Discovering an invalid deduction or a questionable premise can be a great pleasure, especially when it allows us to think that we have out-smarted one of the greats.

We wouldn't want to suggest that this pleasure should never be indulged, but when seeking it becomes the primary motivation for reading a philosophy text, much of what is of value in philosophy is lost. In general we should remember that it is easier to demolish than to build. We are no more the equals of Plato, Descartes, Hume, Mill, Nietzsche and Sartre because we can find faults in their arguments than we are the equals of the great artists because we can spot flaws in their paintings.

But it is not the inflation of the ego which is the main risk when we read philosophy mainly to demolish it. The main victim tends to be understanding itself. Texts often need to be interpreted and they can be interpreted in ways which show them in a better or worse light. If we spot what we think is a glaring error, we should not be triumphalist. Rather, we should ask whether the writer really did make this mistake or whether they have in some way already anticipated it.

Even if it does seem that the philosopher has slipped up, the next stage should be to see whether the error can be remedied rather than gloating over the failure of the argument. Often, adjustments can be made to a philosopher's position to accommodate criticisms, adjustments which preserve the essential nature of the position being argued for. We should consider whether this is possible before we reject the philosopher's position as flawed.

Such a warning is necessary because, unfortunately, much philosophical education seems to be based on the principle that arguments are put up as target practice for students to practise their skills of intellectual demolition. This is without doubt good for honing certain philosophical skills. But a reader who only learns the negative skills of demolition is unlikely to develop the wisdom and insight necessary to get the most out of their philosophising.

In short, it is good practice to employ the principle of charity: always try and interpret an argument in the way which makes it stronger, not weaker. That way you are more likely to hit upon the truth.

Six key texts

The six books selected for this volume represent a broad spread of philosophy's great literature. Three are indisputably classics: Plato's *Republic*, Descartes's *Meditations* and Hume's *Enquiry*. Anyone wishing to read the best works of Western philosophy would be advised to include these texts in their libraries. Mill's *On Liberty* is a seminal contribution to political philosophy and ethics, and represents one of the most influential arguments for liberalism. Nietzsche's *Beyond Good and Evil* and Sartre's *Existentialism and Humanism* however spring from a somewhat different tradition. Western philosophy since the late nineteenth century divides into two divergent traditions: the Anglo-American 'Analytic' school and the European 'Continental' school. Nietzsche can be seen as a forerunner of existentialism and an influence upon elements of the later European 'post-modern' philosophy. Sartre can be seen as a development out of the Franco-German 'phenomenological' school, which began with Husserl and Heidegger. (Be warned that these labels, though helpful, undoubtedly simplify and exaggerate the differences.) However, Nietzsche is notoriously enigmatic, ambiguous and open to interpretation, while Sartre's masterwork, *Being and Nothingness*, is a dense doorstop of a tome. The purpose of this book is therefore to help beginners approach these somewhat daunting thinkers – Nietzsche, through a commentary on arguably his most popular and accessible work, and Sartre, through an exploration of the brief popular account of existentialism which was originally a public lecture.

Having read this book slowly, critically and analytically, our hope is that you will be able to read the original texts themselves in exactly the same way.

1
Plato: *Republic* (*c*.375 BC)

Background

Plato (427–347 BC) may justifiably be considered one of the great philosophers. While he is preceded by a host of substantial thinkers whose ideas are still of interest to us – Heraclitus, Parmenides, Pythagoras, Democritus, and so on – he is the first to present a systematic response to the central problems of philosophy. This is partly due to the fact that the ideas of these predecessors survive only in fragments or second-hand reports – what we wouldn't give for the books of Heraclitus, which might supply a context for his brief, riddling pronouncements. Plato, however, presents us with a body of thought (almost thirty works, and a number of others of debated authenticity), written in a clear, logical form, and through which we can trace the progression of his ideas (though there is still much debate about what he *did* actually think).

Plato's influence has also been extensive. Whilst at times his reputation has been eclipsed by that of his pupil Aristotle, and his philosophy in general has fallen out of favour, few will deny that he did much to establish the general terrain of philosophical enquiry. Add to this that his contributions to numerous areas – ethics, epistemology, politics, aesthetics, metaphysics, philosophy of religion – still form an essential part of any modern introduction to these subjects, and we can be left in no doubt as to his deserved position in the philosophical hall of fame.

As to the man himself, he was born to a wealthy, aristocratic family in the ancient Greek city-state of Athens in around 427 BC. Plato was possibly a nickname (meaning 'broad' – a reference to his stature, perhaps) and his real name was reportedly Aristocles. His early years were overshadowed by the Peloponnesian War (which Athens lost) and political upheavals, some of which his family and friends were involved in. It was quite natural, then, that the young Plato should have gravitated towards politics. However, primarily through the influence of Socrates (*c.*469–399 BC), he was ultimately drawn to philosophy.

Socrates was a controversial figure, whose self-designated role of wandering philosopher was ultimately to bring about his own downfall. While he seems to have written nothing, his general attitude and method of philosophical analysis – *elenchus*, or 'Socratic questioning', as it has become known – was hugely influential upon Plato. Proclaiming his own ignorance on philosophical matters – 'I know that I know nothing' – Socrates developed a form of interrogation that sought to clarify a question, to draw out the knowledge that others professed, or else to reveal his interlocutor's true ignorance and confusion. As such, it was a method guaranteed to humiliate the pompous and make enemies – a key factor, no doubt, in Socrates' ultimate fate. Tried and convicted on arguably trumped-up charges, he was sentenced to death, something he faced with admirable calm and courage.

This injustice played a central role in the formation of Plato's philosophy, and when he comes to compose his own philosophical works, Socrates becomes the lead character in a series of philosophical dramas or *dialogues*. Initially, these recount Socrates' last days, providing opportunity to introduce Socrates' views on life, death, morality, and so on. However, as Plato's own philosophy evolves, the figure of Socrates becomes more and more a mouthpiece for his own ideas. As a consequence, it's sometimes difficult to distinguish between what Socrates actually thought and said, and Plato's extension of his mentor's views.

Following Socrates' death, Plato seems to have travelled and studied, served in the Athenian army, and at a number of points to have attempted to influence the government of Syracuse (missions which ultimately failed). Other than this, his contribution to politics seems to have remained theoretical. At around 386 BC, he established the Academy, a philosophical institution aimed at producing and influencing philosophers and would-be politicians, and spent the last 13 years of his life teaching and writing. He died sometime around 347 BC.

The text

Almost all of Plato's works are in *dialogue* form, each of which may therefore be thought of as a sort of philosophical play, in which a central figure (usually Socrates) debates various philosophical questions with friends, students and adversaries. Some of these are in fact well-known philosophers – Gorgias, Protagoras, Parmenides, Zeno – while others are statesmen or less well known figures (to us, at least). Interestingly, the *Republic* itself contains some of Plato's own family – Adeimantus and Glaucon were his elder brothers, and are chief participants in the dialogue, acting as the main foil to Socrates' questions. Other contributors include Polemarchus, at whose house the debate takes place, his father and brothers, and a handful of other acquaintances. However, aside from Adeimantus and Glaucon, the contribution of these other characters to the dialogue is minimal, and does not extend beyond its early stages.

The *Republic* was probably written around 375–70 BC, and is commonly thought of as part of Plato's 'middle period', during which he seems to push out beyond the concerns of the early dialogues (justice, ethics, etcetera) and toward more abstract problems – primarily, knowledge (epistemology) and the nature of reality (metaphysics). As such, the *Republic* is often taken to represent Plato's own mature views, as opposed to those solely associated with Socrates. He would later come to question and revise some of these theories, but the doctrines that are most commonly thought of as 'Platonic' are to be found here. It is also, of course, where he first reveals his plans for an ideal *constitution* (which is perhaps a better translation of its title than 'republic', which has come to mean a *type* of constitution). In this sense, it may therefore be seen as serving part of the philosophical programme that the Academy was built for: to make rulers into philosophers, or philosophers into kings. But its scope is broad, and the *Republic* has something for everyone, philosophically speaking, and is therefore a good place to start when reading Plato for the first time.

The dialogue itself is often divided into ten 'books' (though these do not reflect Plato's own organisation). However, we've deviated from this slightly by splitting our discussion into sections which we think make more sense thematically and supplied our own section titles in order to help you get a better sense of the topics covered. A common convention is to refer to specific passages in Plato's works using what are called 'Stephanus pages' after the edition of the complete works produced by Henricus Stephanus (Henri Estienne) in 1578. According to this system, each numbered page is divided into five sections, marked *a* through to *e*. So, using the Stephanus numbering, the whole text of the *Republic* runs from 327a to 621d of the Stephanus edition of the complete works. This might seem a bit odd at first, but is a handy way of referring to the same passage when using different editions or translations.

Finally, if you are planning on reading the *Republic* at first hand – and it is highly recommended – then try to get hold of a good modern translation. Plato is surprisingly accessible, and the conversational format helps bring the topics to life. Where we quote, we do so from the Penguin Classics translation by Desmond Lee, which strikes a good balance between precision and readability.

Preliminary discussion: What is justice?
(BK I, 327a – BK II, 367e)

The action, narrated by Socrates, begins with his return from a religious festival. He is politely kidnapped along the way by some old acquaintances, and returns to the house of Polemarchus. He engages in conversation with Cephalus, Polemarchus's father, where they discuss the pros and cons of growing old. Both Cephalus and Socrates agree that what is important in life changes as we get older; our thoughts turn toward death and force us to look back on our lives. Have we been good? Can we face death with a clean conscience? This consideration of what is involved in living a just and moral life leads to a more general question – the central concern of the *Republic* itself: What is justice?

The first thing to note is that the word 'justice' has quite a broad sense here. So, we are not just concerned with political issues or legal judgements, but also moral conduct in general and even religious observances – what we owe to the gods. A just man will therefore adopt the right sort of attitude in every area of life.

Taking over from his father (who toddles off to tend to other affairs), Polemarchus continues to defend what we might call the conventional view of justice: that it involves 'giving someone his due'. In other words, the just man helps his friends and harms his enemies; 'one good turn deserves another' and 'an eye for an eye', perhaps. However, by a process of questioning – what we now call his *Socratic method* – Socrates begins to draw out the problem with this view. It seems natural to assume that a just man is skilled in terms of knowledge and judgement, just as a doctor or a carpenter is skilled in their respective fields. However, to harm an enemy or morally bad person would seem to make him worse, not cure him. Would this be the action of a wise and just individual? Surely, then, this conventional idea of justice is wrong.

Up until now the debate has been a very civil one, but it is rudely interrupted by Thrasymachus, who criticises what he sees as Socrates' cowardly refusal to state the obvious truth: that 'might is right', and goodness and justice are decided by the will of the strongest. It is important to note here that Thrasymachus is a *sophist*, following in the footsteps of such philosophers as Gorgias and Protagoras. The sophists were generally sceptical about the possibility of objective knowledge and truth, and believed that to be right is merely to provide the most convincing arguments. There is therefore no more to truth than winning a debate – by whatever means, fair or foul. As such, many sophists therefore also made a living by teaching others how to reason, argue and speak in order to get on in life (Socrates jokes that he cannot afford to argue with Thrasymachus – literally). The sophists and their doctrines reappear in many of Plato's dialogues, and represent a sort of constant enemy. Whether Plato presents their views fairly is debatable, but for him they represented a real danger, for if we cannot really know truth, then we are all indeed at the mercy of those who are merely more skilful in argument, or even simply stronger and more powerful.

It is easy to see, then, how the sophist's viewpoint can lead directly to the death of morality: right and wrong are merely matters of convention, invented by the weak majority (the 'herd', as Nietzsche will call them) to protect themselves from the naturally stronger minority (the superior sort, cut out for leadership). But does the argument stand up? Thrasymachus's main point is that justice is 'in the interest of the stronger party'. We might say 'the victors write history', for instance. Similarly, then, right and wrong are defined by the ruling classes to reflect their own views on life and to serve their own interests. But here Socrates picks him up on this idea of self-interest. Returning to the analogy with skilled practitioners, Socrates gets Thrasymachus to admit that we measure skill in relation to how it benefits the subject, not the practitioner: the doctor has the patient's health at heart, the shipbuilder is concerned with making a seaworthy vessel, and so on. But, if so, then a ruler cannot serve his own interests, but must serve those of his subjects.

By these and similar methods, Socrates traps Thrasymachus by his own admissions. Thrasymachus tries to save face, and attempts to restate his argument, but again falls into similar pitfalls, for he seems to need to admit that government involves some sort of skill. But skill is never solely a matter of self-interest, or of 'getting one over' on someone else, it is measured according to some sort of standard – the skill of a doctor by the patient's health, the skill of a musician by tuneful melody, and so on. But if Thrasymachus admits the case with doctors and musicians (which he does), then he must also do so with rulers. This is Socratic method in practice – and infuriating it must be to be on the receiving end.

Unhappy with the outcome of the discussion between Thrasymachus and Socrates, Adeimantus and Glaucon take up and enlarge upon the sophist's views – more to provoke Socrates into giving a fuller answer than through any real sympathy with Thrasymachus's position. In doing so, they challenge Socrates' contention that men should love justice for its own sake. Glaucon recalls the myth of the *Ring of Gyges*, which rendered its wearer invisible (and thus able to do anything unde-tected). Wouldn't even a 'just' man succumb to this temptation, free of the fear of capture? Furthermore, isn't it obvious that most people are only *just* because of real (social, legal) or anticipated (otherwordly) rewards or punishments?

By the end of the preliminary discussion, Socrates has seemingly achieved two things: he has shown that there is a problem with the con-ventional idea of justice, and also that the most common alternative – Thrasymachus's view that 'might is right' – is also self-contradictory. Just men are not only more skilled and knowledgeable, but are in fact hap-pier than unjust men, whose pursuit of self-interest ultimately makes them miserable. Justice, it seems, wins out over self-interest (injus-tice) hands down. But the challenge of Glaucon and Adeimantus will force Socrates into a much broader and deeper answer – into discus-sion of moral, political, religious and philosophical topics which in turn develop into a design for an ideal society. However, before we look at that, let's consider some initial problems.

Problems

There are a number of points to take issue with here. Firstly, we might argue that Thrasymachus's case is misrepresented – yes, he is tricked by Socrates' ingenious method of argument, but we might argue that there is still a case to be made for self-interest. A later historical example, of course, is the philosophy of Friedrich Nietzsche (see Chapter 5), whose doctrine of 'will to power' perhaps represents a more sophisticated ver-sion of Thrasymachus's view. Other modern moral theories also argue that self-interest plays an important role in morality, and would look upon Plato's assertion that we can love goodness or justice for its own sake with some scepticism. (We'll come back to this later when we look at Plato's account of how we get such knowledge.)

Another problem perhaps is the parallel that Plato draws between skill and morality. Just because a doctor or a musician measures his skill according to an objective standard (health, tunefulness) does not mean that being moral or just is a similar type of practice. Perhaps Thrasymachus was too quick here to admit the parallel. And of course, the fact that something does not merely serve self-interest does not necessarily mean that it is objective – we might sculpt our physique in the gym to fit an aesthetic ideal, but such an ideal is often a subjective and changing one.

The basis of society (BK II, 368a – 376c)

The first thing Socrates does in response is to draw a parallel between the individual and society. Since, he argues, topics are best viewed on a larger scale (to make things clearer), we may think of society as a sort of individual writ large. So, just as we may talk of a society being well or badly ruled, just or unjust, we may also talk of an individual in the same terms. Justice in the state will therefore mirror justice in the individual, and vice versa.

But to understand society we need first to identify the principles of social organisation. Socrates argues that people are bound together by mutual need, and that the various types of individual within a society are determined both by the range of different natural abilities that people display and by social necessity. You may show an aptitude for carpentry or building, while I may prove a good hunter or fisherman. But it also makes sense to divvy up social roles in this way on grounds of practicality. Things will go more smoothly if I can concentrate solely on becoming an excellent fisherman, rather than having to fish, build, cook, and so on, all by myself.

Out of this seemingly commonsense principle of the division of labour, Plato shows how all the familiar elements of society evolve. There is, as yet, no sense of 'class', as we commonly think of it, but merely one of difference between roles. However, having shown how this principle naturally gives rise to bakers, butchers, market stall vendors, and the like, he muses that as such a simple society grows and prospers, it will naturally come into conflict with other such societies, leading to war. One of the most important roles is therefore that of the 'Guardian', the soldier or protector charged with defending his society from external threat. This type of person is the most important because, of all the various roles identified, it is the one that seems to call for specific character traits and meticulous training. Not only must a Guardian be brave and strong, and possess the necessary military skills, but also be disciplined and moulded by a strict code of ethics – a soldier should not use his martial prowess upon his own civilians, or channel his aggression inappropriately. To do this, of course, he must know right from wrong, which is a philosophical trait. Guardians must therefore be – to an extent – philosophers. From here on, then, Plato concentrates on the education of the Guardian, which will form the backbone of much of the rest of the dialogue.

Problems

The main problem with this picture is the threat it poses to social mobility. If I am forced to specialise in terms of my profession, does that mean that I can never be anything other than a fisherman, or a hunter, etcetera? Perhaps this is fine if all roles are equal, but – as we shall soon see – some are more equal than others, for the Guardians will take pride of place in Plato's ideal society.

It is this division of labour that Karl Marx and Friedrich Engels highlighted as the primary cause of social inequality. In contrast, the ideal communist society would allow an individual to be anything, from day to day – 'to hunt in the morning, fish in the afternoon, rear cattle in the evening, criticise after dinner, just as I have a mind, without ever becoming hunter, fisherman, herdsman or critic' (*The German Ideology*, Part I). Plato would no doubt point out that Marx's ideal is impractical and idealistic, but Plato needs to show how his utopia will avoid such class-based inequalities. (We'll look at his answer shortly.)

Education (BK II, 376d – BK III, 412a)

In educating his Guardians, Plato recognises the importance of starting early, from childhood onwards. In this way, society's future protectors and rulers can be shaped – body, mind and character – into the perfect tools of government service. In this way, not only would Guardians be fit physical specimens, but also be of exemplary ethical character and possessed of a first-rate intellect. To achieve this, he proposes an all-round education, made up of physical training, literary and musical studies, and philosophy and mathematics (the latter, intellectual stages of education, are dealt with in a later section). A point of interest here is represented by Plato's attitude to literature, art and music. He recognised, first of all, that literature could have a profound effect on shaping people's attitudes and opinions – especially children. We must therefore be careful as to what stories, poems, pictures, and so on, we expose their young minds to. Thus, Plato was one of the first philosophers to recognise the positive role of propaganda – and he was not ashamed to use such means to inculcate the correct virtues into his fledgling rulers.

But many common stories and poems were simply unsuitable, either morally or theologically. The famous tales of gods and heroes that the average Greek would be familiar with often presented such figures in an unfavourable light: Zeus overthrew his father and killed him, the gods frequently quarrelled and schemed against one another, Achilles killed prisoners of war, and so on. However, if we are to raise upright citizens, then such stories should either be 'cleaned up', replaced by other more suitable tales, or else – where their purpose was to symbolically convey secret religious doctrines – retained only for select initiates (all common tales should make it clear that the gods are the cause of good). Guardians are thus forbidden from partaking of most forms of poetry and drama, and even from acting out the roles of 'unworthy' characters for fear it might corrupt them! The upshot of all this is that, while Socrates acknowledges the skill of such poets as Homer and Hesiod, he is happy to effectively banish the creative artist and writer from his ideal society – either that, or he becomes merely a tool of the state. Given the affective power of art, he cannot leave it in the irresponsible hands of non-philosophers. (He returns to this subject in Book X.)

Music suffers a similar fate, and musical styles and instruments are banished or allowed in as much as they encourage good or bad qualities respectively. The flute, for instance, with the widest musical range, is considered to allow too much 'licence', but the more humble lyre is fine. Certain musical modes (e.g., the Lydian) encourage listeners toward 'drunkenness, softness or idleness', and are therefore forbidden; others (such as the Dorian and Phrygian) have a martial, upbeat quality, which inculcates courage and discipline. The same is true of rhythm and harmony. In all of this, Socrates argues, 'the object of education is to teach us to love what is beautiful' (403c). For Plato, there was an essential connection between beauty and goodness – not always, of course (Socrates was famously ugly, but possessed a beautiful mind and character), but there was a sense in which he thought that exposure to beautiful and wholesome things – in art, music, literature, and the like – would have a positive effect on psychological development.

Plato's attitude to sex is interesting, for he considers it merely another distraction that is likely to damage the development of good character. Are the Guardians celibate, then? Not really, for Plato seems to have distinguished the sexual act and procreation from a sort of lustful chasing after sexual pleasure. The latter could often take a homosexual form in men, which Plato seems generally to have disapproved of, though (as is clear from other dialogues) he very much approved of a relatively chaste form of romantic love between men (what came to be known as 'Platonic love'). But Plato's attitude is complex and difficult to decide, for the concept of homosexuality, as we have it now, did not strictly exist in ancient Greece. Curiously, romantic heterosexual love seems to have concerned him practically little. (We'll return to matters of sex, family and gender roles in Book IV.)

Finally, having outlined the cultural aspects of the first stage of education, Socrates considers physical education. But his attitude to health and fitness was a balanced one: Guardians should not be athletes, solely concerned with physical prowess, nor should they be merely bookish intellectual types, but rather seek to develop a healthy balance between these extremes through study, good diet and appropriate exercise. Doctors and lawyers would therefore be effectively superfluous, for both the state and its individuals would be 'healthy' through habit and discipline.

Problems

Plato's critique of art is well-known and highly controversial. To a modern Western mind, where creative freedom is so much a part of cultural life, Plato's plan seems nothing less than a form of dictatorial censorship. In seeking to control art, music and literature, Plato's society bears much resemblance to the authoritarian regimes of Soviet Russia and post-revolutionary China – they too had the moral welfare of the people at heart! Plato therefore needs to be careful that his concern for public morals does not merely deteriorate into dictatorship. As Karl Popper argued in his famous critique, *The Open Society and Its Enemies*, the desire to impose a rigid template of the perfect state is a form of *totalitarianism*, and is always at the expense of true freedom, which is a democratic, open-ended process, as individuals work together to evolve a mutual ideal.

On a number of other points, Plato's understanding of art seems simplistic and literal. Is it really true that children 'cannot distinguish between what is allegory and what isn't' (378e)? Plato seems to give too little credit to native intelligence, and too much to individual credulity. We can see here that the ongoing debate as to what sort of influence the content of film, TV, and other forms of media have on young minds began with Plato. Do portrayals of violence make people violent? Plato would have thought so, but – at the very least – it would seem that this is an overly simple view, for there is also good evidence to suggest that it can work the other way (portrayal of violence can put people off, help them realise its dangers, and so on). Another point is that if art becomes unreal and overly censored, then it will cease to be as effective, and may even create resentment. Like the pictures of happy, well-fed workers that belied the drudgery and hardship of Soviet Russia, the picture postcard works to undermine the ideal it is meant to illustrate. There is an assumption here that good art is 'improving' through example. 'Goodies' defeat 'baddies' and the wicked get their just desserts. But, arguably, such a partial picture also falsifies life – is Plato, who rails against falsehood, condoning its use for his own purposes? It would seem so, which Plato himself admits: 'it will be for the rulers of our city...to use falsehood in dealing with citizen or enemy for the good of the state' (389b).

Plato's ideas on music can also seem a bit quaint, with their emphasis on the importance of modes and rhythms – but perhaps not necessarily so. For instance, we may compare his attitude to the suspicion with which Soviet Russia considered Rock and Roll or Jazz. If we look at the social movements that these musical trends accompanied – expressions of decadent Western lifestyles – then his concern with musical expression is perhaps understandable (if not perhaps fully justified). Music, like art and literature, must be strictly controlled and censored because it is such an important tool of indoctrination – I mean, *education*.

Rulers and auxiliaries (BK III, 412b – BK IV, 427c)

Having identified the Guardians as the class from which the society's protectors, rulers and enforcers will be drawn, Plato proceeds to identify how these sub-roles will be established. We must split our Guardians into 'Rulers' – the wisest and most ethical (Guardians proper) – and the 'Auxiliaries' – those who fall short of the highest standards. So, as Guardians grow up, they are subjected to trials and tests – fear, pain and intimidation, but also to the temptations of pleasure and luxury – to see who holds fastest to the central ideal of putting the interests of the community first. Those who can resist such 'witchcraft' (bewitchment of the senses) will be the most eligible for rule; those who fare less well will become policemen, soldiers, civil servants, and so on, and will serve the former.

At this point, Plato introduces a sort of story or 'Noble Myth' (as we may translate it) that is meant to explain to the various classes why and how they are different. When Mother Nature made people, She incorporated different 'metals' into their constitution: Rulers contained elements of 'gold', Auxiliaries of 'silver', and the manual classes of 'iron' and 'bronze'. Mostly, parents of a particular metal would give birth to children of the same – gold to gold, bronze to bronze, and so on – but occasionally, there would be a mix-up, and a 'gold' baby might be born to 'bronze' parents, or vice versa. Therefore, we would need to pay close attention to the skills and abilities of children as they grew up so that they could be promoted or demoted as appropriate.

In order to keep the Rulers on the straight and narrow, Plato proposes that they live communally, possess no private property or wealth, and are supported by the working classes (arrangements for family, child rearing and marriage are dealt with in a later section). In this way, not only are they secured from the commonest form of corruption (desire for wealth) but are free to concentrate solely on the tasks of rulership. When Adeimantus objects that such rulers cannot be happy – what can they have to strive for? – Socrates responds that happiness must be seen in terms of the whole society, not in terms of its parts. If farmers, traders, etcetera, were pampered and made 'happy', they would fail to do their jobs. The wealth of the rulers therefore lies in wisdom and goodness, which they must be fostered to appreciate for its own sake. The Noble Myth plays a role here, giving everyone a reason for playing their part, and Socrates will also shortly return to the analogy between the individual and society in order to explain how it is important that different aspects of a whole work together if there is to be justice.

As regards the specifics of state government, Socrates argues that we need not legislate for every single possible eventuality – rules to do with trade, the rights and wrongs of social conduct, and so forth – because these things will look after themselves. As he puts it 'Good men need no orders' (425e), but can be trusted to employ their good sense and general education and training. As long, that is, as two conditions are met: society remains a unified and functioning whole, and there are no innovations in the scheme of education. The first is important because a society that grows too big will become ungovernable; the second, because – for Plato – education is everything, and having established what he sees as the best principles for its management, any change can only make things worse. Similarly, for religious matters, any tinkering with tradition would be foolish, and all things (founding of temples, etcetera) should be left up to the traditional authority: the Delphic Oracle.

Problems

We can see here Plato's full answer to the problem of social mobility and possible class conflict raised earlier. The various classes are not doomed to their roles forever, but are promoted or demoted appropriately, if they display talent (or lack of it). We might object here that this does not account for late developers, and that it's difficult to develop without educational opportunity (which the manual classes won't have), but Plato's system is perhaps not as rigid as it is sometimes accused of being.

However, there are other aspects of this proposal that are worrying. The stratification of types of people into 'gold', 'silver', and so on calls to mind Aldous Huxley's dystopic novel *Brave New World*, where test-tube babies are genetically engineered to produce Alphas, Betas, Gammas, etcetera. Plato's *eugenics* is not so advanced, but there is still a question to be raised as to whether this sort of 'animal breeding' (as Plato describes it) is the basis for social evolution. Since it is driven by an ideal, we can question whether such a standard is a true one – we need only call to mind the eugenics inspired genocides of Nazi Germany or nineteenth-century African colonisation, which perpetrated atrocities in the name of a false notion of racial superiority. But Huxley's criticism was not so much of the use of eugenics – he believed it necessary – but the extent of control: his fear was that society would become too authoritarian. Huxley, like Plato, feared that democracy would fail because the average man was ill-equipped to participate – though he still held to a democratic ideal. (We'll consider Plato's critique of democracy later.)

Perhaps the most cogent criticism of the idea of the Guardian caste, however, is that it does not fully account for human nature. Yes, they will not be allowed personal property or wealth, thereby defusing the jealousy and resentment that might otherwise arise from their position of power, but won't they be tempted? Won't they see through the Noble Myth – intellectual elite that they are – and start to ask, 'What's in it for me?' As the Roman poet Juvenal later put it, 'Who watches the watchmen?' Who will monitor the powerful? It's a conundrum that has still not really been solved, and persists into modern politics.

Society and the individual (BK IV, 427d – BK IV, 444e)

If Plato's society is a perfect one, then it will arguably possess the requisite qualities. Socrates therefore identifies four 'cardinal virtues', as they have become known, which the state should embody: wisdom, courage, self-discipline and justice. Since wisdom is based on knowledge, then you would expect it to reside with the intellectual elite, the Guardians proper (the Rulers). Courage, similarly, will be embodied by the bravest (the Auxiliaries or soldiers). However, the two remaining virtues – self-discipline and justice – are slightly different, in that they do not belong solely to one part of society, but rather exist in the relationship between the different parts. A person possesses self-discipline when he is 'master of himself' – that is, when his desires and passions are subject to reason. Similarly, then, in society there is good discipline when the most rational (the Guardians) rule the less so (the commoners), who are themselves content to subject themselves to the greater wisdom of their rulers. Each part of society also possesses self-discipline in as much as it recognises the correct social order.

Justice, the final virtue, is also something which is related to the whole. If a farmer were to make laws, or a soldier were to tend sheep and grow crops, then we can imagine that they would both make a hash of things, lacking the skills, knowledge and training to accomplish their respective tasks. However, if the Rulers, Auxiliaries and working class perform their roles properly, then the society will function as it should. A just society is therefore one in which each of the three classes 'does its own job and minds its own business' (434c).

From here Socrates proceeds to show how the structure of society mirrors the psychological structure of the individual. First, he demonstrates that the individual must be made up of different aspects, and is not the expression of a single will. So, we can be in two minds about something, resist or give in to temptation, and so on. Like the state, then, the soul has a tripartite structure: reason, desire and 'spirit'. Reason we are familiar with, for it is just the intellectual capacity; desires and instincts are simply the bodily appetites – hunger, thirst, lust, fear, etcetera. The third aspect, however, is slightly more difficult to pin down. 'Spirit' is a loose translation of *thumos*, which describes a range of feelings, passions and attitudes: anger, pride, self-respect, ambition, courage. We can perhaps best think of these as soldierly qualities, for the man ruled by *thumos* is disciplined, has a 'code' which controls his basic physical urges for some purpose, but does not really possess intellectual talents.

Given this psychological structure, we can therefore conclude that justice in the individual (mirroring the state) occurs when reason rules passion and desire for the good of the whole being. So, each aspect does its job. To make a financial investment based on emotion, or form a romantic relationship solely on rational principles, are equally liable to result in disaster and unhappiness. In another dialogue, *Phaedrus*, Plato pictures this relationship in terms of a charioteer (Reason) controlling two horses (Desire and Spirit). The 'good' horse (Spirit) is more easily controlled and directed than the 'bad' one (Desire), which needs constant whipping! Spirit is therefore a sort of intermediary and helper to reason just as the Auxiliaries are there to do the will of the Rulers.

Problems

We can see now why Plato was so keen on drawing a link between the individual and society, because not only does it help us to see individual psychology 'writ large', but also provides a justification for the structure of the state: society must be this way, because individuals are. But are they? The idea that we are rational beings under the sole direction of reason has come under attack from many sides. Sigmund Freud, founder of psychoanalysis, developed the idea that we are often driven by unconscious and irrational urges; Nietzsche, as we shall see (Chapter 5), similarly thought that it was a desire to exert oneself over others (the 'will to power') that was the true motive of action, but was often masked beneath a more respectable guise (e.g., rationality, morality). Of course, other philosophers may be brought in to bolster Plato's position – Immanuel Kant, for instance, argued that we have a rational duty to be good (what he termed the 'categorical imperative'). Kant and Plato still have their defenders, but many modern philosophers would consider the idea that we are so selflessly and rationally motivated to be a naïve one. So, without going into depth here, we can at least see that Plato's position is a highly controversial, even a besieged one.

Women, marriage and family (BK IV, 445a – BK V, 471c)

Having established the parallel between individual and state, Socrates proceeds to underline its significance by embarking on an analysis of the various ways in which a society/individual can be *unjust*. However, he is immediately interrupted in this task by the whisperings of Adeimantus and Polemarchus, who object to Socrates' too-brief treatment of the Guardians' living conditions. What about marriage, family relations and raising children? In response, Socrates delays his account of injustice, and begins to set out organisational practicalities in more detail.

First, he considers the status of women. In a very progressive move, Socrates proposes that there are only two substantial differences between the sexes: women tend to possess less physical strength than men, and some allowance must also be made for their more arduous role in childbirth. Aside from this, they are otherwise as capable as men in all regards. Thus, not only should women undertake the same training and education as the male Guardians, but they should also be allowed to fight in battle.

However, Plato's notion of equality leads him to take a more controversial position on marriage and child rearing. To be truly disinterested, he argues, Guardians must 'hold all things in common'. This means not only the abolition of private property, but also of other forms of 'ownership', such as marriage and parenthood. In their place, Plato proposes much broader relationships, where the best 'specimens' are encouraged to interbreed with each other (through a sort of rigged lot made to appear random), and any resulting children are considered the property of the Guardian community in general. Actually, the arrangements are slightly more complicated than this, for we must guard against parent-child incest (though not, it seems, between brother and sister). Also, relationships which are not sanctioned by the state are considered illegal, and any resulting children, along with other 'defective' or illegitimate offspring, would be quietly got rid of (of which, more below). However, the main purpose here is to defuse any potential conflict between the interests of the family and the state. No parent would know the identity of its biological child, and all children would have many 'fathers' and 'mothers'.

Having so much in common will provide a source of great social cohesion, and the commonest causes of conflict – traditional notions of family, children, money and possessions – all but disappear. Consequently, there will be little need for litigation, and quarrels and fights – where they infrequently occur – will be minor, and capable of being sorted out 'on the spot' (the odd altercation will even help to keep people fit!).

Finally, since he has discussed the participation of women in battle, Socrates briefly sets out the rules for conduct in war. Children may go to war to observe, the better to accustom themselves to it. The bravest warriors will be showered with rewards and honours, and even affection ('kisses'), the suggestion being that bonds of affection between soldiers will increase courage and performance. The family that fights together stays together. Generally, however, Plato's concern is to lessen the inhumanity of war – to treat prisoners honourably, to refrain from pillage and plunder, and so on.

Problems

There is some controversy here about whether Plato's attitude to 'defective' or illegitimate children in fact amounts to infanticide: the killing of unwanted babies and infants. In some places, he implies that unsuitable children will be farmed out to the third social class. But in others, especially concerning birth abnormalities, he does seem to suggest that infanticide is the best course (for a full discussion of this, see the Desmond Lee translation, pp. 184–6). This would not have been uncommon in ancient Greece, but it would certainly represent a problem now – though we may perhaps tie it in to issues surrounding abortion. But this does highlight another concern with eugenics: in search of 'desirable inheritable qualities', what lengths are we willing to go to? And also, there is great uncertainty surrounding the question of the future 'worth' of an individual only just born. If we were to take action based on screening for genetic defects, for instance, we would be without such individuals as Christopher Nolan, Christy Brown and Stephen Hawking, and other extraordinary people. But human worth is not just about potential artistic or scientific greatness, but is – arguably – a thing we cannot place a definite value on.

Regarding sexual equality, Plato is surprisingly progressive, but he also seems to take away sexual freedom – a fit female Guardian *must* go to war, perform civic duties, etcetera, and there is no option to stay at home to raise children. Which is the other point: she has no children to stay at home to raise, for they are all fostered communally. As in *Brave New World*, the family is abolished as a source of conflict and psychological harm. This is certainly the most controversial aspect of Plato's domestic arrangements, and there are arguments on both sides. Bad families may indeed raise damaged individuals, but not necessarily so; and the same for good families. There are definite positives to the traditional family – close kinship bonds, security and intimacy – which are arguably the basis for other positive social relationships, and which communal rearing may not provide. In George Orwell's 1984 – another futuristic commentary that owes much to the *Republic* – children are raised to put the state before family. Indoctrinated by 'Hitler Youth' type organisations like 'The Spies' and the 'Youth League', children are bred into Party zealots who think nothing of informing on other adults for 'suspicious activity' – even their own parents. Communal rearing therefore may also have a dark, inhuman side.

The philosopher rulers (BK V, 471d – BK VI, 502c)

The justice of the state is reliant upon the possibility of there being the type of philosophical rulers that Plato envisages – but can there be?

Socrates points out that the philosopher ruler – the perfectly just man – is an ideal and not necessarily one that can be fully met in reality. But difficulty in establishing the ideal state or ruler should not stop us from trying, for even if we get close it will be better than that which currently exists. However, we must try, for there will never be true justice until either philosophers gain political power, or rulers become philosophers.

But what is a philosopher? It is someone with a passion to know things. But this is not specific enough: a gossip may desire to hear news, or a glutton may yearn to know what's for dessert, but neither are thereby philosophers. Rather, a philosopher desires knowledge itself. Here Socrates distinguishes between knowledge, ignorance and opinion, the latter of which is intermediate between the first two. Most people are therefore concerned with what *appears* to be the case, which, at best, can only lead to an approximate or uncertain opinion or belief; philosophers, however, are 'lovers of wisdom' (the literal meaning of the word), and their apprehension of knowledge leads to certainty and truth itself. Furthermore, the qualities necessary for being a good philosopher – good memory, facility for learning, having courage, temperance – knit well with those required by the ideal ruler.

At this point, Adeimantus interrupts: given their dubious reputation, why should we trust philosophers to lead our state? Socrates therefore distinguishes between the true philosopher, and the unscrupulous and slippery sophist. Using the analogy of a ship, Socrates asks us to imagine that the Captain who controls the ship, whilst the most powerful, is also shortsighted and lacking knowledge in seamanship. He must therefore be advised and helped – but by whom? The crew, who want to turn their trip into a 'pleasure cruise', will support any man who can persuade the Captain to their will (the sophist), but the wise will support a knowledgeable and trustworthy navigator (the true philosopher). It is therefore symptomatic of Plato's contempt for democracy that he considers the former situation to currently be the case: democratic society is a ship of fools. Most philosophers are therefore not worthy of the name, pandering to the masses like some great fearful beast, having lost their way through pride and flattery, or else being intellectually unfit to begin with. But if a philosopher could become a ruler, or a ruler philosophical, then the public's doubts would be assuaged once they saw the improvement in government. This would obviously require a radical reshaping of society, but it is eminently possible.

The good (BK VI, 502d – BK VII, 521b)

This section contains the philosophical meat of the *Republic*, and it may be fairly argued that the whole feasibility of Plato's vision rests on the success of his arguments here. Moving on to the education of the philosopher, Socrates argues that a philosopher's primary goal is to grasp the ultimate truth, what he terms 'the form of the Good'. Through the dialogue, Plato has occasionally suggested the existence of knowledge which is beyond appearances, but here, for the first time, he makes the nature of such knowledge explicit. He does so by the use of three illustrations: the Sun Simile, the Divided Line analogy, and – most famous of all – the Simile of the Cave.

Socrates first distinguishes goodness from pleasure – there can be bad pleasures, and we can always ask whether pleasure itself is good in a particular context. But what, then, is goodness? Socrates admits that such a definition is beyond him, but – after some coaxing – offers an analogy. In order to have knowledge of the appearance of the physical world, we are reliant upon light in order to see it. The source of this light is the Sun, and we might therefore say that the eye owes its ability to know the world to the Sun itself. In a similar way, if we consider the faculty of the intellect or mind, then it owes its knowledge of the world to truth – as Socrates puts it: 'When the mind's eye is fixed on objects illuminated by truth and reality, it understands and knows them' (508d). So, just as sunlight allows the eye to know physical objects (and the Sun itself), so a similar 'light of truth' guides the mind to know *intelligible* objects. These intelligible objects or pure ideas are what Plato – and subsequent commentators – have called *the Forms*. Examples would include abstract concepts such as those already considered – goodness, justice, courage – but also the ideas which correspond to more mundane things, such as colours, shapes, physical objects, and so on. The *Form of the Good*, however, is the chief Form, the supreme source of knowledge and truth, which allows us to know the other Forms – just as the Sun, whilst itself an object, is the source of the light by which we come to know all other objects. Plato almost seems to become mystical here. The Forms are perfect and unchanging, and therefore, in a sense, must exist 'beyond' time and space. The world of the Forms is therefore completely different to the physical world of flux and impermanence apparent to the senses. However, on the other hand, his point may be simply that the ultimate standards by which we judge knowledge, truth and goodness are not themselves easily defined, or even definable. So, we may to an extent come to know this 'source', but – since it is itself the source of knowledge and truth – not so clearly or completely as we might know other 'objects' (in the same way, perhaps, as the nature of light is mysterious). We simply reach a limit of understanding – or perhaps of expression. The other point to grasp here is that this perspective makes Plato a *rationalist*, for, like René Descartes after him (see Chapter 2), he believes that our knowledge of the world is ultimately based on our apprehension of objective *ideas* (and not built up from sense experience – the position held by later *empiricists*).

The analogy of the Divided Line is meant to develop and clarify the Sun Simile (see table below).

Visible world (opinion based on perception) *doxa*		Intelligible world (knowledge based on understanding) *gnōsis*	
False (illusion based on imagination) *eikasia*	**True** (true belief based on trust) *pistis*	**Indirect** (logic, deduction) *dianoia*	**Direct** (intelligence, dialectic) *noēsis*

We can see here that there are two 'worlds' (the main division of the line): the visible or physical world that we perceive through our senses, and the intelligible world that we understand via our intellect. However, we need not think of this in a dualistic sense – Plato is not necessarily talking of a physical and a 'spiritual' world, but rather of two different aspects to reality: the *sensory* and the *intelligible*, through which we *perceive* and *understand*. The first merely gives us opinion (*doxa*), whilst the second gives us knowledge (*gnōsis*). This attitude to the senses is once again a key component of rationalism, and the idea that we must somehow guarantee sensory knowledge is a concern that is taken up centuries later by Descartes. The senses mislead us, and present us with a picture which is in some way less real or true. For this reason, sensory knowledge can only ever be a form of opinion, which is itself uncertain.

However, the line can be further divided. Firstly, opinion can be true or false. The lowest form of perception is a sort of confused picture made up of shadows and reflections – a complete illusion (*eikasia*). But this may be distinguished from belief or opinion, which – though it is not a form of knowledge – happens to be true (*pistis* - examples of which would be a correct belief based on blind trust without reason to support it). As Plato will later argue in the dialogue *Thaeatetus*, even such true belief is not really knowledge. To gain true understanding we therefore need to consider the intelligible world. This also can be divided into two. Firstly, there is rational or mathematical knowledge (*dianoia*), involving things that can be worked out *indirectly*, using logic or deductive reasoning, but without questioning our basic assumptions (what is often termed *discursive* thinking). Secondly, there is full or *direct* knowledge (*noēsis*). To be a true philosopher we need to apprehend the *Forms* themselves, which is an act of *pure intelligence* or *understanding.* Only in coming face to face with the abstract ideas that make reality intelligible, and which may be arrived at through *dialectic* reasoning or true philosophical method, can we claim true knowledge.

One interesting question which the Divided Line poses for modern readers of the *Republic* is where scientific knowledge fits in. Given that the natural sciences – physics, chemistry, biology – rely heavily on sense experience (collecting data, making observations), we might assume that even seemingly justified scientific theories can only be classed under true belief (*pistis*), and are therefore not true knowledge. From the few comments he makes considering empirical knowledge, it does indeed seem that this was in fact Plato's view. It might be tempting to argue that, since science in ancient Greece was rudimentary, and given the extent that modern scientific theories and statements involve mathematical or logical principles – as most do, in some way – Plato might now change his mind. If rational principles can explain and confirm observation and experiment, then doesn't that make such knowledge certain? In fact, as we'll see later, this is more or less the approach taken by a later rationalist, René Descartes (see Chapter 2, 'The Piece of Wax'). I might *see* an apple fall, but the principles that explain and describe its falling are mathematical and logical. However, of course, a principle or formula can be logically certain but still incorrect as an explanation of physical phenomena – we might still be tricked by our senses or proved wrong by further experience. And, as we shall see later (Chapter 3), some of the principles and assumptions that Descartes thought helped guarantee scientific certainty were perhaps not ultimately rationally justified. Perhaps Plato was right to be conservative.

There is one other further point to note here before we move on. You may notice that the line is divided unequally – not in halves, but in a ratio (3:2, or what is called the *Golden Ratio*). This is probably meant to illustrate how one part is more important than the other, and how the lesser is reliant upon the greater. So, understanding is to reason, as knowledge in general is to opinion.

The final illustration in this section is the most famous: the Simile of the Cave. It is really just a more vivid picture of the concepts already considered, but it does give a more dramatic sense of what the task of the philosopher actually is. Imagine, says Socrates, that you are prisoner in a dark cave, your legs, hands and head bound so that you have no choice but to face the wall in front of you. On the wall, you see flickering shadows and hear strange noises, which are cast by men carrying various strange objects – figures of animals, statues of people, other shapes – which you cannot turn around to see, and probably would not even be aware existed (only the shadows exist for you). Growing up in such conditions (you have been kept this way since a child), it would be natural to assume that you would take the shadows for reality, and make all sorts of false assumptions about their true nature.

This is a very odd image, but perhaps you could replace the picture with someone confined in a room from childhood with only a television (or something like that). Each of the aspects of this picture has an exact parallel in the illustrations already discussed – which Socrates goes on to explain. Firstly, the shadows on the wall represent the false opinions formed from unexamined sense experience; the objects represent true beliefs and opinions; the cave in general then represents the visible world, lit by the fire (a representative of the physical Sun). But now imagine that you are freed from your bonds, and struggle up and out into daylight. You are initially blinded by the true 'Sun' of truth and goodness, and must look at shadows and reflections until your sight adjusts (i.e., you reason about things indirectly until you perceive the Forms themselves). Eventually, you are able to directly perceive the true objects of the world (the intelligible Forms), and finally the Form of the Good itself (the Sun). An interesting implication here is that education is more a 'drawing out' than a 'putting in', for knowledge is innate, or present from birth – or at least, the teaching consists in leading the mind to make its own discoveries. (We'll question this below.)

The precise correspondences of this simile are still disputed, but the general significance is clear: it is a picture of the philosopher's journey, from ignorance and illusion, through intellectual endeavour to full awakening and direct perception of truth and goodness. But wouldn't the philosopher be reluctant to return from such an awakening to the dark cave of ignorance and prejudice (the world of his fellow humans)? And would not his former companions in delusion greet his return with disbelief, scepticism and even hostility? However, it is good that our prospective rulers are reluctant, for it means that they do not desire power, but will rule merely out of duty and a recognition that they are best fitted for it.

Problems

Plato's concept of the Forms is central to his philosophy, but it has been one of the most widely disputed ideas in philosophy. First, it seems to assume the independent existence of rational concepts – a sort of otherworldly realm, where heavenly and perfect ideas live. But how do we know this? Plato argues that our knowledge is a form of recollection from in between previous incarnations when the soul has visited this realm – which may only be a poetic way of saying that such ideas are in some way built-in to the mind or *innate*. This approach, which he shares with later rationalists such as Descartes, has been widely criticised, most notably by John Locke, who simply pointed out that if we had such ideas, then even the uneducated would know them (which they don't seem to). However, the issue is more complicated than this, because there are still aspects of experience which seem to assume a certain order and organisation. In other words, as Kant argued, we seem to see the world in a particular way, make certain types of judgement, because our minds are innately fitted to do so. We might also note that Locke's empiricist alternative – that the mind is a blank slate or *tabula rasa* – is equally problematic, for it would seem to have difficulty in accounting for how our experience takes certain forms. The debate still goes on, in different guises (see Chapter 1 of *Key Themes*), but most would now reject Plato's account as metaphysical wishful thinking.

Another problem, however, concerns the Forms themselves. Don't they assume that, in order for language and thought to make sense, there must exist clear and defined concepts to which they refer? But this too is problematic. For instance, is there one thing that all acts of justice have in common? Arguably, instead of a single or definite set of features, we'll find a complex web of related characteristics. Some acts share some features, others don't, but all are in some way 'related'. The existence of these *universals* (as they're called) is therefore disputed, for language and meaning do not seem to work in that way. Perhaps, then, the very possibility of such *Forms* never really gets off the ground in the first place.

One final point here concerns the definition of the Good. Socrates argues that good isn't the same as pleasure, because we can always question whether certain pleasures are in fact good. I like ice cream, but it makes me fat. This was later called by English philosopher G. E. Moore the Open Question argument: we can always ask if something pleasant, helpful, kind, loving is in fact good, which means that 'good' cannot mean the same as any such generally positive concepts that some seek to define good in terms of. The Good is therefore in some way 'beyond' pleasure. But is it? Some *utilitarians* will argue that all moral acts are in some way determined by pleasure, and what we do when we apparently reject pleasure is to prefer a 'higher' or more refined pleasure – that of looking in the mirror and seeing that you've lost weight, perhaps. But are all our actions driven by 'secret' and refined pleasures? Ultimately, *hedonism* (the idea that pleasure is the only true good) is perhaps no easier to conclusively prove than the existence of the Form of the Good. As a traffic warden, you might claim you are motivated by a sense of duty, whereas I think you secretly enjoy giving out parking tickets – who is right? Should I scan the pleasure centre of your brain (if such a thing truly exists) when you're doing your ticketing? But because pleasure is involved does not necessarily meant that it is a primary motive – it might simply accompany your unimpeachable sense of duty. It's a complex issue.

The education of the philosopher (BK VII, 521c – 541b)

Having suggested in outline the general purpose of philosophical endeavour, Socrates now turns to the specifics of philosophical and intellectual education. The physical and cultural education considered earlier (Books II and III) took care of the body and character respectively, ensuring future Guardians were physically fit, and emotionally and psychologically healthy. The third stage would therefore cater to the mind, consisting of various mathematical disciplines and a grounding in 'dialectic', or philosophical method.

We need not concern ourselves too much with the details of mathematical education, though we can note that Plato seems to have considered maths to underpin virtually all pursuits – from intellectual studies, such as philosophy, to practical activities, such as carpentry and shopkeeping, and even warfare. At the most basic level, everyone needs to count and perform simple calculations just to get by in life. However, Plato's main emphasis is on training the intellect, and mathematical study is a specific use of reasoning, and therefore a first step in philosophy, prompting the mind to move beyond sense experience. As Socrates puts it, 'We are called on to use our reason when our senses receive opposite impressions' (524d). Confusion is the birth of thought!

However, like Pythagoras, who seems to have been a great influence on him, Plato thought that studying mathematical principles was not just useful in practical terms, it was an avenue to deeper truths about the nature of reality. Accordingly, Socrates prescribes five fields of study: arithmetic, plane and solid geometry, astronomy and musical harmony. It might seem odd to include music here, but there is a close relationship between harmony and mathematical ratio – as Pythagoras himself discovered – and one recent theory (that of J. B. Kennedy) even suggests that Plato's dialogues are organised according to a musical scale. For Plato, then, music, number, reason and truth were all linked together in a fundamental way. An understanding of maths was therefore essential training for the philosopher, providing a basis for the final and highest stage of intellectual study, and leading the mind toward ultimate truth.

This last stage is called *dialectic*. In its most general sense, dialectic simply involves investigating a subject by presenting and testing opposing viewpoints, sometimes in the form of a debate or dialogue. The purpose of this is not to win an argument, but to arrive at a deeper understanding, and it is therefore more an investigative than a combative method. In Plato's sense, its more specific purpose is to apprehend the intelligible ideas or Forms, perhaps even the Form of the Good itself (the highest of the Forms, which gives everything its value and meaning). So, returning to the image of the Divided Line, we can see that dialectic is the highest form of intellectual activity in that it leads to direct understanding or *intuition* of these ideas.

Commonly, we use reason and logic to clarify and explain things based on accepted assumptions. In order to determine whether something is 'fair', I must have a working definition of what 'fair' is. Even mathematics and geometry assume such definitions, and therefore represent a lower form of knowledge (*dianoia*) than dialectic (*noēsis*). However, dialectic investigates those assumptions, and questions the ultimate basis of our knowledge. Let's take an example: a jury might be asked to decide whether a man was guilty of a particular crime, and in doing so would reason and argue based on a certain notion of justice. However, the question of what justice is *in itself* (the Form of justice) is a deeper and more philosophical question, one which can only be arrived at through dialectical reasoning. It is the search for 'first principles' – those beyond which we cannot go. Of course, this is similar to the method Socrates himself sometimes uses in seeking to reach the truth through debate, question and answer (as opposed to setting out and defending a position or assumption). However, often, Socrates' method (*elenchus*) is purely negative, in that he uses it to refute opponents by revealing their ignorance (*elenchus* means 'refutation'). At other times, his investigations are inconclusive, and leave us in a state of doubt or confusion (*aporia*). Such a destructive or disconcerting process may of course play a part in a wider, more positive search for knowledge (such as it does in Descartes's *Meditations*, for example – see Chapter 2), and we may therefore think of *elenchus* as a particular form or stage of dialectic. So, though *elenchus* and dialectic aren't completely distinct, what distinguishes the two methods is that, whilst *elenchus* is often intended as a means of refuting opponents or pointing out dead ends, dialectic is intended to lead us to *understanding* as applied to the realm of *pure thought*: the *Forms* or eternal ideas that constitute true reality. The two methods are therefore really a difference in emphasis, and perhaps mark where the historical Socrates differs from the Socrates of the later dialogues. For Plato, dialectic is not about winning an argument or embarrassing an opponent, but arriving at truth. Success in this activity is what marks out the true philosopher.

Socrates finally sums up what is needed for true philosophers (the correct type of character, constitution, etcetera.), and makes some general observations as to the organisation of the curriculum. Compulsory military service takes place between 18 and 20 years old, and at that point some are chosen for higher studies – ten years of maths, and – for the most able and intellectually sturdy – a subsequent five years of dialectic. Having done this, they are then sent back to the military and civil service for 15 years, until finally achieving the status of philosopher ruler. Even then, they will only rule for a period of time, in rotation with others, spending the majority of their time in philosophical studies.

Problems

For dialectic to work (in Plato's sense), we must assume the existence of the Forms (which is, as we've seen, problematic). But perhaps finding truth is not (to use an analogy employed by Socrates in other dialogues) like helping someone give birth. Perhaps, in fact, it is closer to a creative act, or even simply a form of agreement – a sort of compromise. The idea that truth is an objective entity is therefore yet another of Plato's doctrines that has come under attack in relatively recent times. Without it, some of Plato's arguments look like a subtle form of rhetoric, or even outright trickery.

Incidentally, it is in this section (527c) that Plato seems to give his ideal society a name: *Kallipolis* ('Fair City'). Some have taken this to be its official title, so you will often hear it used as such. However, this is its only appearance in the *Republic*, and there is nothing to suggest it is anything other than a playful and fleeting description, not a title.

Unjust societies (BK VIII, 543a – BK IX, 592b)

After the long digression to describe the nature and education of the philosopher ruler, Socrates finally returns to where he left off in Book IV, where he was about to describe the different types of unjust society. The just society (like the just man) is ruled by the wise (reason), assisted by loyal Auxiliaries (spirit), and supported and trusted by law-abiding manual classes (physical desires). However, in an unjust society or individual, this order is upset. Socrates pictures this as various stages of social decline from his ideal state (the best) to a dictatorship (the worst), and traces how the corresponding character to each state arises (which we won't go into).

First of all, the *timarchy* (*timocracy*) or 'ambitious society' is driven by competition and combativeness. Historical examples of this were ancient Sparta and Crete, which were essentially military aristocracies. A perfect society might deteriorate into a timarchy where (through a failure to regulate breeding) an inferior generation of Guardians is born, their 'silver' and 'gold' natures corrupted by 'iron' and 'bronze' (non-rational desire). In this way, they desire private wealth and status, and become the wealthy element in society, leaving the lower classes poor and oppressed. This is a society ruled by a soldier caste, and governed by the principles that they hold dear – courage, honour, ambitious endeavour, and so forth. It is the best of the unjust societies because, whilst it is not governed by reason, it at least succeeds in keeping the worst forms of selfish desire in check in the name of soldierly discipline. However, it will also make bad decisions, because it will distrust intellectual types and thus turn its back on true wisdom. The timarchic character is therefore the caricature of the soldier: harsh on discipline, respectful of authority, fond of physical pursuits, obsessed with reputation, and not overly concerned with intellectual subtleties!

Next comes *oligarchy* or rulership by a wealthy elite. The timarchy declines, corrupted by acquisition of wealth and luxury, and these become the main indications of status and power. Qualification for rulership is through wealth and not wisdom, goodness or even courage and strength. It is a society in which the rich get richer, and the poor poorer. This creates a 'drone' class, who, like the non-honey gathering bees in a hive, are useless to society, and either become beggars or criminals (this is not true of actual drone bees, incidentally, whose main job – unknown to Plato – is to fertilise the queen). The oligarchic character is therefore the archetypal thrifty businessman, concerned only with making money, which – because he loves it so much – he is very careful with. He is also himself prone to criminal behaviour, because he values wealth more than honour or honesty.

Oligarchy slides into *democracy* as the desire for wealth leads the rulers to relax laws and regulations in order to exploit the desires of the masses. But this exploitation causes further resentment, and the poor eventually rise up or force constitutional change. The resulting democracy is therefore a very liberal society, where laws are not strictly enforced and 'anything goes'. The democratic character is correspondingly highly varied and driven by 'unnecessary desires' and whims, knowing no shame, self-discipline or restraint. 'Freedom' and 'equality' are here actually guises for complete licence and lack of respect for tradition and authority – 'all pleasures are equal and should have equal rights' (561c).

The final and worst form of government is *tyranny*. This arises as conflict increases between rich and poor, and the people elect a popular leader or champion, who eventually deposes the property-owning rulers and sets himself up as tyrant. Thus, we go from complete liberty to complete subjection, as the tyrant imposes his will upon the populace – which he does, once his popularity wanes, by force if necessary. The tyrannical man is therefore concerned only with power, at whatever cost, and he is indistinguishable from the criminal type. However, despite his complete authority, he is the unhappiest of men, for, since he has no reason, honour or self-restraint, he is at the mercy of his own most bestial and lawless desires.

Plato goes into a lot of detail regarding the nature and development of these societies and corresponding individuals, which we have only outlined here, but the general point is that the further from rational and wise rulership a society or individual strays, the more unjust and unhappy they become. Finally, then, Socrates completes his answer to Thrasymachus's challenge in Book I regarding why we should be just. The best element in the tyrant – his reason – is enslaved by the worst element – his desires, just as the tyrant himself enslaves the populace, which he treats with fear and distrust. He is also forced to make deals with disreputable types (who else would deal with him?) in order to retain power, and thus, even in his inner circle, is surrounded by enemies. He is in truth the most miserable of men.

The philosopher, on the other hand, is the happiest of the character types. Because he is just, he is ruler of himself, a free man and not a slave to other passions. His life is also the most pleasant, because – having developed all three aspects of character (body, mind and spirit) – he has experienced the best of all three. And lastly, the philosopher's pleasures are the purest and most real, for they are chosen by an intellect which has been trained to recognise truth (and therefore, to distinguish between true and false pleasure). In fact (using an obscure calculation) Socrates declares the philosopher to be 729 times happier than the tyrant! Wrongdoing, then, does not pay, but rather leads to misery. Interestingly, this also shows that, whilst the Good is not itself pleasure or happiness, it may lead to them.

And here, essentially, the account of the ideal society concludes. What follows has the flavour of supplementary material (as we'll see shortly), and Socrates' final words on the matter display a certain sad resignation, for he doubts that his plan for the perfect state will ever in fact be realised, but merely remain 'as a pattern in heaven, where he who wishes it can see it and found it in his own heart' (592b).

Problems

Given Lord Acton's adage that 'absolute power corrupts absolutely', we can perhaps readily accept Socrates' general picture of the all-powerful, all-miserable dictator, hounded by his own desires and living in fear and paranoia – which were in fact features common to both Stalin and Hitler. The link between wrongdoing and unhappiness here is made through knowledge: because the bad person is not ruled by reason, he doesn't actually know what is good for him. Thus, goodness for Plato is ultimately an intellectual matter (and here we are back with the Simile of the Cave), where the highest form of goodness is reached through directly apprehending the Form of the Good. Immoral people, therefore, literally 'know not what they do'.

This is a position which is set out more fully in other dialogues such as *Gorgias*, and it consists in two related views: that good and bad are real features of the world (*moral realism*) and we can therefore hold moral beliefs which can be factually true or false (*cognitivism*). 'Murder is wrong' is true because we can check it against the Form of the Good. Thus, 'murder is wrong' is a fact in much the same sense that 'I have brown hair' is (if in fact I do). There are obviously things about this view which are appealing: it suggests that morality has objective standards which we can aim at – and sometimes miss. It also suggests, as Plato argues, that we learn to be moral, and that there are reasons to be good (it's not just a case of following rules). However, there are also problems. We can wonder what the basis is for this objective standard – we've already seen that the existence of the Forms is metaphysically dubious. Also, the existence of different moral codes in different cultures, or changes in morality over time, suggest that ethical standards are not absolutely fixed. If so, then you might suppose cultures the world over to have evolved the same moral codes – which they haven't. Also, the idea that criminal or immoral behaviour is based on ignorance is questionable. Some wrongdoers will argue that they chose their actions in full consciousness and understanding of what it meant. Furthermore, when wrongdoers have a change of heart, we might argue that emotion or empathy plays a larger role than reason: the violent person suddenly realises the predicament of his victim, perhaps. The cognitivist view, then, whilst attractive in some ways, is also beset by problems.

A more controversial claim, however, given the history of the West, is that democracy is the second-worst form of government, after dictatorship. The basis of this is that, essentially, untrained people are not fit to make political decisions. This is a cynical if not exactly uncommon position, and can still occasionally be found voiced in modern 'democracies' (off the record, perhaps). But what is the alternative? We might argue that, as Churchill said, 'democracy is the worst form of government except all the others that have been tried', and that Plato's ideal state is actually completely impractical.

Of course, modern 'democratic' states aren't actually so in the truest sense (where everyone has a direct say in government), but are really a mixture of limited (representational) democracy moulded by wealthy elites (oligarchies). It is ironic, however, that we often look to ancient Greece with a certain nostalgia, it being the birthplace of 'true' democracy, but Plato, who saw it at first hand, held it in contempt. Was he right? Of course, his personal experiences may have coloured his views somewhat: it was, after all, under a democratic government that Socrates was put to death. We might also note that his contempt for democracy was in part based on the aristocratic values which he wished to preserve – soldierly courage, respect for tradition and the divinely established order. We also have to remember that in 'democratic' Athens, women and slaves – who outnumbered the free – were not permitted to participate, so rule was really by a minority of males (Plato scores high on sexual equality, but possibly not on other forms – he may have permitted slaves in his ideal state). Modern societies, in contrast, are far more likely to value just those things which Plato cautioned against – general liberty, freedom of speech and choice, social mobility and autonomy. Given these differences, would Plato look upon Western democracy with despair, or might he see something new? It's an interesting question.

Art revisited (BK X, 595a – 608b)

The first afterthought sees Plato return to the critique of art from Books II and III, but this time in light of the analogy of the Divided Line considered in Book VI. Imagine, says Socrates, a picture of a bed. Now, this is in a sense a copy of a copy. The original – the idea or *Form* of a bed – is copied by the bedmaker, which is in turn copied by the artist. But only the gods have true knowledge of what the bed is and should be; the bedmaker simply copies other beds, without perhaps a clear idea of the purpose of the design; the artist has even less knowledge, for he does not even know how to make a bed, let alone grasp the essential idea behind it. The point of this analogy is simply to provide another reason for Plato's restriction of the arts. Despite his great respect for such as Homer and Hesiod, Socrates argues that we should trust poets, artists and other makers of representation least of all. In terms of the Divided Line, artworks do not involve knowledge, or even correct opinion, but occupy the last and least category of all: complete illusion.

Socrates illustrates this by arguing that, since art *must* employ illusion to achieve its effects, it is essentially tricking us by appealing to the least rational part of us: our senses. Just as we are fooled by a stick that appears bent in water, so we are by artistic representations of perspective and three-dimensionality. Similarly, a poet or a dramatist will exaggerate things for dramatic effect, and is not primarily concerned with presenting things as they really are or should be. Thus, all arts appeal to the non-rational and worst part of us, and tempt us to imitate bad behaviour. Accordingly, and with regret, until such time as they can make a case for their inclusion, Plato banishes all poets and artists from his ideal society.

Afterlife (BK X, 608c – 621d)

The final section concerns the rewards of goodness, which are presented in the form of a sort of fable, subsequently known as the *Myth of Er*. But before that, Socrates considers the general question of whether the soul is immortal. Physical harm merely affects or destroys the body, he argues, and perpetration of injustice and wickedness – the natural enemies of the soul, as it were – do not destroy the possessor, but in fact merely seem to give it more energy and vigour (bad people are always busy doing wrong). Therefore, a soul which cannot be destroyed must be immortal, and must have always existed.

But what of punishments and rewards? Socrates argues that – whether or not we possess the Ring of Gyges, which would make us invisible – it still pays to be moral and just, for goodness is its own reward. Whilst he is alive, the gods will bless the just man, and any misfortune he does suffer will be for his own good (as punishment for a previous existence, maybe), and the unjust will eventually get their just desserts. What's more, lest it should appear that life is unfair, Socrates claims that greater rewards and punishments are allotted after death. To illustrate this, he recounts the tale of a soldier, Er, who died on the battlefield, but came to life on his own funeral pyre with a tale of a visit to the afterlife. Er's story owes much to traditional ancient conceptions of what the dead were to expect. Judges of the dead send souls up to the skies or down below the earth, whilst others return from both places to choose their next life (Plato believed in reincarnation). Each soul is punished or rewarded in terms of time served, and the very wicked are tortured in Tartarus (the deepest part of the underworld). Er is granted a vision of the cosmos (the seven planets with Earth at the centre), pictured as a 'spindle of necessity' spun by the three fates, and hears the harmonious sound of the 'music of the spheres'. When the souls come to choose their lives, even the good are tempted by power or honour, and only a few are wise enough to choose a life of moderation. Finally, the souls drink from Lethe, the river of forgetfulness (though the wisest not too much – all knowledge being recollection, remember) – all except Er, that is, who is allowed to keep his memory in order to tell his tale on his return.

Problems

The argument for immortality here seems pretty weak and not completely clear. Plato does present better and clearer arguments in *Phaedo* (though arguably still not conclusive) and his position is better evaluated from those.

As for the Myth of Er, there is not much to be said about it, philosophically speaking, except that it is not necessarily presented as a literal account of post-mortem experience. And yet, it is tempting to see it as forming a true part of Plato's idea of morality and justice, for – as is clear from the above – he considered that there were clear rewards and punishments that made right and wrong action the better or worse course. This seems to jar somewhat with his contention that goodness is its own reward, but we might still see him as holding this position. The complaint that wrong doers do not always seem to get their just desserts is of course a common one among atheists: what sort of God would allow that to happen? We might therefore take Plato as providing a form of *compensation* argument, whereby what appears to be injustice or disproportionate suffering is actually remedied in the afterlife. It's difficult to argue against this, of course, since we will only know when the time comes! Consequently, not all philosophers choose to interpret Plato in this way, but Plato does seem to hold this position.

Conclusion

The *Republic* is arguably the greatest work of one of the great philosophers, and deserves still to be studied for that reason. It is perhaps, for modern tastes, a little long-winded in places, but it makes up for this in terms of scope and readability. The broad coverage make it an excellent place to start for anyone embarking on philosophy, and many of the controversies that it has spurred are still ongoing, all of which make it still a vibrant and living text to read.

Summary

The conventional view that justice consists in giving someone their due, either in terms of revenge or reward, must be wrong. Since being just is a form of skill, harming an enemy makes them worse, not better. Nor is it true that 'might is right', for a selfish ruler is necessarily a bad one, like a bad doctor, ignoring the political 'health' of its subjects.

Why should we be just if, as in the myth of the **Ring of Gyges**, we could act as we wished without fear of punishment? Both the individual and society are made up of various parts which must play their correct role if we are to have health/justice. The most important roles are played by the Guardian class, which includes soldiers and other protectors of society, from whom the rulers will be chosen.

To be fit for rule, a Guardian must be properly trained from childhood, through gymnastics and military training, exposure to fitting forms of music and literature, and later on philosophy and mathematics. Unfitting forms of art (poetry especially) are banned, and the educational curriculum is strictly controlled by the State.

Guardians are split into '**Rulers**' and '**Auxiliaries**' according to how they respond to their training. The cleverest and most selfless undergo further training for leadership; the others become civil servants, police, soldiers, and so on. To justify these divisions, we must propagate a '**Noble Myth**' that all people are born consisting of different 'elements' that determine their status in life. Gold and silver are possessed by Guardians, whilst bronze and iron are possessed by the general populace. Close eye must be kept on babies for promotion or demotion between classes (if gold or silver babies are born to bronze or iron parents, and vice versa). The happiness of the rulers consists solely in possession of wisdom and goodness, and serving the State. Laws need not be specified, but left to the expertise of the rulers, who will also ensure that there is no innovation in education and that the society does not become too large and unwieldy.

The ideal state (and individual) possesses four virtues: wisdom, courage, self-discipline and justice. A society ruled by the most intellectually gifted Guardians will be wise, and brave if properly protected and organised by its Auxiliaries (soldiers and ministers). It possesses self-discipline if all parts accept the rule of reason, and justice if they each perform their own role sufficiently well.

Men and women are equal, so must play an equal role in war and government. To ensure their dedication to the State, Guardians will live communally, possess no property or wealth, and all children will be raised in common. There will be no marriage, and no parents, as such, but the best will be encouraged to breed with the best (through a rigged drawing of lots, allowance being made to prevent incest). Children will go to war to observe (but not participate), and conduct within war should be honourable.

The only just ruler is the true philosopher, a person possessing a passion for knowledge for its own sake. Traditional philosophical virtues also make the philosopher an ideal ruler, in contrast with the false philosopher or **sophist**, desiring knowledge only for his own ends.

Goodness is different to pleasure, for we can always ask whether pleasure is good. **The Form of the Good** itself is like the Sun, a 'light of truth' guiding the mind to an apprehension of the perfect ideas or **Forms** that underlie reality. The Divided Line refines this picture: perception leads only to belief (*doxa*), which is either illusion (*eikasia*) or true belief (*pistis*), but to arrive at knowledge (*gnōsis*) we must employ our understanding, either indirectly through logic and reasoning (*dianoia*) or through direct apprehension of the Forms themselves (*noēsis*), the highest grade of knowledge. The Simile of the Cave illustrates this journey from ignorance (the dark cave) to knowledge (the sight of the Sun).

The rulers are trained in mathematics and dialectic (philosophical method). **Dialectic** is not quarrelling or rhetoric, or even Socratic method (*elenchus*), but a collaborative means to arrive at true understanding (the Forms).

One step down from the ideal state is **timarchy**, the ambitious society, dominated by the unintellectual soldier type and the love of status and honour, in which the populace is poor and oppressed. Next down is **oligarchy**, dominated by the businessman type, who values wealth over honour and wisdom and is prone to criminality. It is ruled by a wealthy elite, who make the poor even poorer. Next is **democracy**, which arises as the oppressed force constitutional change. It is a very liberal society lacking restraint. The worst is **tyranny**, where the poor elect a popular champion, giving up liberty for order. Once in power, the tyrant oppresses the populace and is consumed by power and bestial desires. He is the unhappiest of people, indistinguishable from the criminal. The philosopher is the happiest, being free of selfish desire.

Poets and painters are mere peddlers in illusion (***eikasia***), appealing to the least rational part in us, and must be banned from the ideal society. Art and poetry provide distorted copies of physical objects, which are themselves mere copies of ideas (the Forms).

Since the soul cannot be harmed, it is immortal. The good or evil that befalls us in life is deserved, or meant to teach us. The soul's rewards or punishments in the afterlife also show that the gods are just, and that it pays to be moral. This is illustrated by the **Myth of Er**, which relates a soldier's tale of his visit to the afterlife.

Glossary

Auxiliaries   Those *Guardians* who perform secondary roles (soldiers, police, ministers, etcetera) in support of the *Rulers*.

Democracy   Literally, a society ruled by the people.

Dialectic   In the Platonic sense, the method of collaborative philosophical discussion whereby the highest form of truth is uncovered (see also *elenchus*).

Dianoia   Knowledge through logic and deduction; mathematical and geometrical knowledge.

Doxa   Belief, based on perception (can be true or false, but not knowledge).

Eikasia   False belief or illusion, based on perception.

Elenchus   Socratic questioning/method – the means whereby Socrates interrogated others in order to draw out their knowledge (but usually to reveal their ignorance).

Eugenics   The production of ideal physical traits through selective breeding or genetic engineering.

Forms   The Platonic concept of independent, objective, perfect ideas – the ultimate objects of knowledge.

Form of the Good   The highest *Form*, the supreme source of knowledge and truth.

Gnōsis   Knowledge.

Guardians   The general protector class of the ideal society, from which are drawn the *Rulers* and *Auxiliaries*.

Hedonism   The view that pleasure is the ultimate good.

Innate ideas   The view, often associated with rationalists, that the most fundamental concepts are somehow present in the mind from birth.

Myth of Er   The tale of afterlife punishment and reward related by Er, a soldier who is given a near-death vision.

Noble myth   The story told to the populace of the ideal state in order to justify and reinforce social roles.

Noēsis   The highest form of knowledge, involving direct apprehension of the *Forms*.

Oligarchy   A society ruled by a wealthy elite.

Pistis   True belief, based on trust in sense perception, not knowledge.

Ring of Gyges   Greek myth concerning Gyges, who used a ring of invisibility to commit immoral acts with impunity.

Rulers The philosopher kings of the ideal state, the most intelligent, selfless and upright of the *Guardians*.

Sophist In ancient Greece, a form of hired teacher of rhetoric, philosophy and argument. Often used as a disparaging term for someone who holds a form of relativism.

Timarchy/timocracy A society ruled by a military elite.

Tyranny A society ruled by a single individual or tyrant, usually protected by a private army.

Further reading

The Republic, translated by Desmond Lee (Penguin Classics).

Plato and the Republic, by Nickolas Pappas (Routledge). A detailed and readable guide, with good links to other works and further reading. Ideal for someone studying the *Republic* in depth or interested in more thorough analysis.

Plato's Republic: A Biography, by Simon Blackburn (Atlantic Press). A critical discussion of the continued relevance of the Republic and Plato's philosophy in general, written in Blackburn's usual entertaining and engaging manner.

If you want to explore Plato's other works, something like Neel Burton's *Plato's Shadow: A Primer on Plato* (Acheron Press) gives a very readable general summary of almost all the dialogues, together with themes and background, and is a good reference for comparisons between texts. A very good introduction to Plato and his thought is C. J. Rowe's *Plato* (Harvester Press) in the Philosophers in Context series. As for the works themselves, *The Statesman* and *The Laws* present the remainder of Plato's opinions on political matters. *Gorgias* is a good, approachable example of an early-middle Socratic-type dialogue, and *Phaedo* details Plato's arguments concerning the immortality of the soul and his attitude to death. For the more adventurous, *Timaeus* details some of Plato's more mystical, mathematical and obscure doctrines.

Finally, Karl Popper's *The Open Society and its Enemies*, vol. 1, is perhaps the most famous attack on Plato's political views, providing a brilliant and radically alternative reading of Plato's philosophy, the motivation behind the *Republic*, and his relationship with Socrates.

2
René Descartes: *Meditations on First Philosophy* (1641)

Background

Descartes's (1596–1650) *Meditations* is one of the most important works in the rationalist tradition of philosophy. Rationalism is characterised by a belief that all the major problems of philosophy – and perhaps all the major intellectual problems of the world, full stop – can be answered by the application of rational thought alone.

Rationalists believe that one can understand the fundamental nature of reality just by thinking clearly about it and reasoning from 'first principles': self-evident truths that no-one can deny. This reasoning will be deductive in nature. That is to say, arguments will proceed from premises to conclusions by a logically water-tight method. In this way, arguments in philosophy are like sums in mathematics. Just as we add together two numbers to produce a third, so we can add together two propositions (premises), such as 'Lions are mammals' and 'Mammals do not lay eggs' to produce a third proposition (conclusion): 'Lions do not lay eggs'. This method of reasoning is as secure as maths and if we follow it, we can achieve the same degree of certainty in philosophy as we do in arithmetic and geometry.

As we shall see when we look at Hume's *Enquiry concerning Human Understanding*, there are grave difficulties with this rationalist approach. But its attractions should be obvious. For example, many people, from the comfort of their armchairs, consider questions such as the nature of time and wonder if time could have an end. This seems crazy, for if time ended, then there would be something which came after time. But if there is an after-time, then time hasn't ended at all, since the whole notion of 'after' is a temporal one. Therefore, time has no end.

Whenever someone reasons like this, they are reasoning in the spirit of rationalism. However, though such arguments can seem convincing, in the light of contemporary physics we have good reasons not to trust them. The argument about time offered above, for example, is far too simplistic and naïve, despite its intuitive plausibility. It is based on the common-sense idea that there must always be something which comes after something that has ended. But this common sense is contradicted by Einstein's theory of relativity, which argues that the idea of 'after time' makes no sense, since 'after' is itself a temporal notion. The question 'What comes after time?' is therefore meaningless.

The *Meditations* is one of the paradigms of rationalism and its success or failure to a certain degree reflects the success or failure of rationalism. This is what makes it such an interesting text to read, despite the fact that so much of what it argues can seem to be hopelessly wrong. But we should be careful not to dismiss the *Meditations* so easily. It is a remarkably rich text and if one returns to it, one always discovers something new to take away. It is too easy to dismiss it as obviously wrong, for even where Descartes does go astray, his errors are highly instructive and go to the heart of many fundamental issues in the methodology and principles of philosophy.

The text

The *Meditations* is written as if it were a diary written over six consecutive days. This is modelled on the religious retreat, where people would enter a monastery or similar institution for seven days to pray and contemplate. As with the creation myth of *Genesis*, there are six days of work – the meditations themselves – while the seventh day is one of rest.

Of course, the impression that the book was written over six consecutive days is a literary device. One reason for writing the book in this way is that it gives the reader a framework within which to read it. One could, and perhaps should, read the *Meditations* over six nights, making sure that one allows plenty of time to think about the contents of each meditation before moving on to the next. The model of the retreat thus provides a model for the reader, who is encouraged to approach the text with unhurried contemplation.

There are also pragmatic reasons why Descartes might have wanted the structure of the book to echo that of a religious retreat. Many saw his rationalist approach to questions of God's existence and the nature of the soul as heretical and, indeed, the *Meditations* was banned by the Catholic Church for many years. By presenting the book in an essentially religious mode, Descartes perhaps hoped to reassure the religious authorities of its piety.

Descartes took the unusual step of inviting objections to his arguments from eminent colleagues and publishing these, along with his replies, in the book. (The Cambridge University Press edition of the book contains a helpful selection of these.) This reinforces the sense that this is a text for the reader to grapple and argue with for themselves. It is not a treatise to be digested and regurgitated but an argument in which the reader must participate. The book should be read in this spirit.

First meditation

Descartes starts the *Meditations* with an explanation of what motivated him to write it. He believed that 'it was necessary...to demolish everything completely and start again right from the foundations if I wanted to establish anything at all in the sciences that was stable and likely to last.' To reach certain knowledge, it is necessary to eliminate all beliefs that could be doubted and keep only those of which he could be certain. In the objections and replies, he offers a metaphor to explain this idea. If there are some rotten apples in your basket, the best way to eliminate them is to tip out the basket, examine each apple one by one, and only place back into the basket those that are definitely good. Similarly, Descartes will reject all his beliefs, and only accept anew those which prove to be certain. Hence, doubting everything is a *method* of reaching certain truth, a means to an end, not an end in itself. This is an important point to remember, since many casual readers believe Descartes's purpose is to make us more doubtful, rather than to simply use doubt to make us more certain.

Descartes also notes that it is not necessary to consider each of his beliefs one by one if he is to doubt them: 'Once the foundations of a building are undermined, anything built on them collapses of its own accord.' To cast doubt on his beliefs he need only consider the foundations of his beliefs.

Aiming to get at the root of his beliefs, Descartes first considers his senses, which he believes are the source of many of his beliefs. On reflection, it does seem that most, if not all, of our ideas have their origin in what we see, hear, taste, touch or feel. Descartes's argument that all beliefs based on the senses should be considered uncertain can be summarised as:

> 'From time to time I have found that the senses deceive.'
> 'It is prudent never to trust completely those who have deceived us even once.'
> Therefore, it is prudent not to trust our senses completely.

Although this argument appears sound, the conclusion, as it stands, does not justify wholesale doubt. As Descartes puts it, surely only madmen can doubt all everyday sense-based beliefs. All his argument means is that we should not *completely* trust our senses.

However, so long as there is doubt that some of our sense-based beliefs are false and there is no way of telling which of our sense-based beliefs are true and which are false, we are unable to completely trust any particular sense-based belief. It is as though you have 100 coins and know that one is a fake, but not which one. This means that when you pick any coin, you cannot be sure it is genuine. Similarly, once the seed of doubt is sewn, all beliefs become uncertain.

Descartes also confronts the madman objection more directly by claiming that we cannot be sure we are not like madmen ourselves. His argument goes something like this:

> When I sleep, I have sense experiences of things which do not exist.
> 'there are never any sure signs by means of which being awake can be distinguished from being asleep.'
> Therefore, there are no sure means of knowing whether the things I experience through my senses exist or not.

If this is true, then we could be like madmen in that all we take to be true could be illusory, a mere dream. Descartes accepts this argument. Without any way of being sure if we are asleep or awake, there is room for us to doubt that we are awake and hence room for us to suspect that all our waking experience is a lie.

As you will have noticed, the first meditation, like much of the rest of the book, is proceeding like an argument or debate, with Descartes playing the role of both critic and defender. For every argument he puts forward, he considers an objection and then either accepts it or offers a reply. This reinforces the sense of the *Meditations* as a practical course of argument which the reader should engage in.

Continuing with the argument, Descartes considers an objection which suggests his dreaming argument does not justify wholesale doubt.

Though it is true that all the particular things we perceive may not exist, there must exist some general types of things from which our illusions are fashioned. Compare this to a painting of, say, a dragon. Of course, dragons may not exist, but all the elements – heads, eyes, tails, fire and so on – do exist. If they did not, then we would be unable to imagine a creature comprising them all.

But then doubt comes back. Surely any composite thing could be invented. Even an eye can be imagined from the basic raw materials of shape and colour. In our dreams we can imagine almost anything.

However, even when dreaming some things cannot be doubted, such as the basic concepts of arithmetic and geometry: shape and number. The truths of maths and geometry cannot be doubted because they do not depend on whether things really exist or not. Awake or dreaming, $2 + 2 = 4$ must be true.

At this point Descartes introduces the biggest doubt of them all. It is not beyond God's power to make us believe that something is self-evident even if it is false. God could be deceiving us. Nothing could seem more obvious than the fact that $2 + 2 = 4$, but it is within God's power to make the false look obviously true, so we cannot even be sure that we are right about this.

This raises a problem for the very idea of God himself, which can be stated as:

> If God were good, he wouldn't allow me to be deceived.
> I am sometimes deceived. (By my senses – see earlier.)
> Therefore, God is either not good or doesn't exist.

Descartes clearly isn't convinced by this argument and in the sixth meditation he explains why God allows us to be deceived even though he is good. All he is doing here is considering the ultimate – for him – doubt, that God doesn't exist. If this is the case, he believes that there is even more reason to doubt everything, because that means his own existence must have been a result of chance, which is an imperfect cause more likely to lead to imperfections in his intellect.

For some reason, perhaps so as not to appear blasphemous, instead of considering the possibility that God is a deceiver, Descartes introduces the idea of an evil demon which could be deceiving him into thinking falsehoods even about maths and geometry. The specific form of this device is unimportant. We can think of many reasons why a person may believe falsehoods to be definitely true, such as dreaming, drugs, hypnosis or brainwashing.

Descartes ends the first meditation without any firm knowledge at all. Once he allows that anything he can doubt must be rejected as uncertain and therefore not known, it seems nothing can be known at all. Although Descartes takes us through a structured series of doubts, we could arrive at the same conclusion any number of ways. If we ask the question, 'Is there anything so clear and obvious that it cannot be doubted to be true?', the answer is bound to be, 'no,' with one exception, which we will come to in the second meditation. Hence, the idea of a deceiving demon is perhaps unnecessary.

Problems

Having shown that virtually everything can be doubted and is therefore somewhat uncertain, where do we go from here? Descartes moves on to find out the one fact which cannot be doubted and builds up from there. But perhaps the moral of the story should be that if we say that immunity from doubt is required for something to be true or known, then nothing can be true or known. Therefore, maybe we simply have the wrong idea of what it means to know something. Immunity from doubt is simply too strict a requirement for knowledge.

There are other problems caused by the stress Descartes places on truths which are beyond all doubt. Descartes hopes to build foundations which are true, upon which he can build up truth to an all-encompassing system. But how will he know when he has discovered foundations which are true? He will know because these foundations will be indubitable – above all doubt. Although indubitable does not mean the same as true, Descartes does seem to believe that if X is indubitable, then it is true. (Which is not to say if it is dubitable then it is false.) Is this claim credible?

There are difficulties with this approach. To say X is indubitable is to state a psychological fact: certainty and doubt are states of mind in the person who is certain or doubting. To say X is true or that one knows that X, on the other hand, is to state an *epistemological* truth – something about what is actually known or true. Why should we believe that we can move so easily from psychological facts to epistemological ones? This point is put well in the objections. It seems that nothing is so absurd or irrational that someone either asleep or mad could not believe it to be certain and indubitable.

It doesn't seem contradictory to doubt something we know, or be certain of something that turns out to be false. However, there is a long tradition in philosophy of thinking of knowledge as being a particular state of mind. If we question this assumption, then we strike at the *Meditations* at the root. But this invites further questions, particularly: what other tests are there for something to be true?

Some critics have objected to Descartes's idea that the senses deceive, on the grounds that the metaphorical nature of this claim is not fully appreciated. Similarly, when we talk about 'illusions', it is not at all clear that sticks appearing bent in water, or tall objects appearing short in the distance are really illusions at all. Rather, in these cases, things appear to us precisely as they should appear, given the nature of the world and our senses. So perhaps it would be more accurate to talk about 'perceptual errors' rather than illusions and deceptions.

This doesn't eliminate the sceptical doubts, however. The fact that we err about the world and that we cannot easily tell when we are erring is enough to introduce the doubt that our errors could be more general. But now it seems that the error is not necessarily one of our senses, but also of our judgement. If it could be shown that our minds as well as our senses make errors of which they are unaware about the external world, then it is more difficult for Descartes to maintain, as he does, that the mind cannot be in error when it clearly and distinctly perceives ideas. And if the mind is to share the blame with the senses for mistakes, then how can certain knowledge come from the mind?

A further difficulty is that Descartes talks about the senses and our judgments as if these things can be easily separated. But is this really possible? For it to be so would require there to be 'raw sense-data' – perceptions before the mind gets to work on them – and then an interpreting mind. But it is not at all clear that there are such things as raw sense data. Another way to think about this is to ask the question, do we really do two things when we experience the world: perceive *and* judge? If you think we do, try and explain what perceiving without judging is, and how we can do it.

Again, this objection intertwines judgement and sense experience in such a way as to make Descartes's claim that judgement is absolutely distinct from sense experience dubious.

A final difficulty, and one which will be echoed later, is that in order to undertake the meditations, Descartes must be able to distinguish truth and falsehood. He claims that he can, since whatever one clearly and distinctly perceives to be true must be true. Clearly, there must be a difference between what *is* clearly and distinctly perceived and what merely *appears to be* clearly and distinctly perceived. But Descartes does not show what this difference is, and it is hard to see how he could do so.

Second meditation

Having ended the first meditation with no beliefs that are beyond doubt, in the second meditation, Descartes attempts to lay down the foundations which will enable him to rebuild his knowledge on a surer basis. He does this by discovering the one thing that cannot be doubted, and that is that 'I am, I exist'.

Most people are familiar with Descartes's more famous 'I think, therefore I am' (*cogito ergo sum*). But that formulation appears in the *Discourse on Method*, not in the *Meditations*. The difference in wording is significant. 'I think, therefore I am' is in the form of an argument: the fact that 'I am' is deduced from the fact that 'I think'. But 'I am, I exist' is not an argument. Rather, it is an incontrovertible intuition. One directly *apprehends* the fact that one exists as soon as one thinks – one doesn't need to *deduce* that one exists from the fact that one thinks.

Not everyone agrees that one is directly aware of one's own existence in this way. David Hume, in his *Treatise of Human Nature*, for example, argued that when he directed his attention to his own thoughts, all he was aware of were the thoughts themselves. He was not aware of the self which had them. Instead of 'I think, therefore I am', perhaps all Descartes was entitled to deduce was 'I think, therefore there is thought going on'.

Let us suppose that Descartes has established that something – 'I' – exists. What is this 'I'? Descartes has a two-part argument to answer this question. The first can be summarised as:

1. If I can conceive of myself without a property, then that property is not a part of my essential nature.
2. Of all the properties I think I have, such as the having of a body and the thinking of thoughts, only the fact that I think is 'inseparable from me'.
3. Therefore, it is my essential nature to be a thinking thing, no more, and no less.
4. This he takes to establish that his essence is that of a thinking thing. But what sort of thing is this? The second part of the argument aims to provide the answer:
5. This mind cannot be a body, as I can conceive of myself without a body.
6. However, it is clearly not nothing, so it must be something.
7. Hence, it must be a different sort of thing to corporeal things. It must be a purely mental substance.

This is a startling conclusion. Descartes has argued that he is, in essence, a kind of non-material substance which thinks, but has none of the properties of matter. It is singular and indivisible since consciousness is a single centre of thought and as such cannot be divided. In short, he claims to have proved the existence of the soul.

Problems

Descartes's argument is endlessly fascinating but appears to have several major flaws. One is that he appears to think that if two *concepts* are separable, then that implies the *things* to which the concepts apply are always separable. We can see this in the first premise of the argument above, which is the general principle: 'If I can conceive of a thing without a property, then that property is not a part of its essential nature.' For example, although all the cars I know of are made of metal, metallicity is not part of a car's essential nature, as a car which is not made of metal would still be a car. The same appears to be true of mind and body: body cannot be part of the essence of mind, as a mind without a body would still be a mind.

Nevertheless, Descartes draws a dubious conclusion from this. To see why, we have to distinguish between ontological (concerned with being) and conceptual independence or dependence. For example, a husband is ontologically independent from his wife. That is to say, his existence does not depend upon that of his wife. But the *concept* of a husband is dependent upon the concept of a wife. We could not have the concept of a husband if we didn't have a concept of a wife.

Descartes's argument hinges on the claim that because mind is conceptually independent from body, it must also be ontologically independent. This is a very strong claim and is what distinguishes dualism from other theories of the mind. But why should we accept this? For example, the concept of water is arguably independent from the concept of H_2O, but that is not to say we could ever have water that was not H_2O. Similarly, I can imagine myself existing without a body, but that doesn't mean I actually could exist without my body.

This objection is a denial of the first premises in each part of the summary of Descartes's argument above. This illustrates the potential problems of using imagination as a guide to possibility. The fact that we are not aware of anything physical in our essence and so could imagine being non-physical does not prove that we are in fact non-physical in nature. Just as the fact that many are unaware that being H_2O is part of the essence of water, so it may be true that being physical is part of the essence of being a person.

We can push this objection further and ask if it is even possible to have a clear and distinct idea of oneself without a body. If you think about it, imagining oneself without a body tends to be more of a case of imagining oneself invisible, but still basically in space, interacting with objects via various senses and so on. This sounds suspiciously like having a body! The problem with Descartes is that it is not enough to have a vague idea of oneself without a body: unless this idea is clear and distinct, it cannot be taken to be certain and by his own principles, anything uncertain goes the way of the rotten apples.

Another problem is that Descartes's argument appears to blur the distinction between a thing and what it does. If something walks (performs an action), it doesn't mean it is a walk (is an action). So, if something uses its intellect (performs mental tasks), it doesn't mean it is an intellect (is a mental thing). From the fact that I think, the only thing we can conclude is that whatever I am, I have the faculty of thought. But that doesn't prove that the thing which has this faculty is not corporeal (bodily). In other words, Descartes is wrong to infer from the fact that I think to the fact that I am a mental substance. Gilbert Ryle calls this error Descartes's 'category mistake'. Descartes thought that because the mind didn't have the same properties as body, it must be a different sort of thing to body. But there are other explanations. Mind could be a function of body, for example. This is a denial of the fifth premise above: mind is neither a thing nor a nothing, but rather a feature of a thing, probably the embodied brain.

Descartes's view has one very odd consequence. Because he thinks it is our essence to think, it follows that to stop thinking is to cease to exist. But then, how do we explain times when we are not thinking, such as in sleep? There are three possibilities. The first is that we die when we sleep. This is clearly absurd. The second, which Descartes believed, is that we do always think, only we don't always remember that we have. This is implausible. The third is that it is wrong to say that a mind must always be thinking. Rather, a mind must have the capacity to think. In the same way that it is the essence of a knife that it be suitable for cutting with, not that it always will be cutting, so the essence of mind could be that it *can* think, not that it always *is* thinking. But then, if mind is merely something with the capacity to think, why can't a physical object have this capacity? This third option seems to eliminate the need for special mental substances.

A final worry about Descartes's argument is that it doesn't so much provide a positive description of mind as a negative one. We are left with an account of all the things mind is not: not a bodily structure, not air, not a thing which walks and senses, and so on. If we simply list all the things which a mind is not, have we really thereby said what it is?

The piece of wax

Descartes has argued that the only thing he cannot doubt is that he exists, and that he is a thinking thing (*res cogitans*). However, at first sight, there is something that strikes him as odd about this. He seems to have a clear idea of what corporeal objects are like, but no clear idea as to his own nature. But how can his idea of what can be doubted be less clear than his idea of what is certain? To see if this really is the case, he considers a corporeal object, a piece of wax. How does he reach knowledge about the wax's nature?

The first hypothesis he considers is that he knows an object from his sense perceptions of it. Descartes lists all the features of the wax his senses are aware of: its smell, colour, appearance, texture and so on. But then he notes that all these features can change, and yet he is still aware of it as the same piece of wax. This means that it is not the information he gets from his senses which enables him to identify and know the nature of the wax. All the sense information is liable to change, and yet his knowledge that the wax is still there is constant. Therefore, the senses cannot be the source of his knowledge, so he rejects this hypothesis.

The second hypothesis is that imagination is the source of his knowledge of the wax. By imagination Descartes means to mentally represent sense perceptions (e.g. to picture something). Even though the sense-dependent features such as colour, smell and so on of the wax can change, we also have an idea of it as something extended, flexible and changeable. But imagination cannot give us this idea, because the imagination cannot run through all the possible changes the wax may undergo. Our understanding of what would constitute a piece of wax is wider than all those particular examples we can imagine. So this hypothesis, too, is found wanting.

This leads him to his third hypothesis, that the mind is the source of his knowledge. It is our minds which have an idea of what the wax is and which comprehend its true nature, and this knowledge is far superior to that provided by the senses or imagination. So the mind alone is the source of our knowledge about the world. The mind can conceive of what the wax is, and this goes further than either sensing or imagining can.

So, what I literally perceive is not a piece of wax, or a person, for example. What I perceive are merely collections of shapes, colours, smells and sounds. It is only through the mind that these can be understood as the objects which they are, so it is really more true to say that it is the mind which perceives the wax: the senses merely report the sensible qualities of the wax (its 'incidents'), which are not enough to reveal its true nature. Compare this to a camera. A camera merely records colours, it doesn't interpret what these various colours represent. Similarly, our senses merely report sense information: our minds interpret it.

His considerations about the piece of wax persuade Descartes that, in fact, he does know his own mind more perfectly than corporeal things. The mind is primary – it comes before knowledge of material things – because without the mind we could not even recognise material objects and the fact that we perceive at all confirms that we exist. Both these are reasons for saying that the mind is better known than corporeal objects, despite first appearances suggesting the contrary.

Descartes's conclusion is a little puzzling, because although his reflections do indeed seem to confirm that sense perception depends upon his having a mind, it doesn't seem to illuminate the nature of that mind. Certainly, it establishes that he exists and thinks, but it doesn't seem to reveal anything more about his existence. The discussion of the wax does not seem to add to our understanding of what kind of thing we really are.

It is also unclear how our understanding of the wax is truly independent of our awareness of its incidents – its smell, colour, shape and so on. If you take away the 'incidents' of the wax, just what is it that you have a clear understanding of? Do we really have a clear idea of a piece of wax that doesn't involve reference to these incidents? Perhaps this shows how our understanding is not quite as independent of our senses as Descartes believes.

Third meditation

The first four paragraphs of this meditation reveal something interesting about Descartes's idea of clear and distinct perception, summarise the argument so far and explain why an argument proving God's existence and non-deceiving nature is required if the *Meditations* are to progress.

Descartes has been searching for knowledge that is certain and indubitable. In order to search for something, though, you must be able to recognise it when you find it! So Descartes must have been working with an idea or a feeling of what certain knowledge is like. He claims to know that he exists when he thinks. So how can he know this? Because there is a 'clear and distinct perception' of his own existence. This is not sense perception, but more like mental apprehension. Could this having of a clear and distinct perception be what knowing something for certain is? Descartes thinks so and we can follow through his thinking to complete an implicit deduction to this conclusion:

> '[A clear and distinct perception] would not be enough to make me certain... if it could ever turn out that something which I perceived with such clarity and distinctness was false.'
> Clear and distinct perception is enough to make me certain
> Something clearly and distinctly perceived cannot be false.

This argument is certainly valid, but it is not sound because it is circular. The first premise is true if the conclusion is true, but the conclusion can only be deduced if we accept the first premise. But is the first premise true? Surely it is possible for something to be clear and make me certain of it, and yet be false? At least some people must have thought that nothing could be more obvious than that the world was flat, and yet they were wrong. Things can appear clear and make a person certain, and yet be false.

Descartes now has a problem. He has resolved only to accept those things that are certain. But things clearly and distinctly perceived are not certain. Indeed, he hasn't managed to explain how we can tell the difference between *really* clearly and distinctly perceiving and only *seeming* to do so. So what is certain to be true? Nothing, it seems, except the fact that he exists. It seems that Descartes has led himself down the dark and narrow path to solipsism – the belief that only my own existence is certain.

Descartes himself thinks there is a way out of this dark hole. The obstacle to overcome is that though he clearly and distinctly perceives that he exists, that $2+3=5$ and so on, he admits that if God were a deceiver, he could be wrong even here. In other words, if God deceives, then even what he clearly and distinctly perceives could be false. So in order to move ahead with absolute certainty, he must discover whether God exists and whether he is a deceiver. It is vital to realise how important this is for Descartes's project.

The existence of God

Descartes now attempts his first proof for the existence of God. He starts with considerations about ideas (which also include sensations and perceptions) and how many have their source outside of us. For example, when I feel heat from a fire, it is clear that the source of this perception is not something within me and under my control. I feel the heat whether I like it or not.

The problem is that, although many ideas have their source outside of me, I cannot be sure that the ideas I have truly resemble their causes. For example, a person can be made to feel a burning sensation if they are told something hot is going to be pushed against their back and an ice cube is then placed there. So we cannot learn anything about the cause of our ideas just by considering the ideas themselves.

Nonetheless, Descartes does go on to construct an argument for the existence of God based on ideas and their causes. He does this by invoking what we might call the causal reality principle: a principle which Descartes believes is evidently true by 'the natural light'. The natural light is an odd phrase in Descartes. It sounds like something mysterious and mystical, but is generally used to refer to things which are so clear and self-evidently true that they cannot be doubted. The causal reality principle is one such truth and it states that 'there must be at least as much reality in the efficient and total cause as in the effect of that cause'. Put more simply: 'Something cannot arise from nothing, and...what is more perfect...cannot arise from what is less perfect.'

Descartes's terminology can make things appear more complex than they are. For instance, he talks about the 'efficient' cause, which in Aristotle's terminology is the event which begins the change that produces the effect. But since he also talks about the 'total' cause, the principle is not narrowed by talk of efficient causes after all. He also talks about ideas or things containing 'more reality', but for our purposes we can take this simply to mean that these things are more perfect or more complete.

Of course, these technical distinctions are important in high-level scholarly debate about Descartes. But for the reader new to the *Meditations*, the causal reality principle can be simply understood as the idea that an effect can never be more than its cause: you only get out what you put in.

How do we get from this principle to God? Well, although almost all our ideas are of things which are no greater than we are, we have one idea which is of something far greater than ourselves: God. By God, Descartes means something which is 'infinite, independent, supremely intelligent, supremely powerful and which created both myself and everything else...which exists'. Such an idea could not possibly have originated in Descartes himself, so it must have originated in something as great as the idea itself: God. Therefore, God must exist.

This argument seems too quick. Yet despite the slow build up, it is all indeed found in one short paragraph of the *Meditations*. To see if it stands up, we need to unpack it carefully, as Descartes himself does in the remainder of the third meditation, anticipating objections to clarify the argument.

The most obvious objection is that you do not need an infinite being to exist to give you the idea of the infinite. We can arrive at the idea of the infinite by merely negating the idea of the finite. For example, we all know what a piece of string with an end is like. All we need to do is to imagine such a piece of string *without* an end and we have the idea of infinity.

Descartes's response to this is rather unsatisfactory. Since, he claims, the idea of the infinite contains 'more reality' than the idea of the finite, it must be prior to the idea of the finite. This response really lays bare the main weakness of the argument. Descartes's response here is really little more than a reaffirmation of the causal reality principle. This principle states that something less perfect can only be caused by something at least as perfect, and therefore the idea of the finite must have as its cause the idea of the infinite and not vice-versa. But what the piece of string objection really says is that the causal reality principle itself is false. It offers a counter-example. It shows us that, in fact, there is no problem at all in seeing how a greater idea can spring from a lesser one. It is no good turning around and saying this can't be true because of the causal reality principle: the whole point of the counter-example is to show that the causal reality principle is false.

This is the problem of the remainder of the meditation. Descartes considered many objections, but they are all dealt with on the assumption that the causal reality principle is true. So, for example, he argues that the idea of God can't be caused by nothing because nothing can be caused by nothing. Similarly, Descartes considers and rejects the possibility that he is the cause of these ideas because he is greater than he thinks. This is an attempt to offer an alternative explanation of how we get the idea of God within the framework of the causal reality principle.

None of these objections get to the root of the problem, perhaps because Descartes is so convinced that the causal reality principle is manifest by the natural light that he thinks it has no need of any further justification. But there are at least two ways of attacking the principle.

The first is to draw upon the distinction between ideas and things. We might accept it is true that something lesser cannot be the cause of something greater. But that may not mean that something lesser cannot create the *idea* of something greater. For example, maybe I cannot produce something which manifests more intelligence than I have. But I can have the idea of something more intelligent than myself. We are not so limited in our ideas that we cannot conceive of many things greater than ourselves. The causal reality principle has some plausibility when it comes to physical causation, but seems less plausible when applied to the creation of ideas.

The second objection is to question the general truth of the principle itself. The main problem is that the principle is evidently not true if taken at face value. For instance, current scientific theory states that everything around us is the effect of a big bang that heralded the beginning of time and space. In many ways, this complex universe with its manifold life forms is greater than the simple explosion of energy that occurred at the big bang. Yet if the causal reality principle were true, we could never have got from the big bang to here.

It is true that most scientists believe that the total sum of energy in the universe must remain constant. In this sense it is true that nothing comes of nothing. But the causal reality principle seems to imply something broader: that the more complex cannot be caused by the less complex; that the less intelligent can never give rise to the more intelligent; that the smaller can never give rise to the larger; and so on. All these specific claims are contradicted by current science.

Interestingly, even the idea that nothing can come from nothing is being challenged by science. Baffling though it may sound, it is believed that the amount of matter in the universe is exactly balanced by the amount of anti-matter. In other words, subtract anti-matter from matter and you get zero. This means that the big bang could indeed have come out of nothing – as the net amount of matter in the universe is zero!

The argument Descartes offers is therefore on very shaky ground. It is based entirely on a principle which Descartes believes to be self-evidently true, but which, on reflection, seems much less secure. If Descartes requires a proof for the existence of God for his project to succeed, he needs another one. In the fifth meditation he does indeed try once more. But first, he turns to the question of truth and falsity.

Fourth meditation

In the philosophy of religion, a major issue is the so-called problem of evil: why, if God is all-good and all-powerful, does God allow suffering and evil in the world? Attempts to resolve this problem are known as theodicies. In the fourth meditation, Descartes offers a kind of theodicy to answer the problem of evil's kid brother – the problem of error.

Here, the problem is, if God is all-good and all-powerful, why does he allow people to be so mistaken about the nature of reality and his existence? If he does this – which surely he does – it seems he is wilfully allowing the truth to be hidden from us. Why would God want to do that?

Descartes is convinced that whatever the explanation, it cannot be because God wants to deceive us, since trickery and deception involve a lack of perfection and this is contrary to God's nature (which, after the third meditation, he claims to perceive clearly and distinctly). We could question why Descartes is so sure that deception is contrary to God's nature, but at the very least, if God is a deceiver then he is very different to how we usually take him to be.

Descartes's first solution to this problem does not entirely satisfy him. He considers the possibility that it is because his rational capacities are not infinite. In his rather odd language, if God is the supreme being and his opposite is non-being, then Descartes, as a mortal human, lies somewhere in between.

The reason this answer does not suffice is that error is not simply a matter of *negation:* of the person in error lacking something. It is also a matter of *privation*: their not having something – knowledge – which they could otherwise have been given. To give an analogy, if a person in a wheelchair cannot reach the buttons on an elevator, then we could say this is because they are not tall enough to reach it. There is a negation – something they lack – which explains why they can't reach the buttons. But surely it is more accurate to say that this is a case of privation: they could have reached the buttons if the designer had placed them lower. In the same way, our error seems not solely to be explained in terms of our limits, but also in terms of what our creator has deliberately made it possible for us to not have.

Before giving another, better explanation, Descartes first builds in some caveats. First, it is not surprising if he doesn't fully understand God's ways, for he is not God. Second, although our error may appear to be a fault in the universe, perhaps if we looked at the universe as a whole, we would see it as essential to its perfect workings. This may seem a bit like cheating, as it implies that even if Descartes fails to explain why God allows error, we shouldn't worry. We just need to trust that God knows best. How we respond to this depends on how we approach this part of the *Meditations*. For people who already believe in God, it can serve as a piece of apologetics: that is to say, it gives a rational account of how the idea of God can be reconciled with the doubts reason produces. If this is how we read it, it only has to find a place for faith within a rational framework, not to justify faith by reason. But if we approach the text as non-believers, these caveats will seem only to be fudges.

So how does Descartes finally explain error? He does so by explaining the different roles of the faculty of knowledge and the faculty of will. These are very different. As finite beings, our knowledge is limited. For this we cannot blame God, for finite beings must have finite intellect. In addition to this faculty, God also gave us free will. Unlike knowledge, however, a free will is not something which admits of greater or lesser degrees. You either have free will or you do not. God does not have more free will than humans in the same way as he has more knowledge. Again, we cannot blame God for this, since if he were to give us free will at all, he had to give it to us all or nothing. We should rather be grateful that he gave it to us at all.

But what happens when you combine a finite intellect with an unlimited freedom? What happens is that humans fail to limit their freedom so it corresponds to the scope of their intellect. On occasions where they should refrain from assenting or dissenting because they don't have the knowledge to make a proper judgement, they sometimes assent or dissent anyway and thus fall into error. Hence, the way to avoid error is to refuse to make any judgement unless one perceives that something is clearly and distinctly true.

Error is thus the improper use of our free will to make judgements that go beyond what we know. This implies no criticism of God because in granting us finite intellect and unlimited will, he gave us as much as he could. Rather, it is our fault if we overextend ourselves by making judgements about things we do not have clear knowledge about.

Nonetheless, there is still a problem: couldn't God have built in a few safety mechanisms? For example, could he not have given us a kind of instinct that made us refrain from overextending our will in this way? Could he not have created us so that we were naturally cautious when making judgements about things not clearly and distinctly perceived to be true, rather than making us the way we are – all too prone to make such errors?

Descartes considers these objections and then pulls from out of his sleeve the 'get out of jail free' cards he showed us earlier: maybe in the grand scheme of things it is better this way and I have no right to question God's reasons for making me the way I am. For the religious believer, such explanations may suffice. But for the person who remains to be convinced, this is a disappointing answer to a major problem with Descartes's argument.

Fifth meditation

As we saw in the third meditation, Descartes needs to prove that God exists, and that he is not a deceiver, in order to remove the doubt that he could be wrong even about such truths as those of mathematics. He made one attempt at this in the third meditation and tries again here, using a different strategy. The type of argument used is known as the ontological argument for God's existence.

Descartes's approach is to consider God's essence and try to show how God's essence necessitates his existence. He claims to be able to do this without presupposing God exists. How is this done? Descartes starts by considering geometric shapes; in particular, a triangle. An essential property of a triangle is that all its internal angles add up to 180 degrees, and this would be true even if no triangles existed. Further, these properties are objective, and therefore in some sense real. I do not invent them, but they are 'ones which I...recognize whether I want to or not.' So, although there may in fact be no triangles in the world, one is nonetheless able to deduce the essential nature of triangles from the clear idea we have of them. From this example, he draws the general principle that 'The mere fact that I can produce from my thought the idea of something entails that everything which I clearly and distinctly perceive to belong to that thing really does belong to it,' *whether or not that thing actually exists.* In other words, everything has an essence (essential properties), even if that thing doesn't actually exist. The inventor of the paper clip, for example, knew the essence of paper-clips before he or she had actually created one.

The idea of God is just as clear and distinct as that of a triangle. Therefore, it should be equally possible to deduce God's essence, without presupposing that God exists. Whatever is found to be a part of God's essence is as certain a part of his essence as the properties of a triangle are part of a triangle's essence.

So what is God's essence? The properties which cannot be separated from the idea of God are the properties of having all perfections, hence supreme perfection is God's essence. 'Since existence is one of the perfections', the idea that God exists cannot be separated from his essence. Therefore, God must exist. Existence can no more be separated from God's essence as three-sidedness can be separated from a triangle's essence, and both facts can be known with equal *a priori* certainty. Note that God is unique in this sense. Normally, existence is not part of a thing's essence. But if something is supremely perfect, it must exist, for were it not to exist, it would be less perfect than something identical to it, but existing. But then, it cannot be less perfect than anything, or it would not be supremely perfect. Hence, it exists.

We can consider the argument in another way. Descartes says he has 'countless ideas that, though they may not exist outside of me, still cannot be called nothing, and although not invented by me still have their own nature'. A triangle is one example: it may not exist out of his own mind, but it cannot be called nothing, is not invented by him and has its own nature. God is another such idea, which also may not (at least not be presupposed to) exist outside of him, but is not nothing, is not invented by him and has its own true nature. But with God, as his nature is supreme perfection, he must actually exist.

Descartes illustrates his argument with an analogy. Just as the idea of a mountain cannot be separated from the idea of a valley, so the idea of God cannot be separated from the idea of his existence. Put simply, 'I am not free to think of God without existence', as this would be to think of 'a supremely perfect being without a supreme perfection', which is logically impossible. It is not an assumption that God has all perfections – it is simply a fact which follows from the idea of God itself. Once Descartes has found the clear and distinct idea of God, it is as certain as any other clear and distinct idea.

We can summarise Descartes's argument as follows:

> Everything that is clearly and distinctly perceived to belong to a thing really does belong to it.
> One cannot think of God except as existing (i.e., one clearly and distinctly perceives that existence is part of God's essence).
> Therefore, God must exist.

Descartes is convinced this is true and though when his mind is on other things he may lose sight of the force of the argument, all he needs to do is to bring it to mind to see without doubt that it works. Further, since the argument is based on reason and not on the objects of this experience, the conclusion is true whether he is awake or asleep. In this way, the argument bypasses all his sceptical doubts.

Problems

One common type of objection to this argument was first raised by Immanuel Kant. Although the precise form of the objection varies, what they all have in common is the claim that Descartes is not entitled to deduce that God exists merely from his essence, as existence is not one of those things which can be counted as a property or perfection.

Descartes includes existence among the properties of God, claiming it is one of God's perfections. However, if something doesn't exist, surely it doesn't *lack* a perfection or property; rather it has *no* perfections or properties. If I have 100 real coins and 100 imaginary coins, it seems bizarre to say that the real coins have all the properties of the imaginary ones plus the property of existing. It is more accurate to say that the imaginary coins have no properties at all. This is a way of saying that existence is not a 'perfection' or a 'property'.

Descartes responds by just denying this and saying that necessary existence is very much a property of God since it defines what he is. But if existence is a property of God as a perfect being, then it can be attributed to other perfect beings, such as the perfect heffalump. Since the perfect heffalump has as one of its properties perfection, and perfection implies existence, then surely the perfect heffalump must exist. But that would mean, by the same logic, that the perfect everything must exist, which is surely absurd. (However, it should be noted that Plato's theory of the Forms seems to imply just this conclusion.)

Descartes's reply would be to say that God is different because he is supremely perfect, whereas the perfect heffalump is only perfect in certain respects. This is why existence is part of God's perfection, but not that of the perfect heffalump. But it seems that the heffalump argument is enough to show that existence is not a perfection at all, so it is irrelevant that God is supremely perfect – existence just hasn't got anything to do with perfection.

A second type of objection owes its origin to Hume (see Chapter 3 on his *Enquiry concerning Human Understanding*). Descartes's argument is *a priori* – it is not based on facts gleaned from experience, but on first principles of logic. Many philosophers believe that all *a priori* arguments about matters of actual existence are hypothetical: they tell us what must be true *if* certain premises are true. But whether or not the premises are true is either a matter of fact – and therefore they need to be established by observation not logic – or purely logical, and therefore not a matter of fact or existence.

This point is illustrated by an objection raised by Thomas Aquinas to an earlier version of the argument. Aquinas argued that the fact that the concept of existence is inseparably linked to the concept of a supreme being only tells us about the *concept* of God. It does not follow from this that the existence of God is anything actual. One cannot deduce anything about existence from mere concepts.

This objection is supported by close consideration of Descartes's analogy with mountains and valleys, which perhaps doesn't deliver the conclusion Descartes thought it did. The argument about mountains runs something like this:

A mountain without a valley is a (logical) contradiction.
That which is (logically) contradictory cannot exist.
Therefore, a mountain cannot exist without a valley.

However, if you now replace 'mountain' and 'valley' with 'God' and 'existence', this is what you get:

God without existence is a (logical) contradiction.
That which is (logically) contradictory cannot exist.
God without existence cannot exist.

This is true, but it doesn't show that God must exist. It only shows that if God exists, he exists, which is a tautology. This supports the objection that the ontological argument cannot get beyond facts about the concept of God to facts about the real existence of God.

But perhaps the most famous objection to Descartes's particular use of the ontological argument is known as the Cartesian circle. We are sure that what we clearly and distinctly perceive is true only if God exists. But we can be sure that God exists only if we clearly and distinctly perceive this to be true. But what we clearly and distinctly perceive is true only if God exists, and so on. This creates a vicious circle.

Set out more formally, we can see the circle in action:

1. How do I know God exists?
2. Because I clearly and distinctly perceive he exists.
3. How do I know what I clearly and distinctly perceive is true?
4. Because God exists.
5. How do I know God exists?
   . . .

We need to prove God exists to be sure that we are not mistaken even about apparently self-evident truths. But we cannot prove God exists unless we assume apparently self-evident truths are true. If Descartes is to consistently apply his method of doubt, then he has no right to suspend his doubt that even what he clearly and distinctly perceives is true in order to prove God exists.

Descartes does have a reply. He claims that what he doubts is 'knowledge of conclusions *recalled* when we are no longer aware of them', and that he doesn't doubt things he clearly and distinctly perceives *now*, in other words, self-evident truths, at the time he is aware of them. This is certainly not what he appeared to be saying in the first meditation, and one must ask why self-evident truths that you are currently aware of should be made immune from doubt. His justification for this seems to come in the third meditation, but it is not a convincing one.

We should consider one final, brief objection. Descartes's argument hinges on the fact that the idea of God is as clear and distinct as that of a triangle. This is highly doubtful. Two rational people cannot meaningfully disagree about what a triangle is, such is the clarity of the idea of a triangle. The fact that God's nature is a matter of debate shows that it is not so clear and distinct. The idea of God may also differ from that of a triangle, as it may be invented, which the idea of a triangle isn't.

Sixth meditation

Descartes completes his project of reconstructing his beliefs about the world by turning to material objects. Descartes begins his account with some preliminary remarks concerning the difference between imagination and understanding.

Descartes understands what a triangle is, and when he considers a triangle, he usually imagines a triangle at the same time. But this imagination is not required for understanding. For example, he understands what a chiliagon is (a 1,000 sided object), but what he imagines when he thinks of a chiliagon does not form part of that understanding. This can be seen from the fact that his mental image of a chiliagon is not distinct from his mental image of a 10,000-sided myriagon. It is merely a vague mental picture of a many-sided shape. Imagining, which we can define as 'the mental representation of sense experiences' is thus distinct from understanding, which is 'to comprehend, or grasp an idea intellectually'.

Descartes has already argued that it is his essence to think, and now he has shown that imagination is not a necessary part of this thinking. As he can thus have a clear and distinct idea of himself as a thinking thing without imagination, it therefore follows that the faculty of imagination is not a part of his essence. Descartes then makes a 'probable conjecture' that he has been endowed with the faculty of imagination because his body exists, and that this gives him ideas of corporeal things, which are the subject matter of imagination. In other words, existent bodies are the most likely source of the contents of his imagination.

But Descartes is not satisfied with this probability and seeks out more certainty. His argument draws together many of the threads that have run through the *Meditations* and can be summarised as follows:

1. Material things can be clearly and distinctly understood, and thus it is within God's power to make them exist.
2. My essence is as a purely thinking thing, which does not have extension as one of its properties.
3. The ideas given to me by sense perception and imagination cannot be understood without the idea of extension.
4. My faculty of sense perception is passive (i.e., I cannot control the nature of what it is I perceive).
5. Therefore, there must be some active faculty producing the ideas given to me in sense perception.
6. This faculty must be external to me, because of (2) and (4).
7. The source of my ideas of material things must either (a) 'contain formally everything which is to be found objectively in the ideas' (i.e., it will actually have the properties of material objects) or (b) 'contain eminently whatever is to be found in the ideas' (i.e., it merely causes the ideas without having the properties of the material objects; a virtual reality machine would be one such cause).
8. Nature leads me to believe (a).
9. Nature is God's creation, and if nature is misleading me into believing (a), then God is deceiving me.
10. God is not a deceiver.
11. Therefore the cause of my ideas of material objects is really existing material objects themselves.

This argument has a beautiful elegance and following its elaborate chain of reasoning can be challenging, but it is ultimately rewarding.

Problems

The main problem with this argument is that it relies heavily on the idea that God is not a deceiver. Unless we can prove this (and it is not clear that Descartes has proved anything about the necessary existence of God), then we cannot conclude that we do not live in a virtual reality environment created by a deceiving demon or a mad scientist.

Also, unless it is true that our essence is that of a purely thinking thing, it is not necessary to suppose that our ideas of material things cannot be the product of our own imaginations, although Descartes does seem right to say that there must be some external cause for our ideas of material objects in general, if not in specific cases.

So to sum up, this is an elegantly constructed, probably valid argument. Its weak links are premise (2), which rests on the arguments of the second meditation, and premises (9) and (10), which rest on the arguments of the fifth meditation. The most telling criticisms of this argument therefore do not concern its structure and presentation in the sixth meditation, but the earlier meditations upon which it rests.

Outstanding problems

It would seem to be a problem for Descartes that his argument relies on God not being a deceiver, because if God is not a deceiver, why in fact are we deceived so often? Descartes argues that this is an inevitable result of two facts. First, we are finite in our intelligence, so we cannot always be right. Second, the mind is only connected to the body via a small part of the brain (the pineal gland), so the information it gets from the body comes indirectly, via the various nerves in the body. For every sense perception, there is a series of causes. Nerve A will send the signal to nerve B and so on until it finally reaches the mind at, say, Z. Imagine such a sequence: A–B–D–G–M–Z. If the sequence starts at D but continues the same, the mind will receive a signal identical to that which would normally be sent when the series starts at A. In such a case, if A is the end of my toe, I will feel as though the end of my toe is in pain, even though it has not been touched. Descartes says there is no way around this: it is an inevitable result of the way in which our minds are connected to our bodies. We should just be grateful that God has given us a way of sensing which is in normal circumstances reliable.

However, it must be said that while Descartes explains well why we do make mistakes, he hasn't really answered the question of why God didn't see fit to design us a little better. The possibility of error does seem to be inevitable, but only because of the way we happen to have been designed. God must surely take ultimate responsibility for this and, as a consequence, also for our errors.

One final matter outstanding is a solution to the dreaming argument. Descartes now declares – contrary to his pronouncements in the first meditation – that there is a feature which distinguishes dreaming from waking: dream experiences are not linked by memory to other experiences. This raises two questions, one serious, one less so. First, dream experiences do *seem* to be part of a connected series of memories, so can't we be dreaming and it only *seem* to us that our experiences are connected by memory to other experiences? The new answer to the dreaming problem doesn't seem to provide a convincing solution. Second, if it is so easy to refute the dreaming argument in this way, why did he not do so in the first place!

Conclusion

Descartes has come to the end of his project. There is a symmetry in the *Meditations*. He starts the book as someone who carries with him a body of beliefs he thinks he knows. He slowly attacks these until he is left with nothing but the certainty of his own existence. Then, he slowly builds up his beliefs once more until he ends up back where he started – convinced of the existence of himself, God and the material world, but this time convinced on the basis of what he takes to be sound foundations.

The book is in some ways a metaphor for a lot of philosophy. It leaves the world as it is, while at the same time utterly transforming it. Philosophers often believe much the same things as everyone else. But their reflections lead them to base these beliefs on considerations that others are often unaware of, or to see the world in a slightly different way.

In this and many other ways, the *Meditations* is an exemplary philosophical text. You may disagree with almost all of it, but when you've finished reading it, you will almost certainly understand yourself, the world and philosophy better.

Summary

Descartes's goal in the *Meditations* is to establish a sure and certain **foundation** for his knowledge. To do this he follows the **method of doubt**. He decides to disregard all beliefs which he can doubt until he is left only with something certain. He rejects the evidence of his senses because they have in the past deceived him and have thus proven to be an unreliable source of knowledge. He also considers the possibility that he is dreaming and therefore may be tricked into thinking that everything that he thinks is real is just a chimera.

In dreams, at least some basic truths are beyond doubt. But if God were a deceiver, or if a powerful **evil demon** were deceiving him, he could be wrong even about this.

The only thing Descartes can't doubt is that he thinks and he exists. Reflecting on this, he concludes that he must be in **essence** a thinking, rather than physical thing, because although the idea of body can be separated from his existence, the idea of thought cannot. He confirms this by considering a piece of wax and concluding that it is his intellect which allows him to know its essence, not his senses. This shows that the intellect is primary.

Descartes knows that he exists because he **clearly and distinctly perceives** this to be true. Such perceptions would not make him certain, he concludes, unless they were true. Armed with this hallmark of certainty, he tries to establish whether God exists, for if he does, he can be sure he is not being deceived about even the most basic truths.

His first attempted proof of God is based on the **causal reality principle**: since the cause of the idea of God must be at least as perfect as the idea itself, so God must exist.

But then, why does God allow him to be in error? This is purely because God has made us as best he can: he has given us a finite **intellect**, but the **will** does not admit of degree so we had to have it complete. We err when our will asserts things to be true or false which are beyond the capacity of our intellect to accurately judge.

Descartes's second proof of the existence of God is a version of the **ontological argument**. This attempts to show that a non-existent God is a contradiction in terms and that therefore God must exist as certainly as a triangle must have three sides.

Descartes concludes the *Meditations* by arguing that material objects must exist. This is because the idea of material things comes from something outside of himself. This must be material things themselves or something else. Because nature leads him to expect the former and God would not deceive him, he can be sure that material objects exist. This completes the re-establishment of all Descartes's beliefs on a surer foundation – or so he believes . . .

Glossary

Causal reality principle   The principle that nothing less perfect or complete can be the cause of something more perfect or complete.

Clear and distinct perception   When the mind apprehends something so evident that its truth cannot be doubted.

Essence   The essential nature of a thing – that which cannot be separated from the idea of it.

Evil demon   A device used to personify the possibility that we are constantly being deceived about even the simplest of apparent truths.

Intellect   The faculty with which we reason and which is finite in us, but infinite in God.

Foundationalism   An approach to philosophy which seeks to establish truth on a secure and certain basis.

Method of doubt   The systematic doubt of all beliefs in order to arrive at truths which are certain and indubitable.

Ontological argument   An argument that seeks to show that we can know God exists purely by thinking about what the idea or concept of God entails.

Will   The faculty which allows us to make free choices, which is single, indivisible and does not admit of degrees.

Further reading

John Cottingham's translation of the *Meditations on First Philosophy* (Cambridge University Press) is highly recommended especially since it comes accompanied by a selection of the objections and replies. Other than the *Meditations*, *The Discourse on Method* is the next most important work by Descartes and is available in many editions, including F. E. Sutcliffe's translation (Penguin), which also includes the *Meditations*.

Cottingham also contributed the *Descartes* volume to the *Great Philosophers* series (Phoenix). The book manages to be clear while at the same time presenting a fresh picture of the sometimes tired, caricatured figure of Descartes. The book also appears as part of the anthology, *The Great Philosophers*, edited by Ray Monk and Fredric Raphael (Phoenix). Gareth Southwell's *A Beginner's Guide to Descartes's Meditations* (Blackwell) is a comprehensive and accessible introduction.

3

David Hume: *An Enquiry concerning Human Understanding* (1748)

Background

Perhaps the simplest way into Hume's (1711–1776) *Enquiry concerning Human Understanding* (1748) is to contrast the author's empiricist approach with that of his rationalist predecessors, such as Descartes (see Chapter 2 on the *Meditations*). To put it rather crudely, empiricists believe that all knowledge is derived from experience, and there is nothing which can be understood by the mind alone. Without experience, the mind is, as Locke put it, a 'blank slate' (*tabula rasa*), incapable of thinking of anything.

This contrasts with the approach of rationalists such as Descartes, who believed that fundamental truths about reality could be discovered purely by thinking, without any reference to experience. Rationalists have high hopes for the power of *a priori* reasoning – reasoning that starts from basic principles of logic and rationality which can be known to be true without reference to experience.

The distinction between rationalism and empiricism can easily descend into caricature. It is not that rationalists see all experience as irrelevant and empiricists believe experience justifies all our beliefs. What one actually finds on reading these philosophers is that Descartes does base some of his arguments on the evidence of experience and Hume argues that some of the principles of thought we employ are not justified by experience. The major difference is that Descartes believed rationality was the ultimate underpinning of all our knowledge, whereas for Hume, experience, custom and habit are at least as important and often more so.

While distinctions such as that between rationalists and empiricists can help us get to grips with unfamiliar philosophy, when reading any work it is important not to allow preconceived notions about which school a philosopher is coming from to get in the way of understanding the arguments they actually put forward. This is particularly true for Hume, whose empiricism is far subtler than broad-brushed generalisations about empiricism would suggest were possible.

The text

The story of Hume's *Enquiry* provides encouragement for anyone who has struggled to find an audience for their work. The book is effectively a rewrite of Part I of Hume's earlier *A Treatise of Human Nature* (1738). Although now regarded as a masterpiece, Hume recalls in his short memoir, *My Own Life*: 'Never literary attempt was more unfortunate than my *Treatise of Human Nature*. It fell dead-born from the press without reaching such distinction, as even to excite a murmur among the zealots.'

Hume believed the failure to be due to the manner rather than the matter of the book, and so several years after its failure he revisited Part I of the *Treatise* and the *Enquiry* was born. Alas, it was not much more successful. It would be many years before Hume would be acknowledged as perhaps the greatest British philosopher.

Hume himself saw the *Enquiry* as the superior, more polished work. Nevertheless, one often finds scholarly debate focuses on the longer *Treatise*. It would be a pity if this trend were to put people off reading the *Enquiry*, since it is a lucid, clear and compelling work, in many ways easier to navigate one's mind through than the lengthy *Treatise*.

I   Of the Different Species of Philosophy

The first section of the *Enquiry* sits apart from the remainder of the text. What follows is a sustained argument, leading into a detailed application of the principles Hume establishes to various areas of philosophy. Section I does not introduce either the main argument or these later themes, but rather reflects on the general nature of philosophy itself.

The dangers of reading a text two and a half centuries after it was written are evident in the book's first two words: 'moral philosophy'. Nowadays, we would take that to refer specifically to ethics, or the philosophy of judging the rights and wrongs of human conduct. However, for Hume the term simply contrasts with natural philosophy, which we would now call physical science. So what Hume goes on to say applies to most, if not all, of what we would now consider philosophy, not just ethics.

Hume distinguishes between two types of philosophy, that which considers humanity (or man, as Hume called it) as 'chiefly born for action' and that which considers it 'in the light of a reasonable rather than an active being'. The distinction Hume is really making is between two approaches to treating the subject of humanity: the evocative, emotional and pleasing on the one hand, and the analytic, rational and reasoned on the other.

What Hume means by the second type is easy to see, since it simply describes the philosophical approach to human nature. This approach seeks to understand humanity by cool, calm and careful reasoning. It aims to establish the most general principles possible which enable us to understand our place in the world. It doesn't seek to discover just *what* we know, but *how* we know it and what justifies the claim that we do know, rather than merely believe. It doesn't seek simply to distinguish right from wrong but to establish the principles which allow us to judge between right and wrong. It doesn't seek merely to represent the huge edifice of human nature, creativity, ethics and intellect, but to understand the foundations on which it rests.

So noble an enterprise may seem beyond reproach. But in a way, the whole of this first section is a pre-emptive defence of philosophy against its critics. The problem, as Hume explains, is that this kind of approach to human nature leads us into difficult arguments and abstract reasoning. From a distance, the relevance of these arguments may be hard to discern. Philosophers can look like strange eccentrics who are obsessed by matters of irrelevant detail. Compared to the poet's treatment of human loss and triumph, for example, philosophy can appear sterile, dry and irrelevant. It appears to have no use or purpose to anyone other than aficionados of abstract reasoning.

In contrast, the first type of philosophy Hume describes is obviously relevant to the concerns of people in general. This kind of philosophy never strays too far from everyday concerns, since it aims merely to 'represent the common sense of mankind in more beautiful and engaging colours'. Although Hume's description makes this sound more like poetry than philosophy, the examples he gives of practitioners of this art are all essayists, if not fully-fledged philosophers. Cicero, La Bruyère and Addison are identified as authors of this lesser style of philosophy, while Aristotle, Malebranche and Locke are exemplars of the better, though less obviously engaging style. Interestingly, the philosophers

Hume identifies as being greater, but less well thought of, are now considered giants of philosophy, whereas the popular thinkers of his time have largely been forgotten. Posterity, it seems, has been a better judge of quality in philosophy than Hume's peers.

Hume is describing a dispute which still continues today. It is basically about the accusation that philosophy is removed from the concerns of everyday life and much poorer for it. For instance, the noted journalist Simon Jenkins wrote, of the great twentieth-century philosopher W. V. O. Quine: 'Quine's work was not a window on the Great Beyond but an intellectual microscope applied to games he played with others' (*The Times*, 3 January 2001). As evidence, Jenkins points out that he had 'understood hardly a word' of Quine's obituary.

Hume's defence of what he thought of as the best philosophy could be used in response to Jenkins today. Hume argues that such philosophy relies on making very careful and subtle arguments. Hence, its practitioners are likely to get it wrong often, and thus can easily be made to look stupid. Also, because their reasoning goes into great depth and it is many stages removed from the point at which the questions first arise in the general population, it is easy for their work to appear abstract and irrelevant. Even its practitioners find that their reasonings do not apply directly to everyday life and can separate out their philosophical reflections from daily living.

Philosophy matters because only careful and thorough thought can lead us to reject the many false beliefs and ideas we would otherwise be encumbered with. Philosophy is also important because the questions it considers are so fundamental. Only philosophy turns the eye of enquiry inwards on to the mind of the thinker itself, for instance, enabling us to understand not just how to categorise objects in the world, but also the 'operations of the mind'. It is a shallow thinker who rejects such concerns as irrelevant.

Hume's defence does, however, grant something to the other species of philosophy he criticises. That does at least have the virtue of being clear, engaging and accessible. Hume's hope is that his own work will combine the rigour of the best form of philosophy with the colour and vitality of its more vulgar relation. Many would say he succeeded.

II   Of the Origin of Ideas

The starting point of the *Enquiry* proper is an investigation into the fundamental basis of knowledge. In this respect, Hume follows the same 'foundationalist' strategy as Descartes. The difference is that whereas

Descartes searched for these foundations within his own mind, Hume looked for them in his experience of the world.

Hume, like Locke, believed that knowledge starts with what we are directly aware of, which are the contents of our own mind – what he called the 'perceptions of the mind'. Hume puts these perceptions into two categories: ideas and impressions. Impressions are what we perceive when we look at an object, feel a sensation or emotion, touch something and so on. Impressions can thus be of things external or internal to ourselves. Ideas are what we perceive when we imagine, think of, or remember something. Impressions, he says, are 'forcible and lively', whilst ideas are 'faint and dull'. In common speech, we may refer to 'ideas' as 'thoughts' and 'impressions' as 'sensations' (though note Hume's particular definitions of each). 'The most lively thought', he claims, 'is still inferior to the dullest sensation.'

Here, Hume could mean one of two things. Firstly, he could mean that *all* ideas are less lively than *all* impressions. This seems clearly false. I can just catch sight of something in the distance through the fog and have a very faint impression of it, whilst I can dream something very vividly indeed. What Hume more likely means is that any particular idea will always be less vivid than the impression from which it originally derived (as he claims all ideas are derived from impressions). But even this may be false on occasion. In a traumatic experience, I may not be aware of many things going on around me as I struggle to survive. However, once the original trauma has passed, these things may return in my memories more vividly than my original experience of them.

This problem highlights a general difficulty in Hume's account. It seems that by making vivacity and liveliness what distinguishes an idea from an impression, he has not selected the defining distinguishing features of either. Although it is true that most ideas are less vivid than impressions, this does not capture their essential nature, but is rather a consequence of their essential nature. What truly distinguishes them is that impressions are the raw data of experience, and ideas are later copies of this data. Usually, a copy is less vivid than the original. But it is not this feature which distinguishes a copy from an original. A copy of an old painting may, for example, be more vivid. So Hume seems to make two mistakes. First, he confuses typical features of ideas and impressions with their natures. But second, if vivacity is how we are supposed to distinguish ideas from impressions, he also turns a useful rule of thumb (copies are *usually* less detailed than originals) into a strict rule (copies are *always* less detailed than originals).

Why did Hume do this? The reason is probably that he wanted to be able to distinguish ideas and impressions and *then* make the claim that all ideas are derived from impressions. If he simply *defined* ideas as copies of impressions, he would be beginning his theory with a bold hypothesis, rather than with facts based clearly on experience.

Whatever his errors, is he right to claim that all ideas derive from impressions? We can see how ideas of dragons and other fanciful creatures can be amalgams of parts we have already experienced. But what about ideas such as that of God? Hume claims this is just made up of ideas from experience augmented. For example, the idea of God's infinite goodness comes from impressions of limited goodness, which we then just imagine without end. This makes it clear that ideas are not simply copies of impressions. They are impressions copied, augmented, modified and/or rearranged. It is difficult to think of an idea which *could not* be explained in this way. But the question is, *are* they formed in such a way? It is possible, for example, to derive the idea of atoms by simply adapting impressions, but is that actually how the idea arose? It is very difficult, if not impossible to tell. So whilst Hume could be right, he hasn't given us convincing reasons to believe he must be right.

There are other problems too. Bertrand Russell points out how the so called 'rules of thought', the principles of logic and induction, are not given to us by experience, but are *a priori*. In this case, at least some ideas are not derived from experience. Hume returns to induction later.

The final problem is one Hume himself considers. If we were to arrange all the shades of blue in a row, remove one, and show them to someone who had never seen that shade, could she not imagine what that missing shade would look like? Hume concedes she could, but claims 'this instance is so singular, that it is scarcely worth our observing'. This may seem to be a poor response, because it is clear that one counter-example is enough to destroy a claim of the sort 'all Xs are Ys'. However, it is revealing, because it suggests that Hume is not bothered that he hasn't got an exceptionless rule. He seems content enough to have discovered regularities in nature that hold for the most part. For an empiricist, who seeks to understand the world as it is given to experience, it would perhaps be foolish to assume that all regularities have to be exceptionless. If experience shows they are not, experience wins, not prior suppositions.

One might think an easy way to solve the problem of the missing shade is to say that it is a modification of the other shades rather than a distinct idea. But this would not do, since by that reasoning all colours can be placed in a spectrum and be seen as mere modifications of the next shade, and so all colours would be modifications of one colour. This seems absurd.

Hume's basic claim that all ideas derive from impressions thus faces serious difficulties. First, his idea-impression distinction seems to be wrongly characterised as hinging on the distinction between the liveliness and dullness of these 'perceptions of the mind'. Second, his claim that all ideas derive from impressions also seems to have several counter-examples. Perhaps Hume needs to say more about the relation between experience and ideas, or maybe his theory is more fundamentally flawed.

III   Of the Association of Ideas

Hume claims that there is clearly some 'principle of connexion between the different thoughts or ideas of the mind' (note that 'connexion' here is simply an old spelling of 'connection' – I'll stick to the latter except when quoting). Thoughts do not come from nowhere. No matter how loosely our thoughts appear to flow, there is always some hidden connection between them. Hume believed there are only three basic types of connection: resemblance, contiguity (closeness) in time or place, and cause or effect. If we examine the flow of our ideas, it will always be possible to explain the jump from one to another in terms of one of these relations.

This is a hard claim to deny or verify. We can probably work out some connection between any two ideas based on these three principles, but how can we know whether that is the actual connection? This is a problem shared with the impressions–ideas theory, which again is plausible, but almost impossible to test. It is perhaps ironic that we have already found two major planks of Hume's theory that seem to be untestable when the most common characterisation of empiricism is that it is based on the principle that ideas can be tested against experience.

IV   Sceptical Doubts Concerning the Operations of the Understanding

Part I

The principle which opens this section has come to be known as Hume's Fork. This is a distinction which Hume believed should be made (but which often is not) between two fundamentally different objects of reason: relations of ideas and matters of fact. Relations of ideas include algebra, geometry and logic – all those areas of knowledge where affirmations can be demonstrably true and certain, because they are basically no more than affirmations about the relations of ideas: $1 + 1 = 2$ can never be wrong, because no matter how the world is, the ideas represented in this sum are such that they have to be related in this way.

Matters of fact include propositions such as, 'the cat on the mat is fat,' and 'the world began with a big bang'. The truth or falsity of these ideas cannot be ascertained merely by attending to the ideas contained in the proposition. No matter how long one considers the idea of the world, one will never reach *a priori* the conclusion that it must have begun with a big bang. Hence, it is a feature of statements of fact that their opposites are always logically possible and contain no contradiction. 'The sun won't rise tomorrow' is not a self-contradictory statement; $1 + 1 = 3$ is.

Hume next claims that: 'All reasoning concerning matters of fact seems to be founded on the relation of cause and effect.' In this he seems to be correct. Our belief that the sun will rise tomorrow rests on the assumption that the forces which caused it to rise yesterday will operate again tomorrow. Even the belief that the cat on the mat is fat depends upon the assumption that the cat's appearance is an effect of the way it actually is.

The next question therefore is, 'How do we arrive at the knowledge of cause and effect?' The answer is, 'not by reason, but by experience'. There is no way that we could, just by observing a sequence of events, deduce *a priori* that earlier events were causing later ones, or that an object with certain properties also has other causal properties (for example, that clear water can cause a person to suffocate). Again, this can be demonstrated by the fact that there is no logical contradiction in imagining events occurring without or with different causes or effects. If apples defying gravity is not a logical contradiction, then it cannot be by logic that we conclude they must obey gravity. If clouds forming for no reason is not a logical contradiction, then it cannot be by logic that we conclude clouds must form for a reason. Therefore, it is experience alone that gives us knowledge of cause and effect, and not reason.

Part II

Hume has concluded that all reasoning concerning matters of fact depends upon the relation of cause and effect and that our knowledge of the relation of cause and effect is founded on experience, not reason. The next question, then, must be: 'What is the foundation of all conclusions from experience?'

Hume's answer is largely negative: conclusions from experience are not founded on reasoning. This is a mightily sceptical claim. It means that the ideas that bread nourishes, water freezes at zero degrees centigrade, and all men are mortal and so on are not based on reason. Why does Hume believe this? Objects in nature, he claims, have certain powers which are hidden from us. Bread has the power to nourish, for example, but we cannot in any sense observe that power. We can only find that it has it when we eat it. No matter how much bread we have eaten, when we see a new loaf, we cannot observe that power to nourish. We assume it has it, but this is just an assumption based on past experience. It is not based on reasoning.

This is a surprising claim, but Hume supports it by asking us to consider the nature of arguments based on experience, such as this one:

> I have found that such an object has always been attended with such an effect.
> I foresee that other objects, which are, in appearance, similar will be attended with similar effects.

This is clearly not a valid deduction – the conclusion in the second sentence does not follow from the premise in the first. In order to make the argument valid, a second premise is required, along the lines of:

> Whenever such an object has always been attended with such an effect, objects which are, in appearance, similar will continue to be attended with a similar effect.

This is a premise which Hume claims neither reason nor experience can ever justify. Experience, being confined to the past, can never provide proof for what the future will be like. Nor can reason justify this premise, since it is not contrary to reason to deny that it is true. The gap is just as gaping if we attempt to show that the conclusion of this argument is probable.

Just because Hume cannot provide the missing premise, it doesn't prove that no-one ever could. However, as even animals, idiots and children learn from experience, and clearly don't employ anything like this missing premise when they do so, it seems clear that no such deductive argument is employed in our actual learning from experience.

However, we certainly do reason along the lines of the invalid argument set out above, which is an example of *induction*. How we do so is the subject of the next section.

V   Sceptical Solution of these Doubts

Part I

After extolling the virtues of sceptical philosophy (by which Hume means what we would call modern Western philosophy), Hume considers how we reason concerning matters of fact. He observes that our philosophical reasonings are incapable of undermining our 'reasonings of common life'. For example, nothing Hume has said so far has stopped him believing the sun *will* rise tomorrow, even though there are no strictly rational reasons for believing this. It seems that nature, of which human beings are for Hume very much a part, has made sure of this. To find out how nature does this, Hume conducts a thought experiment.

Imagine someone were brought into the world for the first time, fully equipped with all the normal faculties of reason and reflection. Looking around, he would see a succession of events, but would never be able to see the causal powers which link them nor form a rational argument that would show that earlier events cause later ones. This merely repeats Hume's earlier point about the inability of reason and observation to tell us anything about causation. But, if this person were to continue to garner more experience and had observed similar objects or events to constantly follow each other, he would soon begin to infer the existence of one object from the appearance of the other. Yet it is not by reason that he infers this, but by custom or habit. Repetition makes him expect the 'effect' to follow the 'cause', not any process of rational thought. Custom is nature's great teacher, without which we would be lost.

It follows from all this that 'all belief of matter of fact or real existence is derived merely from some object, present to the memory or senses, and a customary conjunction between that and some other object'. Belief in cause and effect therefore depends upon the psychological effect of witnessing constant conjunction – two objects or events repeatedly following one another, or being found together. It is not something we either directly observe or discover by a rational process.

Part II

Hume now turns to the nature of beliefs and the customary conjunctions between them. The mind is free to think of ideas in any way it sees fit. You can imagine a winged horse as easily as a normal one. But what the mind is not free to do is to imagine a winged horse and really believe it to have existed. So although the ideas of winged and normal horses can just as easily be thought of as each other, there is a certain *feeling* attached to *genuine beliefs* which is absent in *ideas of fictions*. Ideas which we truly believe are involuntary, strong, immediate and are held by force of custom. Ideas of fiction are weaker, and there is no necessity to our having them. So it is the *manner* in which we have ideas, rather than the ideas themselves, which distinguishes beliefs from mere fictions. Whether or not our beliefs are true or not is, however, another question.

From where does this strong manner in which we have beliefs derive? Hume claims it comes from custom. Nature, as he has said, has established connections among particular ideas, namely those of contiguity, resemblance and cause and effect. When objects are presented to the senses or memory, these connections are strengthened, such that they are stronger than they could be if they were just imagined. And the more the objects are presented to us, the stronger the associations will be. Various examples show this. If I look at a picture of someone I know, then there is my idea of the person, the present impression of the picture and the relation of resemblance between them. Where there is a good likeness in the picture, my idea of that person is strengthened by this resemblance, whereas if there is little likeness, my idea of the person will be more faint. Thus it is that the vivacity of our ideas and the strength of the relations between them are both increased by objects presented to the senses much more than they can by mere imagination. *How* this is so, we do not know, but Hume is sure *that* it is so.

However, it should be pointed out that error can occur. Two objects can be presented together and associated in my mind with all the forcefulness of a belief, even though those objects have no real relation at all. Such is often the case with phobias. If we come to associate a harmless object with something fearful, we will begin to fear the harmless object. In this case, we can form a false belief that something harmless is dangerous. Thus, we cannot know if our beliefs are true by their vivacity and the strength of their association in our mind, and Hume doesn't here provide an alternative test of truth and falsehood, although he does return to this issue in Section VII.

Hume has thus provided us with an explanation of how we reason concerning matters of fact through custom, not reason, and shown us why this is necessary. Whether this is enough to dispel the scepticism of Section IV is for us to decide, but even if it is not, he has some more interesting things to say on the subject after he deals with the question of probability.

VI   Of Probability

Locke distinguished between demonstrative and probable arguments. Demonstrative arguments concern maths, geometry and so on, whilst probable arguments concern things such as the rising of the sun. This distinction mirrors the two prongs of Hume's fork. Hume, however, wishes to divide matters of fact into two categories: proofs and probabilities. Those matters of fact of which there can be no doubt (even though they are not logically demonstrable), such as the existence of gravity, are considered proven. Probability concerns matters of fact for which such proofs are not possible because of a lack of constant conjunction.

So what is probability? If chance means that an effect is not the inevitable result of its cause, then Hume says chance does not exist. In cases of apparent chance, there is merely an ignorance of the real cause. So chance or probability arises when *apparently* identical causes have a number of different effects. Consider rolling a die. In truth, no one roll is identical to any other, but they appear to be basically the same. What we have found is that, over time, each result of the roll occurs one in six times. In saying, then, that there is a six-to-one chance of rolling a particular number in the future, we are merely projecting into the future the past proportion of outcomes. But for any given roll, it is inevitable, given the way the die was rolled, that the number ends up showing as it does.

What Hume is thus doing in this section is showing how, even though matters of fact are not logically demonstrable, we can distinguish between proofs and probabilities whilst at the same time retaining the idea that every occurrence is the determinate outcome of its cause.

VII   Of the Idea of Necessary Connexion

Part I

All our ideas, Hume claims, come from an antecedent (prior) impression. And in order to fully understand that idea, we need to know what impression(s) it comes from. For example, knowing that the idea of a unicorn is a combination of impressions and that the idea of a tiger comes from whole impressions is part of what enables us to know one is a fiction and one is a fact (thus completing the unfinished account of this difference in Section V). So in order to fully understand the idea of necessary connection, we need to locate the impression from which it derives. Hume has already argued that we do not perceive necessary connection in the external world: all we perceive there is a series of constant conjunctions. So where does the idea come from? Hume considers three likely sounding candidates.

First, Hume considers the possibility that we directly observe the power of necessary connection when we are aware of the power of our minds over our bodies. The thesis is that 'we are every moment conscious of internal power; while we feel that, by the simple command of our will, we can move the organs of our body'. Hume rejects this for three reasons. First, how can we directly observe this power when, in fact, the union of mind and body is the most mysterious thing in the entire universe? Second, we cannot move all parts of our body at will, and what is more, we discover which parts we can control and those we cannot by experience, not by any direct awareness of our power over them. Third, when we move an arm, for example, we in fact move various muscles and nerves between the arm and the brain first. Now, if we were directly aware of the power we had, we would have known this intuitively, whereas in fact we have to learn this from anatomy.

A second possibility is that we can feel the power of the mind over its own ideas. Every time we conjure up a new idea, we feel the power of necessary connection. Hume also rejects this for three reasons. First, if we know a cause, we must know what power in the cause produces the effect. But we know so little about the mind that we cannot pretend to know any such thing in this case. Second, the power of the mind over its ideas is limited, and those limits are only known by experience. (Compare this to the argument concerning the mind's power over the body.) Third, our power over our ideas varies according to our state of mind, health and so on. The only reasons we can offer for this fact are from experience, which again shows that the power itself is not known to us.

A third possibility, which Hume gives short shrift, is the theory of occasionalism. This is the idea that God is the cause of all events and is thus the power which makes a cause always produce an effect. This is a kind of non-explanation and Hume dismisses it because he cannot see how any chain of reasoning could lead us to this conclusion, as it would take us way beyond what we can justly infer from experience.

Part II

This part of the *Enquiry* is absolutely crucial. Many readers miss its significance, including those who should know better. At this point, we are left with the puzzle about where the idea of necessary connection comes from. Hume has stressed that all ideas come from impressions and has so far failed to locate the impression which is the source of the idea of necessary connection. This leads some to think that Hume is really saying we do not have an idea of necessary connection at all, or that it is a fiction, since it has no corresponding impression. But, right here, Hume says explicitly what the impression is.

Nature has instilled in us the capacity to form the idea of necessary connection from constant conjunction. How is this done? When we observe a constant conjunction, the idea or impression of the first event always conveys to our minds the idea of the subsequent event. The mind is carried from the idea of the cause to that of the effect. This is something which just happens to us, without our will. It is thus this necessity of moving from one thought to the other which gives us the impression from which the idea of necessary connection derives. 'This connexion, therefore, which we feel in the mind, this customary transition of the imagination from one object to its usual attendant, is the sentiment or impression from which we form the idea of power or necessary connexion.' (I once had to show this sentence to a colleague writing a scholarly book on Hume to prove to him that Hume does locate an impression from which the idea of necessary connection arises, so don't be surprised if you come across people writing on Hume who neglect this!)

This is important. It shows that the impression of necessary connection arises in the mind. What we do is project this idea out on to the world and believe that there is necessary connection in the world itself. It should also be noted that nowhere does Hume question that we are right to believe that there is such a thing as necessary connection in the world – only that the origin of that idea comes from our own minds, not the world. Indeed, many of his arguments elsewhere depend upon the reality of cause and effect. This is also important, since some commentators claim that Hume denies the reality of causation. Hume seems to believe that the impression in the mind he has located is simply nature's way of teaching us about cause and effect. He does not deny that there is cause and effect in the world itself and that it is not just in the mind.

However, critics would argue that once Hume locates the source of our idea of cause and effect as the operation of the mind, the door to scepticism is wide open, and it would seem natural to doubt the objective reality of cause and effect. One way out for Hume would be to admit, which he does not for the reasons already given, that we do have some direct experience of physical necessity. Perhaps Hume's claim that all experience must be of particular impressions is at fault here. It may be possible to explain how we observe the power of causation in some way which does not require there to be a particular impression of this power.

VIII   Of Liberty and Necessity

Part I

Hume notes there is a continued disagreement over whether or not human action is free or not. He concludes that the only reason for this disagreement is that the terms themselves, 'freedom', 'liberty', 'necessity' and so on are not properly defined. He wagers that if we could all agree on what these terms mean, all our apparent disagreements would disappear. Hume thus claims the controversy is merely verbal, rather than factual.

The meaning of a word, for Hume, is given by the idea in the mind to which the word is attached. This is a very contentious theory, since if meanings are determined by ideas private to each individual, how can we have shared meanings for words which make communication possible? However, we should not worry too much about this since Hume's basic claim that the disagreement is verbal does not depend on his particular theory of meaning.

Hume first considers necessity and reminds us that it is constant conjunction which gives us this idea. In the affairs of people, he argues, we also observe constant conjunctions. There is uniformity in human behaviour and action over time and place, so strong that if we were to be told of a society hugely different from ours, where people were not jealous, ambitious and so on, we would disbelieve it as much as we would stories about dragons and monsters. The differences in human behaviour also teach us the influence of factors such as age, sex and culture have on behaviour, in just the same way that differences in the behaviour of matter teach us about the influences of temperature, air pressure and so on.

It is true that human behaviour is unpredictable. But this is not, as the 'vulgar' believe, a result of any uncertainty in the cause, but rather 'the secret opposition of contrary causes'. This is the same in persons as it is in matter. If a telephone explodes, we believe it was caused by something not usually operative in telephones, and if a patient man gets angry, we assume there is some reason for this which is not usually operative.

Hume gives more examples to support his case and concludes: 'The conjunction between motives and voluntary actions is as regular and uniform as that between the cause and effect in any part of nature', a fact, he claims, which 'has been universally acknowledged'. We do not think that people act randomly, but that their actions are explained by their motives, dispositions, desires and so on.

But does this resolve the dispute as he claimed it would? Perhaps not. The real dispute is not over whether motives cause action, but whether motives and so on are themselves effects of other causes. If this is the case, then the originating causes of actions lie not within our own minds, but in our environment and our genes. This is what determinists believe, and not everyone agrees with them. We might agree that desires and motives are part of what cause actions, but disagree about whether these themselves are chosen or whether, in addition to these, there is an extra faculty of 'free will' which makes the final choice. Hume's argument is therefore incomplete. However, Hume does outline the basis of the compatibilist approach to determinism. That is to say, it is claimed that the fact that all human actions are effects of motives, character and so on, which are in turn effects of other causes, *ad infinitum*, does not contradict the principle of human freedom, which is that we have '*a power of acting or not acting, according to the determinations of the will*; that is, if we choose to remain at rest, we may; if we choose to move, we may also.' However, if we take the more usual definition of human freedom, which is that 'men are free only if they could have done otherwise', Hume has not shown we are free in this way, although there are problems with this notion.

If, as Hume claims, no-one fundamentally disagrees as to the facts of the matter, why do we seem to disagree? Hume's explanation is that we tend to reason (perhaps not consciously) as follows:

1. We perceive necessary connection in nature.
2. We do not perceive any necessity forcing our own actions.
3. Therefore, we have a liberty of action which nature does not.

Hume, as we have seen, denies (1). We do not perceive any necessary connection in nature, only a constant conjunction. And, as Hume has eloquently argued, such constant conjunctions are to be found in human action as well. To disagree with Hume we could either reject his account of causation, or reject his claim that human behaviour is as regular as the behaviour of bodies in nature.

Part II

What are the consequences of accepting this position? Does it mean that no one is to blame for their actions? Even if the theory did have dangerous consequences, that would not in itself refute the theory. But Hume claims that it does not have such consequences anyway. He believes that without the causal link between motives, character and action, we would have no basis for punishment, blame or the idea of repentance. It only makes sense to punish someone if their character is somehow the cause of their actions. If it were not, then there would be nothing to punish or reform. So Hume argues that we actually need the idea of necessary connection to apply to human action to justify our morality.

The other main problem is that if everything is an effect, eventually God will be found to be the initial cause. As there are many bad things done in the world, this either means God is to blame for everything or he is not wholly good. One way to avoid this is to claim that as a whole, the universe is good, even though individual parts may seem bad. Though Hume acknowledges that psychologically this belief fails, in that it provides no comfort for a person suffering, nonetheless philosophically it makes sense. As regards the idea that God is the author of all things bad, Hume dodges the issue, arguing that 'there are mysteries, which mere natural and unassisted reason is very unfit to handle'. But in a way, Hume's evasion is justified. After all, he has consistently argued that matters of fact can only be known from experience. God's authorship of the universe is a matter of fact which cannot be known *a priori*. And as we have no direct experience of God either, we are unfit to reason about him in any detail.

Of course, this argument not only saves God from being blamed as the author of all sin, but it also prevents his nature and existence being the just subject of philosophy too, a consequence the tactful Hume fails to point out. It should also be noted that in Hume's time it was prudent not to question too vigorously orthodox religious doctrine.

IX   Of the Reason of Animals

Do animals reason? To answer this, as with any other question concerning matters of fact, we have to use a combination of experience and analogy. If we discover that an animal has a heart, for example, and that such an organ circulates the blood in all other animals we have studied, we should reason until shown otherwise that this is also the function of the heart in this animal. In the same way, we should conclude that animals do reason.

There are two facts which together suggest animals do have the power of reason. First, animals learn from experience. This shows, according to Hume, that animals, like humans, reach conclusions about more than they are actually aware of in sense experience, and that this process of inference is a matter of using experience of the past as a guide to what will happen in the future. In other words, animals reason as we do.

Second, this reasoning cannot be based on any process of argument. Seeing as Hume has already claimed that we do not use any such principle of argument in our reasoning concerning experience, it is hard to suppose that an animal, a less sophisticated creature, has access to this form of reasoning that eludes us.

Hume is aware that people ascribe much animal behaviour to instinct. Hume's answer here is that we too have instinct: our capacity to learn from experience is itself an instinct, which we do not need to be taught about and, indeed, has no logical basis.

The differences between animal intelligence and our own are explained in the same way as differences in human intelligence are. These are factors such as capacity for attention, memory, distinguishing a number of causes, ability to carry a chain of reasoning further and so on. Hume provides a comprehensive list at the end of this section. The key point is that the difference between human and animal reasoning is a difference in degree, not of kind.

Much of what Hume said was ahead of its time. But in other respects, it may be a little crude. Modern psychology has shown there are many ways of learning, such as simple conditioning, whereas Hume supposes all learning from experience is a species of induction. However, in emphasising how much we have in common with animals, Hume anticipated much of what later came to be received opinion.

X   Of Miracles

Part I

In all matters of fact, where there is disagreement, we must simply balance up the evidence for the one belief against the evidence for the other. 'A weaker evidence cannot destroy a stronger.' If gravity appears to always operate, we cannot deny the truth of gravity just because an illusionist like David Copperfield appears to be flying around the theatre.

The testimony of people is no exception to this rule. A person's testimony, though we may have no reason to believe that person to be a liar, must be balanced against all the evidence which contradicts what they say, which includes the testimony of others, experience and the character of the teller. Of course, sometimes we may be wrong, but this is always possible with matters of fact. Hume points out that the fabled Indian, who didn't believe in the stories of ice which he was told about, reasoned justly, as all of his experience of water and the effect of cooling on matter told against the idea that water would expand and solidify at one crucial temperature. He was wrong, but he reasoned as best as he could, given the information available to him.

However, even in this case, ice was something merely extraordinary, not truly miraculous. Ice was beyond his experience, but not contrary to it. For something to be miraculous, it must be 'a violation of the laws of nature'. Not everyone would agree with Hume. Many modern Christians would believe that a miracle can be merely a highly unlikely event occurring at a particularly apt time, even though it is not contrary to the laws of nature. For example, there are explanations of how the Red Sea could have parted according to natural laws, but is it not still a miracle that it happened just when Moses and the Israelites needed it to? But this is not satisfactory. To distinguish a remarkable coincidence from a miracle, we need some kind of idea of God's intervention. And if God intervened, it meant that he must have altered the progress of nature. And to do this, he must in some sense break the laws of nature, as nature alone would not have provided sufficient cause for the miracle. So Hume does seem to be right.

We can therefore have no reason to accept a miracle unless evidence for the miracle is greater than the evidence against it. Note, however, that we could still believe in miracles as an act of faith, one which would actually be contrary to reason. This makes the act of faith that much harder.

Part II

Hume continues his argument by claiming that, as a matter of fact, no miracle can ever be supported by reason. He gives four explanations for this. They all hinge on the key idea that the evidence for a law of nature, supported by all experience, can never be outweighed by a few conflicting experiences or testimonies. First, there is no-one so virtuous that they could never be free from the suspicion that they were deceiving. Second, the emotions of surprise and wonder are very strong, and such is their effect that we really want to believe in the extraordinary. Thus, humans are very susceptible to belief in apparent miracles. (This is important, because so far, Hume has based his argument against miracles on facts concerning how we actually do reason from experience. But as people clearly do believe in miracles, he has to explain why they do so when it is contrary to their normal method of reasoning.) Third, it is no coincidence that tales of miracles are most rife in 'primitive' and 'ignorant' societies (or, indeed, that aliens only seem to visit isolated farmhouses!). The more advanced we are in our intelligence and science, the less we believe in such things. Fourth, against the witnesses of any miracle, we can balance up an infinite number of witnesses to events which uphold the laws of nature. As laws of nature are by their very nature exceptionless, the whole of human history is, in effect, testimony against the reality of miracles.

Hume follows this up with a lengthy, interesting, though philosophically unimportant series of anecdotes to back up his arguments. He considers various reported cases of miracles, applies his ideas to them and discredits them. His conclusions, though, are worth noting. He argues that 'a miracle can never be proved so as to be the foundation of a system of religion'. Although he concludes that faith may yet provide a basis for belief in miracles and religion, since belief in the former is contrary to reason, the implication is clearly that belief in miracles has no place in religion.

XI   Of a Particular Providence and of a Future State

In this section, Hume suddenly becomes coy, presenting his argument as if it were simply the recollection of what his friend attributes to be the thoughts of Epicurus (341–270 BCE). The odd-sounding title of this section refers to the belief that the world has been designed, with a particular purpose, by God. Hume argues that there is no *philosophical* justification for this belief. In doing so, he claims not to be undermining the foundations of society, but arguing for principles which any person arguing consistently must accept to be true.

Hume's target is the so-called 'argument from design' or 'teleological' argument for God's existence, which really contains three steps. The first is the observation that there is order in nature. The second is that this order contains the marks of intelligence and design, and that mere chance or the 'blind and unguided force of matter' is not causally sufficient to create this order. The conclusion is that therefore it must be God who created the world. Just as one infers the existence of a watchmaker from the order one finds in a watch, so one infers a creator from the order one finds in the universe.

Hume criticises this argument on the grounds that 'when we infer any particular cause from an effect, we must proportion the one to the other, and can never be allowed to ascribe to the cause any qualities, but what are exactly sufficient to produce the effect'. In other words, we can only infer a cause sufficient to produce the effect. For example, if a hole is blasted through a wall, we may only infer that the blast was sufficient to produce that hole. Though it *may* have been greater, we have no reason to claim that it *was* greater.

So, if we allow that the gods created the universe, we can only ascribe to them those powers sufficient to create the universe and no more. However, what the argument from design does is to claim that the existence of the universe points to an all-powerful, all-knowing, all-loving God. This is to endow God with more properties than are required to create the universe. (Now, with advances in physics, it is considered possible to ascribe *nothing* to the cause of the universe, it could actually be a *causa sui* – a cause of itself.) People make the mistake of positing the creator, and then becoming so enamoured of their own idea that they attribute many other qualities to it.

So, in essence, what Hume's argument does is not to attack the basic premise that there is order in the universe, but that from this order we can infer that God is its creator. He attacks this supposition as 'uncertain and useless'. Uncertain, because it goes beyond what we can reasonably infer from human experience, and useless, because it is based entirely on the order of nature, so we cannot use the 'discovery' that God exists to understand this order more. God's existence is derived from this order, so to attempt to derive new facts about this order from God's existence would be to reason in a circle.

Now, he considers a counter-argument from analogy. If it is right to infer from a half-finished building that there has been a builder, or from one footprint in the sand that someone has been walking there and the other prints must have been washed away, isn't it just as valid to argue from the order of the universe to an intelligent creator? Hume replies that we can infer in the analogous cases, because we know from experience the relation between human artefacts and human artisans, footprints and people. As all knowledge of matters of fact is based on experience, this is how we justify our inferences. But where we have seen only one example of something, with no previous knowledge of who or what created it, little or nothing can justly be drawn from experience about the nature of its creator. As there is some wisdom and goodness in nature, these can be ascribed to the creator, and so on. But we are very limited in how much we can ascribe to the creator, as we have no experience of other of its creations.

Later, Hume suggests that even this would be to ascribe too much. As we have no experience of God at all, and as the universe is a singular, unique thing, we cannot reason anything about its creator, as this would be to go way beyond how we can justly reason concerning matters of fact. Without experience of the universe's cause, there is no basis for any inference about it.

A final point is that just because reasonings such as the argument from design *should not* influence people's thoughts, that doesn't mean they *do not* influence them. The argument from design had, and still has, many supporters, despite Hume's devastating and seemingly unanswerable objections.

XII   Of the Academical or Sceptical Philosophy

In this final section, Hume attempts to find the right role for scepticism in philosophy and avoid some of scepticism's more negative features. In Part I he considers scepticism concerning the existence of external objects. In Part II, he considers scepticism concerning our reasoning in matters of fact. In Part III he draws out what he believes are the right consequences of mitigated scepticism.

Part I

Hume distinguishes between antecedent and consequent scepticism. Antecedent scepticism, like that of Descartes, begins with universal doubt and then attempts to build up knowledge from those principles which are certain and cannot be doubted (see Chapter 2 on the *Meditations*.) This fails because, first, there are no such indubitable principles, and second, even if such a principle could be found, nothing could be built on it without using those faculties (reason, et cetera) which we are supposed to already doubt.

Consequent scepticism is when we become sceptical because, having already reasoned, we discover faults and errors in our faculties, be they mental or perceptual. Perceptual error in itself does not justify universal doubt, as all this shows is that we must not trust our senses alone. Nor can this scepticism convince us that the external world does not exist.

However, Hume thinks 'the slightest philosophy' can destroy our certainty about external objects, as it teaches us that 'nothing can ever be present to the mind but an image of perception'. In other words, he believes reason leads to the belief that we do not directly perceive objects in the world. It is impossible to show that our perceptions resemble real objects, as we can only reason from experience, and experience is only ever of these perceptions. Nor can belief in God help us. Clearly, God does not make sure we are never deceived by our senses, so if sensory deception is OK by God, then we cannot argue from the fact of his goodness to the veracity of our experiences.

This antecedent scepticism is also reinforced by the collapse of the primary and secondary qualities distinction. Locke argued that, though secondary qualities such as smell, colour and taste were dependent on our senses, primary qualities such as extension, hardness and so on were not. But Hume rightly points out that knowledge of even these primary qualities depends on our senses, so we cannot consistently claim that primary qualities are independent of us if we say this is not true of secondary qualities.

Hume concludes by claiming that the belief in external objects faces a two-pronged challenge. If it rests on natural instinct, it is contrary to reason, as reason shows we do not directly perceive external objects. If it rests on reason, it is contrary to natural instinct, and at the same time fails to find this rational support, as there are no reasonable grounds for believing we experience external objects. What we are then left with is the view that such a belief is contrary to reason, and that all we are aware of are sensible qualities (i.e. qualities we perceived), and that once we take these away, there are no other properties left which we can ascribe to matter. It is merely, as Berkeley put it, 'something, I know not what'.

Part II

Hume now turns to attack the use of abstract reason to discover properties of reality, such as space and time. Hume shows that, if we try and reason about matters of fact just by using our powers of reason, we end up with contradictions. For instance, Zeno's famous paradoxes of motion seem to show that if space and time are infinitely divisible, it would be impossible for anything to move. But if we suppose they are not infinitely divisible, we have to suppose that each point of space is 'infinitely less than any real part of extension', since if this were not true, they would be divisible. But this is absurd, as an infinite number of non-extended points cannot be extended, yet space and time are extended.

Hume uses these examples to show how using pure logic to solve questions concerning real existence leads to absurdity and contradiction.

In matters of fact, he claims there are no real abstract ideas, 'only particular ones, attached to a general term'. Abstract ideas belong to the realm of the relations of ideas.

This seems to open up another route for scepticism. Popular scepticism just claims we are fallible, so we should be sceptical, and so is a weak form of scepticism. But philosophical scepticism reasons that matters of fact are only known through experience, and experiences depend upon cause and effect, which is in itself not supported by experience. In short, the sceptic reasons as Hume does, but concludes that this means our reasonings concerning matters of fact are worthless. Hume, on the other hand, believes that this view cannot result in any good, and therefore it is useless. Hume advocates just accepting how we reason and not giving in to excessive scepticism. Hume's argument is not a logical one, but a psychological and pragmatic one. As the complete suspension of belief advocated by the sceptic is neither possible nor desirable, we should simply carry on, aware of how we reason concerning matters of fact. This way of answering scepticism would also apply to the conclusions of Part I.

Part III

Hume calls this mitigated scepticism, that is, scepticism tempered by pragmatism. He believes this scepticism is useful for two reasons. First, it prevents dogmatism. Second, it will generally lead us to 'enquiries to such subjects as are best adapted to the narrow capacity of human understanding'. We shall not waste our time attempting to argue over things we have not the ability to argue justly about, such as the existence of God.

This leads neatly to Hume's concluding paragraphs, in which he states again the two fit areas of human enquiry, matters of fact and relations of ideas. One new feature is explained here, concerning the role of definition in the relation of ideas. It is often said that truths such as $231 - 165 = 66$ are true by definition, but nevertheless we can understand all the terms in this sum and yet the correctness or otherwise of the answer may not be immediately obvious to us. On the other hand, if we understand 'husband' and 'wife', then the sentence 'every husband has a wife' is not only true by definition, but is transparently true. This makes it clear that not everything 'true by definition' is known in the same way.

The last paragraph of the *Enquiry* is a classic of philosophy, though somewhat hyperbolic. In it, Hume restates his 'fork' and distils the consequence of his theory for the future study of mankind. As a conclusion, it cannot be surpassed, so it is with Hume's rather than my own words that we leave this chapter:

> When we run over libraries, persuaded of these principles, what havoc must we make? If we take in our hand any volume of divinity or school metaphysics, for instance; let us ask, *Does it contain any abstract reasoning concerning quantity or number?* No. *Does it contain any experimental reasoning concerning matter of fact or existence?* No. Commit it then to the flames: for it can contain nothing but sophistry and illusion.

Summary

Hume argues that all we are directly aware of are the 'perceptions of the mind', which he divides into **ideas** and **impressions**. All ideas are copies – sometimes altered or amalgamated – of impressions, which are more or less sensations. There are three forms of connection of ideas in the mind: Resemblance, contiguity (closeness) in time or place, and cause or effect.

Ideas and impressions are the building blocks of knowledge, which comes in two distinct forms: knowledge of **matters of fact**, which concerns what happens in the actual world; and knowledge of the **relations of ideas**, which concerns abstract reasoning of mathematics and logic, as well as things which are true by definition.

All reasoning concerning matters of fact is based on the idea of cause and effect, which in turn is explained in terms of the **necessary connection** between the effect and its cause. But if we try to locate the impression which gives rise to this idea of necessary connection in the world itself, we look in vain. The impression of necessary connection is rather found within the mind itself. When we frequently observe one event to accompany or be followed by another, we are led by **custom and habit** to expect the latter when we experience the former. Hence, through habit, a necessary connection is forged in the mind between what we call the cause and the effect. Our **inductive** reasoning, therefore, is not based on rationality but on habit.

Hume goes on to apply this general theory to several particular issues. He claims that **probability**, strictly speaking, does not exist. We say something is probable when we do not know enough about its causes to be able to predict with accuracy when it will occur, but we know from past experience what proportion of similar causes leads to the effect.

Human action is as much caused as anything else in the world, yet we do have free will. This is the **compatibilist** thesis that all freedom requires is that we act without external coercion or compulsion.

On Hume's view, we have no reason to say that animals do not reason, since they too expect future events to follow the pattern of past ones by the same non-rational mechanisms that we do.

We have no reason to suppose **miracles** ever occur, since we have more experience that tells us the laws of nature are never broken than the few testimonies which claim that they have been. Neither can we argue from the fact that the world has order to the fact that a designer God must exist, since such reasoning goes beyond the evidence of experience.

The upshot of Hume's arguments is that we should have a mitigated **scepticism**. This means accepting that there are no certain proofs for most everyday beliefs but accepting that this is just a result of inescapable limitations on human thought and no reason to doubt everything. It should, however, make us undogmatic and stop us from speculating about matters our minds are ill equipped to think about.

Glossary

Compatibilism   The view that humans have free will as long as there are no external forces making them act the way they do, even though ultimately all actions are as much subject to cause and effect as events in the natural world.

Custom and habit   The way we learn from repeated experience, rather than by logical reasoning.

Empiricism   The view that all knowledge is derived from experience, rather than from the independent operation of the intellect.

Ideas   Weaker, fainter copies of impressions. Ideas are the basic building blocks of thought and imagination.

Impressions   Sensations, feelings and emotions from which all our ideas are derived.

Induction   Reasoning from one or more particular past experiences to conclusions about the future or the general nature of the world. Such reasoning cannot proceed according to rational principles, claims Hume.

Matters of fact   Statements and beliefs about the world which are based on experience, not reason.

Miracles   Breaches of the laws of nature by divine intervention, which Hume argued we can never have reason to suppose occur.

Necessary connection   The power which links cause and effect. The existence of necessary connection is not established by reason or by our experience of the external world.

Probability   The likelihood we ascribe to an event happening when we do not know enough about its cause to be able to predict with certainty when it does or does not occur.

Rationalism   The view, contrary to empiricism, which states that knowledge is acquired through the rigorous use of reason alone, without any need for the data of experience.

Relations of ideas   Statements and beliefs about concepts or number, the truth of which does not depend upon facts about the actual world.

Scepticism   The view that nothing can be known for certain.

Further reading

Many editions of the *Enquiry concerning Human Understanding* are available and there is little to distinguish them other than presentation and cost. The Open Court edition, edited by Antony Flew, has some useful extra material packaged in with it, including Hume's fascinating but brief autobiographical essay.

The Enquiry concerning the Principles of Morals and the *Dialogues concerning Natural Religion* are the natural next steps for those wanting to read more Hume and are available in many editions.

A. J. Ayer's introduction to *Hume* is still a classic and is another text to be reissued as part of Oxford University Press's series of *Very Short Introductions*.

Hume on Knowledge by Harold Noonan is another worthy member of the Routledge GuideBook series.

4
John Stuart Mill: *On Liberty* (1859)

Background

John Stuart Mill (1806–1873) was one of the most influential thinkers of the nineteenth century. His philosophical and political writings, his involvement in the great social causes of the time – the abolition of slavery, female emancipation – ensure his place in history. However, his reputation as a philosopher is sometimes underplayed. A man of many opinions and enthusiasms, it is said that he failed to found them on any sufficiently rigorous doctrine. But this is an unfair picture, and a close reading of his work reveals a coherent and deeply thought-out view of life.

He was the first-born son of James Mill (1773–1836), a Scottish economist, political philosopher and historian. James was also a friend of Jeremy Bentham (1748–1832), the English utilitarian philosopher, and it was the influence of these two men that was to shape the young Mill's life. In line with the empiricist view that we acquire all knowledge through experience, James hot-housed his son: by three, he was reading Greek; by eight, Latin. Mill's childhood was therefore an experiment, conducted to prove that genius was not innate. This ordeal left Mill with various psychological scars, resulted in a mental crisis at 20, and was something that he later reproached his father for in his autobiography. However, the experiment itself proved to be a remarkable success, and we might argue that Mill's prodigious career owes itself to his father's somewhat arduous parental discipline.

Whilst he eventually came to criticise James' role, his father's views remained a great influence upon him throughout this life. As well as an empiricist, James Mill was a classical liberal and a utilitarian, views which his son continued to profess. Classical liberalism favoured the individual, arguing that minimal government involvement in business and private affairs would enable both person and society to flourish. Jeremy Bentham, the father of utilitarianism, had argued that everyone was primarily driven by a desire for pleasure, which was in fact the chief good – what is called hedonistic utilitarianism. Therefore, all acts are good in as much as they increase pleasure, and bad in as much as they decrease it or result in pain. In terms of society, the general good was therefore that which caused the greatest happiness for the greatest number.

While initially Mill agreed with Bentham's system, he eventually came to see problems with it. If ten people are made happy by beating up two people, then what the ten people want is 'good' by sheer weight of numbers (ten amounts of happiness being more than two amounts of misery). This is obviously unjust (by traditional standards), and it seems that, if we define what is good simply in terms of specific acts which produce quantifiable amounts of happiness, then utilitarianism will always face problems. Therefore, Mill proposed a more sophisticated version of utilitarianism in which he attempted to marry it with a concern for liberty and the rights of the individual. We'll consider just how successful Mill was in due course.

The text

On Liberty was written in 1859, and was – according to Mill – a joint work with his wife, Harriet Taylor. Although the majority of critics have tended to consider Taylor's input negligible, a significant number believe she played a major role and would have been a notable philosopher in her own right, were it not for the sexist culture of the time. Mill considered it to be one of his most important works, and one that would perhaps best survive the test of time. This is undoubtedly true, and after a period during the twentieth century where its reputation dipped, there is now renewed enthusiasm and respect for the work. Mill is, above all, a consistent thinker – not without flaws, but one at least whose work forms a coherent whole. There are therefore links between this and his other works – the *System of Logic* and *Utilitarianism* especially – which, taken together, provide an intriguing picture of what Mill was trying to accomplish.

The text itself is relatively straight forward, consisting of five chapters that develop Mill's thesis clearly through different areas. The first chapter introduces the central concern for liberty, and the principle of harm; the second applies this to freedom of thought and discussion; the third to the importance of fostering individuality; the fourth concerns the principles as they relate to government involvement in individual actions; and the final chapter considers various applications of these principles.

In terms of style, Mill is a very clear and engaging writer, though his sentences are occasionally overlong for modern taste. However, *On Liberty* was purposely written for the general reader, and is an enjoyable and stimulating read that is remarkably free of intimidating technical vocabulary and jargon, so we do encourage you to search out the original text.

I   Introductory

The first chapter of *On Liberty* introduces the central issue of the essay, which is not the 'liberty of the Will' (whether our actions are freely chosen or causally determined), but the liberty of action (*how* we may act) – what Mill terms 'Civil or Social liberty'. The question therefore concerns the limits of authority: To what extent can society legitimately regulate our thoughts, speech and actions? Most people would consider that you are not free to avenge the defeat of your football team by assaulting randomly chosen opposing fans, or by responding to the refusal of your loan application by setting the bank on fire. Such actions are harmful to people or property and seem to have insufficient cause for such violence. But what if you wanted to ride your bike through the town centre on a Saturday wearing nothing but a smile? Or fill your greenhouse with cannabis plants for private consumption? We may all have opinions on these matters, but is there something that we can appeal to in order to settle them? Mill thinks there is, and claims that there is a single rational principle that can determine these matters to the greatest benefit of all.

To begin with, Mill provides some historical and cultural background. In early societies, laws protecting individual liberty were as much concerned with shielding the people from the sovereign, or from each other, as from outside aggressors. However, as more democratic political systems evolved, the rulers were first restricted (for instance, a king's commands required ratification by parliament), and eventually made subject to popular vote. Rulers became the servants of the people.

But the replacement of monarchy or aristocratic rule by democracy does not in itself mean that all common interests are automatically served. Even democratic rule selectively favours a particular portion of society – the 'norm' – and we must therefore be on our guard against what Mill terms 'the tyranny of the majority'. This is an important issue, especially for utilitarianism, involving situations where minority interests are ignored or even harmed in favour of what most people want. Since utilitarianism is traditionally defined in terms of 'what most people want', then if Mill can establish a principle of liberty that avoids this sort of injustice, he will kill two birds with one stone: rescue utilitarianism from a common criticism, and protect social liberty.

But in what way is the majority tyrannical? First, Mill states that it can make laws that can (directly or indirectly) oppress minorities; or it can, less formally, influence the conduct of individuals by popular opinions and attitudes. To use a modern illustration, it's not against the law for a woman to work on a building site, but wolf whistles and boorish behaviour might make her uncomfortable enough to seek other work. We need therefore not only to ensure that minority interests are not politically oppressed, but also that freedoms are not restricted by more subtle means, such as attitudes in the media, at the pub, in the home or the workplace.

But liberty is a double-edged sword. We should be free to act in legitimate ways, but not free to restrict others' legitimate actions; free to speak, but not always to condemn or persecute. Laws should therefore protect both individual freedom and society itself, whilst opinion can be used to combat prejudice as well as influence behaviour. But what makes actions or opinions legitimate or illegitimate? We are still missing a principle.

The problem, as Mill sees it, is that few seem to have recognised the need for one. Even though customs and attitudes differ greatly between countries and cultures, it's commonly assumed that people mostly agree about things. But this is just a prejudice. People often keep unpopular or eccentric opinions to themselves out of fear, and it's likely that not everyone will agree on what is acceptable behaviour. Furthermore, notions of acceptability are often influenced by non-rational factors – prejudice, superstition, personal desire – the common attitude being that feelings ('gut reaction') make a rational, thought-out position unnecessary. 'I mean, *everyone* knows *that*, don't they?!' Often, social class or religious allegiance will dictate our views. Even in religion a *principle* of tolerance has only developed through self-interest. For instance, Mill points out, as various protestant sects broke away from the Catholic Church during the Reformation, tolerance became a means of survival: these new 'minorities, seeing that they had no chance of becoming majorities, were under the necessity of pleading to those whom they could not convert, for permission to differ.' So, even in religion, where non-judgementalism and forgiveness supposedly abound, tolerance is limited, reluctantly employed and selective.

In England, Mill argues, there has long been a deep-seated resentment of government interference in individual life. But this is based once again on feeling and not on rational grounds, and the government is applauded or condemned for its behaviour without any clear sense of what the principle of its actions should be. What is needed, then, is a clear and rational principle of the regulation of conduct – as to whether and where the authorities can step in to regulate the free choices of individuals, or public opinion can be made to influence it.

And here, having made the case for the need for such a standard, Mill introduces what has become known as his *principle of harm*.

> the only purpose for which power can be rightfully exercised over any member of a civilised community, against his will, is to prevent harm to others. His own good, either physical or moral, is not sufficient warrant.

Immediately, there are some important things for us to note here, and a number of questions which arise. First, prevention of harm does not extend to the moral or physical good of the individual as perceived by others: a man might fritter his money away on gambling or drink, he might enjoy hitting himself over the head with a cricket bat, but if any of these things do not involve harm to others, then we cannot interfere with his freely chosen pastimes, attitudes or opinions. We can of course seek to persuade him not to have those opinions or perform those actions, but they are his free choices – what Mill later terms his 'self-regarding' actions: 'Over himself, over his own body and mind, the individual is sovereign.' Second, an authority may not generally interfere with the actions of *sane*, *adult* members of a *civilised community*. So, the insane, the temporarily unhinged, children, and those who exist in what Mill terms 'backward states of society' (that is, so-called 'primitive' societies) can all be legitimately 'guided' by wiser hands. We should also be aware here that Mill is primarily concerned with harm in terms of *interests*. We overstep moral boundaries not just when we damage individuals or their property, but when we restrict their ability to follow their own legitimate goals. Just what this means will come out more fully in the course of the essay.

But what sort of thing is the principle of harm? It is not, Mill states, 'an abstract right', possessed innately or objectively by all people (such as we find in the philosophy of Immanuel Kant), but rather springs from the *principle of utility* – that is, 'utility in the largest sense, grounded on the permanent interests of man as a progressive being'. So, abiding by the principle of harm will ultimately lead to greater happiness and social evolution. It is a utilitarian principle, as a result of which, Mill implies, human society will become more rational, democratic, tolerant and peaceful – 'happier' in general.

Concerning the things regarding which a man may be legally compelled or socially influenced, Mill is keen to stress that these may involve both acts and omissions; injury to others and also failure to perform duties which would be beneficial to others. Refusal to give evidence in court or to stop someone jumping off a bridge (if possible), are both punishable offences – though omission in general is a lesser evil, and should have lesser penalties.

But in what respect, then, is a person free? It is here that Mill is most radical. First, a person should be free to have thoughts and hold opinions on any subject, 'practical or speculative, scientific, moral or theological'. For instance, you may think the Earth is flat, that children should be beaten, that we are all subject to the Giant Turnip, but – as long as your views do not cause harm to others – you are free to hold and express them. They are only views, not actions (your advocacy of child-beating may merely remain an opinion). Second, you should have 'liberty of tastes and pursuits'. This means 'doing as we like', so long as no one else is hurt, even though others 'think our conduct foolish, perverse, or wrong'. This, obviously, will include a wide range of practices that express personal preference – sexual inclination, hobbies and pastimes – which are all the expression of individual free choice. The third aspect of individual freedom concerns our relationship to others. We may get together with other adults to whatever purpose we see fit, as long as we are all freely consenting and not deceived in the matter. It would not be permissible for some leather-clad dominatrix to force or deceive someone into being her personal slave, but there is nothing to stop two people forming such a relationship in full and conscious expression of personal desire – as long as it is not *literal* slavery, of course, which Mill has something to say about later on.

And yet, despite the rational appeal of this principle, it is, Mill writes, in almost direct opposition to the spirit of the times. He considers that the conditions which perhaps once merited the invasive intervention of the state in individual affairs (protection from foreign threat) are greatly lessened in modern democracies. Yet even so authorities persist in such meddling – the secular no less than the religious, who are both driven by a concern to impose their moral values on others. (Mill cites French sociologist Auguste Comte (1798–1857) as an example, see below.) So, unless something is done – unless, that is, Mill's recommendations are adopted – this mischief will continue to increase.

Problems

The first problem that strikes us is that Mill's principle provides selective freedoms. As already noted, 'backward' or 'primitive' societies are considered incapable of rational self-government. Mill is primarily thinking here of non-Western, less technologically developed societies where science and rationality have not yet taken as firm a hold as they have in the West. So, the British rule of India (in which both Mills played a part) resulted in a general attempt to 'improve' and revise laws and customs in line with Western values. For instance, the traditional practice of *Sati*, where a widow might voluntarily (or involuntarily) join her husband's funeral pyre, was eventually outlawed and eradicated. We might agree with this, but such changes were arguably driven by a more general desire to impose Christianity and democracy out of an assumption of their superiority. In a world where you can walk into a McDonald's in Manchester or Mumbai, there is a growing backlash against such 'cultural imperialism', and we are now more sensitive to the global spread of Western values, and the presumption that Mill's view implies.

On the other hand, Mill surely has a point when he argues that freedom requires 'free and equal discussion', hence rationality, and cultures which do not value this cannot develop true liberty or justice. In view of this, he says 'Despotism is a legitimate mode of government in dealing with barbarians, provided the end be their improvement, and the means justified by actually effecting that end.' But we must be *very* sure of our values to justify such totalitarian rule – and can we be? In response, we may argue that Mill is in fact very concerned with *not* imposing our values on others. Mill's mention of Auguste Comte is relevant here. The two were friends, and Mill was heavily influenced by Comte's *positivism*, the idea that all theories should as far as possible be based on the evidence of sense experience. As the father of sociology, Comte was keen to apply this approach to society and culture, but – in Mill's eyes – he went too far, seeking to impose a new 'religion of humanity' that would revolutionise society. In contrast, Mill may be thought of as an *ethical minimalist*: we have minimal duties to others and society in general, but outside of that, we are completely free, and should not try to impose on others' free development. Mill's concern for 'backward' societies was therefore restricted to establishing the minimum conditions necessary for such free choice to exist. This is still to impose a value, of course, but it is perhaps only cultural imperialism *lite*.

II   On the Liberty of Thought and Discussion

Having argued the need for a principle to regulate the relationship between the individual and society, and outlined it in general, Mill now proceeds to consider its first aspect: the freedom of thought and discussion. Mill first argues that all moves to silence or limit free speech are illegitimate, for either what is expressed is correct, and society loses out by suppressing a valuable opinion; or else it is mistaken, and exposure to it thereby helps us to clarify why we are right in disagreeing with it. So, even if a controversial opinion is only held by a single individual, and the government and the rest of society are in agreement against it, suppressing it is as wrong as if that single individual were to suppress the view of the majority (which would be a form of tyranny).

Mill then proceeds to defend each of these points in detail. First, what if we inadvertently suppress truth? As Mill argues, 'All silencing of discussion is an assumption of infallibility.' We need only look back to other ages or to different cultures to see how certainty of opinion is often relative to one's culture or background. But, someone might object, does this, then, mean that we can never enforce an opinion for fear of being wrong? No. Just because there have been unjust wars or taxes, we should not refrain either from just war or taxation. Our certainty may not be absolute, but we must still do what we consider right.

But Mill's point is that the strength of our convictions can only come from the freedom of others to contest them. The existence of rational opinions and conduct owes itself not to the fact that we are often right – we often aren't! – but to our ability to correct our mistakes, in which discussion and openness to experience play a central role. To possess sound judgement one must therefore possess an open mind. Even the Catholic Church, Mill says, which he considers 'the most intolerant of churches', allowed a Devil's Advocate to argue against a candidate for Sainthood. (Or at least it did up until 1983, when the function was revoked by John Paul II.) The greatest certainty we can aspire to is therefore to be found in opinions which have best resisted all challengers, not those which have never been in the ring. We must therefore guard against selective free speech, which allows questioning, but only up to a limit, or to the exclusion of certain topics. To hold certain opinions as sacred cows is to fear that questioning may undermine them – which is the very thing we should like to know if it *were* the case: if there *are* such weaknesses, we would want to know them. We see here an illustration of Mill's scientific attitude. He is not sceptical as to the existence of truth, but, as an empiricist, recognises that we do not have infallible access to it. Since knowledge comes from experience, *new* experience may cause us to revise our views.

But aren't we entitled to protect certain opinions because they are *useful* to society? No, Mill replies, because their usefulness should be just as open to question as their truth, and the only way we can truly determine this is through testing it.

Mill argues that, even if we take the most certain and socially useful doctrines – moral or religious beliefs – the problem is not that we consider them certain, but that we decide their truth for others by forbidding expression of opposition; we assume infallibility. In other words, Mill is not being relativist (all our values and opinions are equally valid), or even sceptical (we can never know the truth), but simply pointing out, more moderately, that suppressing dissent in the name of supposed good has in the past led to terrible mistakes. Here, he cites two noted examples: Socrates (see Chapter 1), executed by the Athenian government for supposed impiety and immorality, denying the gods and corrupting the youth; and Jesus, who was crucified by the Roman authorities on the charge of blasphemy – both of whom, posterity agrees, were the *opposite* of the type of men who might have deserved such treatment. And, lest we assume that the people responsible for these injustices were abnormally wicked or intolerant, Mill asks us to recall that St Paul was himself among those who persecuted and stoned the first Christian martyrs. An occasional blindness to truth is something that even the best may share.

Mill also cites the Roman emperor Marcus Aurelius as an illustration of how even great wisdom and learning does not guarantee infallibility. Despite being, in spirit if not in doctrine, 'a better Christian...than almost any of the ostensibly Christian sovereigns who have since reigned', Aurelius nonetheless persecuted Christianity, which he saw as a threat to the traditional social order. And who among us, Mill asks, can claim that he is of greater intellect, learning or wisdom than Marcus Aurelius was in his time?

Perhaps, then, intolerance and persecution is a necessary rite of passage for truth, a sort of ordeal that tests its mettle? If your opinion is true, we might argue, then it will survive. But Mill rejects this also, for it would seem to be unjust to the advocates of newly discovered truths, whom this argument would seem to condone treating with persecution and intolerance. And is it always the case that truth survives? No. Mill says we need only look at, for instance, the fact that the Reformation was put down again and again before it finally succeeded under Martin Luther. (He is obviously siding with the Protestant cause here, but we need only take it as an example of how hard it may be to make unpopular opinions heard.) It did eventually succeed, but it might not have done, and only ultimately prevailed through sheer momentum. As Mill puts it: 'Persecution has always succeeded, save where the heretics were too strong a party to be effectually persecuted.' But this will not be the case with all truths. Of course, if something is in fact true, then, whilst it may be suppressed and persecuted time and time again, there will always be those who will rediscover it. This makes it more likely that a true opinion will ultimately prevail, but not certain, which is why we need to protect *all* opinion from persecution, in case one turns out to be true.

While Mill's times were relatively tolerant of diverse opinion, there were still legal penalties for holding certain opinions. For instance, atheists were still debarred from giving evidence in court. (This changed in the United Kingdom with the Evidence Amendment Act of 1859, though discrimination is still current in some countries, and atheists still have no legal status in Iran, for instance.) Paradoxically, Mill observes, in considering all atheists untrustworthy, such a rule forces atheists to lie in order to give testimony, and excludes those honourable enough to refuse to hide their unbelief. As for atheism and blasphemy, so for other forms of unpopular opinion, no one of which should be the cause of discrimination or suppression of free speech. Mill admits that things are much better now than they were – people are no longer burnt for heresy (the last was in 1721 during the Spanish Inquisition, though others continued to be killed, tortured and imprisoned for other crimes). But we may still do serious harm to freedom by more civilised means of repression, and there is no guarantee that such persecution will not return, and bigotry and intolerance are forever just below the surface. Moreover, while there may not be legal restraints, there is still the oppressive influence of common opinion, which may affect a person's livelihood. In other words, to express or be known to hold certain opinions may be frowned upon to the extent that you are discriminated against socially – passed over for jobs, mocked or bullied, and so on. The fear of this therefore forces would-be dissenters to stay quiet in order merely to make a living. Thus, although this keeps expression of dissent at a minimum, Mill sees society as harmed by being robbed of the challenging opinions of 'the most active and inquiring intellects', which, even if false, would serve to broaden our minds and deepen our understanding. But, as it is, such minds must craftily further their ambitions by more stealthy means, thus fostering an atmosphere of dishonesty. Also, where such hidden opinions may be false, they remain unchallenged and uncured. But the greatest damage is to the orthodox, whose mental development is stunted by fear of heresy. Such freedom is necessary not only for the development of great minds, but for the general health of society, and he argues that Europe would not have developed to its current level of civilisation were it not for periodic relaxation of dogmatic and authoritarian rule (for instance, following the Reformation).

Having pointed out that popular opinion may be false, Mill now considers the benefits of free speech even where received opinion is true. Unless tested and questioned, a true opinion can only ever be a 'dead dogma'. In this way, truth becomes a mere prejudice or superstition, armoured against all rational objections. But, it may be argued, one doesn't have to hear opinions contradicted in order to understand them: when we learn geometry, we learn the grounds for the conclusion without hearing them argued against. True, admits Mill, but the parallel is a false one: no difference of opinion is *possible* in maths (well, given the most straight-forward demonstrations, perhaps – but we can see Mill's point). Even scientific matters admit of many possible forms of interpretation, and we cannot progress scientifically without showing how one theory is better than another. What greater reason, then, to foster debate where there is much greater possibility of variance and error – such as in religion, morals and social policy. Opinions most benefit from the greatest familiarity with the objections of those who sincerely oppose them, for it is only in this way that we can know the strongest reasons for holding our beliefs, and defend them rationally against opponents.

Isn't it enough that there are experts who know and can respond to all the objections? We needn't trouble the average person with these, who is ill-equipped to defend himself. But, Mill responds, how are such experts to be made aware of all possible objections? This in itself seems to require freedom of opinion. In Catholicism, he points out, priests are allowed to read banned books, not, however, with an open mind but merely to generate counter-arguments to heretical views. Ordinary believers are not even allowed that, but must accept religious doctrine on trust. In Protestantism, where individuals are responsible for their own salvation, restriction of free opinion presents a greater problem. What's more, these opinions, uninvestigated, lose much of their original spirit and intent, and become in danger of being misapplied or misconstrued. What these points illustrate, Mill argues, is that when

it originates, and whilst it fights for existence, a new creed or doctrine is actively explored and defended; but once it becomes established,
and becomes the majority view, such vigorous defence is no longer
considered necessary, and the believer becomes lazy and dull.

An example of this can be found in the common form of Christian
belief. Mill argues that most believers hold to the principles of
Christianity loosely, whilst the majority of their views stem from common attitudes in society. They say and believe one thing, and do
another. Thus, their belief is not a living faith or guide to action, but
something they pay lip service to and adhere to when it suits them.
This was not so with the early Christians, he says, for they had to defend
their controversial faith against others. Discussion is therefore essential
to the vitality of a doctrine: 'Both teachers and learners go to sleep at
their post, as soon as there is no enemy in the field.' But Mill is not singling out Christianity here – the same point may be made regarding any
set of ethical principles or beliefs. It often takes some harsh experience
to wake us up to the truth of some opinion that we've long held, or been
aware of, but if we were more accustomed to debating these principles,
then this would not be the case.

Does this mean, then, that true knowledge is only to be obtained
through continuous dissent and questioning? Is unanimous opinion
necessarily a bad thing? No, Mill says, for progress may partly be measured in the extent to which people agree about important issues, even
though there are also drawbacks, as we've seen. A compromise is therefore for those learning such opinions not to swallow them uncritically,
but to reconsider past objections in order to arrive at the accepted doctrines afresh (what may be termed the *dialectic* approach). We find this
attitude alive in the dialogues of Plato, or the philosophy of the Middle
Ages, but Mill considered it to be lacking in his time, with the result
that it was common even among intellectuals to hold opinions with
little awareness of possible objections or how to defend against them.
Modern times are not greatly different, perhaps.

However, aside from the possibility that a suppressed opinion might
be true, or the benefits of having true opinions challenged, Mill presents
a third argument in favour of free speech: the truth may exist somewhere in between two views, or be shared between them. Heretical
views often in an exaggerated way reveal aspects of conventional truth
that the majority ignores. Mill's example here is the French philosopher Jean-Jacques Rousseau (1712–1778), whose critique of the artificial
nature of contemporary society was in a sense further from the truth
than the conventional view, Mill thought, but nonetheless highlighted

important values that the mainstream had neglected. A modern illustration could be the radical Green movement, which might not have a fully viable alternative model for how to run a modern society, but has arguably already generated enough support for mainstream parties to change their attitudes to the environment. So, Mill concludes, until such a time as a ruling group or individual can hold such opposing attitudes in balance, and can weigh up the opposing virtues of co-operation and competition, liberty and discipline, luxury and abstinence, and so on, then we must always accord minority views the freedom to express themselves.

But what of Christianity? Is that to be considered a 'half-truth'? Mill's attitude here is interesting. Some have interpreted him as an atheist, stifled from expressing his unbelief by the spirit of the times. However, there are good reasons for thinking him a religious sceptic or agnostic. He was not anti-religion, but merely against common religious trappings, and the authoritarianism, intolerance and repression that often seem to go hand in hand with Christian culture. Accordingly, he argues that we must distinguish between the teachings of Christ and Christian morality, the latter being influenced by Greek and Roman culture, and moulded by the Catholic Church for its own political purposes (i.e., to suppress and supplant paganism). Also, he says, we should not assume that the original Christian teaching was meant to provide a complete ethical doctrine, for it leaves out many important things. Any ethics solely erected on a narrow reading of Christian doctrine can only *detract* from moral goodness. Christian morality needs to be supplemented by secular ethics and must develop a tolerance of free speech and unorthodox opinion if the whole truth is to be revealed. Free discussion will admittedly not eradicate religious conflict, Mill says, but the less partisan will benefit, for 'there is always hope when people are forced to listen to both sides; it is when they attend only to one that errors harden into prejudices.'

Mill ends this chapter by summarising the four main benefits of free opinion and expression. First, suppression of opinion assumes infallibility, for the suppressed opinion may be true. Second, even if wrong, the suppressed opinion may contain some truth, and the conventional opinion not the whole truth; free discussion is therefore necessary to arrive at a truer opinion. Third, even if the majority opinion is the whole truth, it will remain only a prejudice unless it is constantly tested by vigorous opposition. And lastly, this suppression will result in the essential meaning of a true doctrine being lost, for conflict brings deeper understanding.

Problems

Mill's position here on free speech and tolerance springs from a philosophical position known as *fallibilism*, the general view that any of our beliefs could be wrong. We may consider this a broadly scientific view, since science is generally thought to advance by the proposal and testing of hypotheses, which are held provisionally until disproved by data, when better models are then adopted. Similarly, then, Mill's argument for allowing unpopular opinions or even religious heresy is that it can only benefit us: either it helps us deepen our knowledge of what we already take to be true, or it helps correct our mistakes.

The problem with this is that it seems to leave the door open to scepticism. If we can never really know whether our beliefs are true, then it is possible that we will always be mistaken – and not know it. But Mill is not a sceptic, so how can he justify believing in truth? Mill's response is close to what may be termed *pragmatism*: truth is what seems to work or fit. This doesn't mean that *whatever* works or fits is *true*, for that would leave open the possibility that there are multiple 'truths'. Rather, truth refers to what seems to best fit given our current knowledge. We call it truth – it may turn out not to be – but that is just because our knowledge is relative to experience. To hang on to an absolute and fixed certainty is therefore to deliberately blind oneself. We need to test truth in order to ensure that it is still 'true'. So, whilst this uncertainty may make some people uncomfortable, it is the most honest and beneficial approach.

A good illustration here is the contemporary debate surrounding intelligent design (a form of religious creationism). Whilst Darwin's theory of evolution by natural selection is widely accepted and supported by scientific evidence, certain religious believers persist in arguing that the world was in some way created or shows evidence of divine design. Since, they argue, evolution is 'only a theory', the theory of intelligent design should also be taught in schools. Many scientists are against this: why should we promote error? Mill's take on this would therefore be interesting. Allowing people to consider both views can only strengthen their ability to reason and evaluate. Even if some form of creationism has nothing at all to contribute to our understanding of evolution (it is 100 per cent false), we will learn more about how to prove that point rationally. If, however, there are elements of truth in some form of creationism, then we will also benefit. It's win-win.

Or is it? It may be argued that many of us are not capable of arriving at a correct understanding of these issues – most are not trained in biology, palaeontology or genetics. We might therefore arrive at the wrong conclusion. There is a point here, but it is also a potentially patronising one. We can see this if we put the boot on the other foot. Certain religious fundamentalists will argue that we gain nothing from tolerance of heresy and unbelief, which only harm believers. We should therefore protect religious doctrines from criticism. Atheists and agnostics would criticise this, and suggest that such restriction stems from fear. And where religious views affect public opinion or legislation – abortion, stem cell research, and so on – then the public interest is served in questioning and challenging these attitudes. But then, that would apply to the creationism debate also: are some scientists afraid that people simply aren't rational, or that they won't arrive at the 'correct' opinion? The underlying issue is a deep one, that of *paternalism*, or the idea that the state should protect its citizens, even from 'false' opinion. It also concerns the very purpose of education. Are we teaching people the truth, or to find the truth for themselves? We'll come back to this issue.

III   Of Individuality, as One of the Elements of Well-Being

Having established the benefits of freedom of opinion and expression, Mill now turns to action: should people be free to act as they see fit 'so long as it is at their own risk and peril'? Even opinions must be regulated where they might lead to directly harmful actions – such as inciting a mob to riot. Mill therefore arrives at a general principle of free action. An individual

> must not make himself a nuisance to other people. But if he refrains from molesting others in what concerns them, and merely acts according to his own inclination and judgement in things which concern himself, the same reasons which show that opinion should be free, prove also that he should be allowed, without molestation, to carry his opinions into practice at his own cost.

In other words, you are responsible for your own actions, and as long as you don't bother anyone, and accept the consequences, you can do what you like. Others might disapprove, but it's none of their business. Knock yourself out – just 'don't do it in the street and frighten the horses', as the actress Beatrice Campbell once famously put it. The same factors that favour free opinion and expression considered in the last chapter (fallibility, social progress) therefore also apply here (with some reservations).

However, Mill argues, the problem is that not everyone considers minimally regulated freedom to be a good thing, and many simply don't understand why we all don't share the majority view. Most people simply do not seem to value freedom highly enough to allow others the full liberty of such 'self-regarding actions'. Why then *should* we value such freedom? Citing the German philosopher Wilhelm von Humboldt (1767–1835), Mill argues that, for an individual to reach their highest potential and achieve true originality, there must be freedom to choose and act. But there is a balance that needs to be made: no one thinks that happiness lies in *always* following the herd in or conforming in *everything*, and nor, on the other hand, should we ignore all past opinions and attitudes. Thus, Mill argues that education should teach children what is generally thought to be right according to current consensus, with the proviso that, once they become adults, they will have the right to question and explore things for themselves. This is because the conventional wisdom dished out in schools, whilst valuable during development, may ultimately prove too narrow, be revealed to be based on false assumptions, or in some way prove unsuitable to the individual in question (who may be 'unusual' in some way). Customs accepted without question also do not serve to produce genuine principles, Mill argues, for we learn better from mistakes based on our own conscious choice or desire, which involve more skill, knowledge, will power and reason than mere dumb acceptance. Even if machines could accomplish all that humans currently do, Mill says, we should not prefer a mechanised world, because it would thereby deprive us of the means to develop ourselves. This is an especially interesting point for our technologically-rich twenty-first-century societies. Thus, education and government should not seek to impose a single ideal upon all individuals, but simply provide the basis for free organic growth. Mill puts it beautifully:

> Human nature is not a machine to be built after a model, and set to do exactly the work prescribed for it, but a tree, which requires to grow and develop itself on all sides, according to the tendency of the inward forces which make it a living thing.

People will admit that freedom to explore and question is generally better than blind allegiance, even where such liberty occasionally allows us to go wrong. However, Mill says, people also generally disapprove of eccentric behaviour or strong passion, something which may be less true today than it was in his time. And yet, he says, to have strong desires is not wrong in itself, for 'Strong impulses are but another name for energy', and can be used for great good as well as immorality. Love of virtue and self-control are also driven by impulses, albeit disciplined ones. When such impulses form part of a controlled and disciplined character they are vital to any society.

Once, Mill argues, society struggled to control the strong impulses of emperors, generals and other powerful men, but Mill believed that in his own Victorian society the opposite was the case: society restricted individual passion and spontaneity to the detriment of the common good. All opinion and action was censored. People did not act in accordance with what would most benefit them or allow them to develop, but out of a sense of what was 'proper'. This left most people without strong feelings or opinions, and with no developed capacities for free thought or deliberation. Today we are all still deeply affected by public opinion and disapproval. Is this what we want?

The attitude Mill is criticising may be termed Calvinist (after the Puritan theologian John Calvin), though it is also broadly shared by many whose cultures have been influenced by Calvinism. It involves the belief that human free will is corrupt, and that to live a virtuous life we must turn our back on all 'pagan' impulses and follow the dictates of Christian authority without question. However, Mill argues, this rejection of paganism, which includes Greek and Roman culture, is shortsighted, and secular attitudes are vital if we are to be moral in its fullest sense. Fostering individuality allows the higher growth of humanity and even strengthens social ties, for each person becomes more valuable and worthy of respect, both to himself and others. As Mill puts it: 'when there is more life in the units there is more in the mass which is composed of them.' When anti-social tendencies are repressed, this improves the individual, and makes him more social; but repression of private impulses only creates weak, ineffective individuals, or strengthens those more inclined to rebel.

But, for some, Mill concedes, the benefit to self-development that springs from freedom will not be in itself enough, and we must show that there are other benefits. First, originality might lead to new discoveries – geniuses are rare, can seldom fit within accepted social norms, and require freedom to grow. However, though people will admire genius in abstract, or in the form of a painter or an exceptional poet, they like it less when it describes a more general originality of thought, action or lifestyle. But we all have to admit, he says, even if we cannot see what 'use' this or that person has, that such originality is necessary to discover such truths as are yet to be known.

Mill saw his own age as a time when the masses ruled, when individuality was completely under the yoke of mediocrity. Those individuals who did influence public opinion were often mediocre, themselves drawn from the masses, and not exceptional or original. This, he says, is the nature of democracy or rulership by majority, which does not aim at producing originality but equality. However, this is not in itself a flaw, merely a common consequence of democracy, and Mill is not arguing for some tyrant to rise up and impose his will by force (which would be worse). However, it does mean that, unless individuality is fostered and protected, originality is suppressed. In this sense, at times of great conformity, non-conformity itself becomes a virtue. Mill therefore concludes that eccentricity should be considered a sign of a society's mental health – and where it is lacking, a sign of danger.

But, Mill argues, individuality should not be encouraged solely to test out unusual practices, or to suit the development of geniuses, but simply because individuals are not sheep – and even sheep are not all alike. People differ in all manner of ways, and require different conditions in order to develop. But Mill considered that his own society lacked such freedom: to engage in pursuits which were substantially different from those the masses preferred was to risk not only social disapproval but, in some cases, being branded a 'lunatic' and locked up. Mill cites contemporary examples of this, including atheists being considered 'insane'.

Mill also cites another reason for why people distrust eccentricity. Because the vast majority have common tastes, they simply do not understand those who differ. In addition to this, Mill saw the programmes of social and moral reform current at the time as attempting to impose a single standard of behaviour, treating everyone as if they were the same. (This is arguably still true, to a degree.) Mill saw such attitudes as having a harmful effect on those possessing the sort of extraordinary energy and spirit required for great enterprises. Stifling the development of such individuals, he argues, produces a state of cultural decline (such as England then found itself in, Mill claims). Liberty and the attempt to improve people don't always go together, but true improvement only has its fullest expression when it is joined to liberty. But both improvement and liberty are in opposition to custom, which is historically responsible for stagnation: cultures evolve to a point and do not advance beyond it. Mill wonders whether this will also happen in Europe. Mill did not see his own society as stagnant – there was, in a sense, constant change and technological and scientific progress. But there was also a great lessening of individuality, and even progress was increasingly measured in terms of making everyone conform to a single ideal (both in terms of education and morality).

Mill cites China as a warning here, a country he saw as possessing a rich cultural tradition, but which had nonetheless succeeded in suppressing individuality by imposing a uniform template upon its population, a structure which hadn't changed in thousands of years and which could only subsequently be altered through outside forces. And yet, he says, this is what England's reformers are heading toward. The recipe for avoiding stagnation is therefore to prize individuality, diversity of character, and other things which spring from freedom of thought and behaviour. It is to this diversity, and the failure of any one power to impose a single ideal, that he says Europe owes it richness of culture and advanced development. Referring back to his earlier discussion of Humboldt, Mill reiterates the need for two conditions essential to personal development, 'freedom, and variety of situations'. All current social forces, he says – movements in politics and education; greater ease of communication, trade and travel – work toward the assimilation of people into one type. These social levellers are the signs of the increased influence of public opinion within the state, as support for non-conformity continues to diminish. The time to resist such a development is now, he argues, and this can only be done through convincing the intelligent portion of society of the value of difference.

Problems

Mill's remarks here may be quite surprising for those who view him as the great spokesman for democracy. But the truth is that, whilst he was a democrat, he was also wary of the dangers of democratic society. The ones he lists here – the loss of true individuality, conformity and oppression, the fostering of a mediocre type of person as the norm – are all sentiments that we find in Nietzsche (see Chapter 5), with whom he actually shares a surprising amount of common ground.

Mill's remarks therefore highlight just how radical he actually was. He was a controversial figure in his day – anti-slavery, pro-sexual equality, in favour of enfranchisement (the widening of voting rights), none of which were exactly popular views at the time. Whilst prominent and influential, he saw himself as an outsider, an agitator whose job was to criticise the status quo and provoke change.

His advocacy of individualism and other 'pagan' values stems in part from his childhood education, where his models were the great philosophers and statesmen of Greece and Rome. Measured against these, contemporary individuals seemed small to him. Mill therefore shared the classical liberalism held by his father and Jeremy Bentham, where government should mostly leave the individual alone to do his own thing and discover his own path.

The principle which regulates individual expression, as already noted, is the principle of harm. But there is a deep tension here: how can Mill promote individualism *and* social responsibility? This is in fact a tension between freedom and justice. As a utilitarian, Mill would prescribe those actions which promote happiness (specially defined). However, a limit on freedom would seem to *reduce* happiness, for, as already noted, there must be situations where a minority of individuals could have their freedom or rights interfered with to the greater happiness of the majority. Executing a murderer might serve no other purpose than pleasing the public's thirst for revenge. If the only reason here is to make the public happy, then we might consider it an injustice, and yet, in traditional utilitarian terms, 'making the majority happy' is what constitutes right. Mill would reject this course of action, but in doing so, does he not cease to be a utilitarian? Some have argued that he is trying here to have his cake and eat it: to define 'good' in terms of happiness or utility, whilst at the same time employing a principle which protects and promotes liberty. He can't have both – can he?

In answering this question, we need to appreciate just how Mill's utilitarianism is different from that of his mentor, Jeremy Bentham. Firstly, he argued, the good is not simply a matter of one type of pleasure. Bentham had famously declared that 'Push-pin [a simple pub game of the time] is as good as poetry.' But to Mill, there were higher and lower pleasures, and we should generally prefer the former to the latter. As Mill put it, 'It is better to be a human dissatisfied than a pig satisfied; better to be Socrates dissatisfied than a fool satisfied.' Refining the notion of pleasure in this way allows Mill to translate utilitarianism into more common moral terms. So, being just, courageous, truthful, or professing other traditional moral qualities, can be seen from a utilitarian perspective as enjoying higher, or perhaps broader pleasures – a more sophisticated account of 'happiness'. What's more, Mill rejects act utilitarianism, whereby we must calculate the greater good for every single action, in favour of more general rules of thumb: if we do x, then, overtime, we will increase our happiness. The principle of harm is therefore a general utilitarian rule which, if followed, will result in the greatest overall happiness. Acting in such ways results in greater 'happiness', not in the short term, perhaps, or on all occasions, and not in the same way as eating a burger, but in a more sophisticated sense, which takes into account our long-term ambitions and allows for individual self-development.

The reason why Mill emphasises the importance of liberty is thus that it allows for individuality to flourish, something he considers central to his broader notion of happiness. Liberty and self-fulfilment were therefore what might be termed *secondary principles*, or things which might not always make us happy *in themselves*, but form part of a more general 'happiness strategy', as we might call it. We might therefore, along with John Gray, term Mill an 'indirect utilitarian'. He aims not at maximising pleasure for short-term goals, or at subjecting each act to a utilitarian calculation, but at long-term goals that have a broader overall benefit. Respecting liberty and fostering individuality are means to an end, and that end is happiness – or, as Aristotle would have termed it, *eudaimonia* ('human flourishing').

There are, however, problems with this approach. First, some may argue that, in refining 'happiness' in this way, Mill is actually moving away from true utilitarianism and toward some sort of *ideal* utilitarianism. If 'happiness' can mean freedom, or moral justice, or any other ideal, then this is far from Bentham's definition, and we might argue that such things need to be cashed out in more basic terms in order to be legitimate – that is, freedom must at some point produce more happiness. But does it? We might question this, or argue that the same old utilitarian problem resurfaces, in that there might be situations in which *restricting* people's freedom might in fact result in greater overall happiness.

Since the majority of Western societies are heavily influenced by liberalism, we might look to them as a test of Mill's principle: has greater freedom and tolerance produced more happiness and human 'flourishing'? Although measures of happiness and well-being are controversial, some international studies suggest that people in more prosperous, democratic and equal societies are happier than others. There are some, however, who question whether our apparently greater freedom to speak and act is an illusion, and that what we actually have is a subtler form of control. Individuality and self-expression, it is argued, are increasingly shaped by consumerism. We are all individuals in as much as we are all consumer units. This is most evident in something like Japanese 'street fashion', where young people may choose from a colourful array of affiliations – Lolita Goth, Ganguro, Visual Kei – all kitted out with tailor-made uniforms and apparel, and catered to by merchandise brands, fashion houses, computer games and TV programmes. The West has its equivalents, of course – surfers, skaters, jocks and geeks – but the point is that, where even teenage rebellion and the search for identity is exploited for financial gain, isn't such freedom as we apparently possess illusory? I don't think this is really what Mill envisaged. Has greater liberty therefore led to greater shallowness? Is the sort of personal liberty which Mill promoted therefore insufficient for true self-development?

IV   Of the Limits to the Authority of Society over the Individual

The previous chapter highlighted the value of individuality, and the harm that the general tendency toward uniformity has upon the formation of unique individuals. In this chapter, Mill goes into the possible tension between the need for individual freedom and the apparent need for society to occasionally regulate that freedom. When is it legitimate for authorities to intervene in matters of personal conduct?

The principle which Mill employs here may be described as 'to each its own': Society, he says, has rights over those actions which affect it; the individual over those which do not affect society. However, Mill rejects the idea that this relationship is some form of 'social contract' – an implicit agreement between individuals and society to abide by certain laws in return for protection and security (we find this view in the philosophy of Rousseau, John Locke and Thomas Hobbes). Rather, Mill argues, the relationship must be defined in terms of utility – what is best for both individual and society. The individual benefits from living in society, and thereby owes a duty to behave in certain ways and not in others; society in general benefits when there is peace and security for its members. First, then, in behaviour and expression of opinion, a person must respect the rights and interests of other people. Second, each individual must help defend society and its members from harm (in times of war, for instance). In both these cases, the authorities may compel individuals to comply by force of law. But there are subtler forms of oppression and harm which do not concern the law, and which must therefore be regulated by opinion. For instance, it is not illegal for one person to determine what everyone in the family watches on television – you wouldn't call the police because you were forced to watch *The Weakest Link* (probably). However, since Mill is also concerned here with when society may exert pressure on others through the expression of opinion – that is, through disapproval – then he argues that it may do so when the harm involved is not a violation of rights. No one has the legal right to choose what to watch on television, but each individual is free to complain about another's preference, and the remainder of the family may rise up in protest at TV dictatorship. Society is therefore allowed to intervene in personal choice – whether through law or merely opinion – when that choice affects another person's interests. (The exceptions here, mentioned in the first chapter, concern minors, 'primitives' and the mentally ill.)

But, Mill is keen to point out, this is not a *laissez-faire* doctrine of self-interest, merely one that looks to non-coercive methods to promote the good. People need encouragement and persuasion to develop the 'self-regarding virtues' required for personal improvement, but neither society in general nor other individuals has the right to tell someone what he may or may not do with his life. He must be left to himself because he is the person whom his decisions most affect, who knows his own heart, and the interests of others can never match that. Others may advise or seek to persuade, but – as long as his actions do not affect society – he must be the final judge. All errors he makes are much better than the evil of external coercion, for at least he may learn from them. However, Mill says, this doesn't mean that we can't express distaste or disapproval regarding his personal qualities and preferences – in fact, if we do so politely and out of genuine concern, then we perhaps *ought* to. We may also act on our personal opinion – avoid his company, warn others about him, pass him over for jobs where the qualities in question make him unsuitable, and so on. Therefore, if a person behaves in a way that others disapprove of, then he has only himself to blame. For instance, your friend might drink excessively (in your opinion), and you tell her that she should drink more moderately. But this is not a moral concern – she doesn't drink and drive, neglect her job, or become violent – but merely arises out of a concern for her character, which you would like to persuade her to improve, good friend that you are.

In addition to criticising those acts which have a direct bearing on the rights of others, Mill argues that we may also consider immoral the qualities of character which act as tendencies toward the performance of those acts – bad temper, malice, envy, cruelty, being domineering, and so on. Unlike the self-regarding faults (over-fondness for alcohol, laziness or poor personal hygiene), Mill considers these as 'moral vices' because they *potentially* involve a 'breach of duty to others'. The distinction between expression of displeasure or distaste, on the one hand, and moral disapproval on the other is an important one here. For example, you can dislike your friend's manners or the company she keeps, her taste in music, and so on, and can tell her, but you should not pressure her, suggest that she *must* change or that her choices are simply 'wrong'. But immoral character traits are different: you *can* strongly disapprove of her capacity to lie, her tendency toward sadism, or any behaviour which affects (or could affect) others. However, while you should try to help rather than punish someone who you consider to be ruining her life, at the end of the day it's none of your business: it's her life.

Not everyone will admit this distinction between self- and other-regarding actions. Mill considers a number of possible objections. First, how can we divorce private actions from the society of which every individual is a part? If you damage your own property, for instance, what of the people who depend on that property in some way? Your family who live in the house you own, for example, or the people you employ in your business. If you damage your health, you also lessen your ability to pay your debt to society in terms of being useful, and become a burden to others. Furthermore, if you lead such a dissolute life, you set a bad example which may mislead others. We can also question whether society should leave such obviously flawed individuals to govern themselves in such matters. Shouldn't the law intervene in these cases also, even if it only affects an individual's own self, especially concerning those things which generations have agreed are to be avoided?

In answer, Mill argues that where such personal choices do indeed lead to some morally reprehensible wrong, then it is the wrong that should be censured, not the habit. So, for instance, if you are a policeman or doctor with a fondness for drink, you should only be judged where you are drunk on duty. But other than that, society should accept that personal vices are the price we pay for social freedom, and should therefore be borne for the sake of the greater good. What's more, Mill points out, society has had all an individual's youth to impose its values on him and to attempt to mould him into an upright citizen, and if it has failed to do so, then this is a sign that it should concentrate on doing its job better, not extending its interference into adulthood. Wouldn't it be better to look to the next generation, and seek to do a better job there? Society's powers are sufficient. Besides, such coercion of rational and autonomous adults would only make rebels worse. As for setting a bad example, Mill retorts, it may be argued that such examples are in fact a warning to others, since they also harm the perpetrator.

However, the strongest argument against interference is that the public is not fit to judge on these matters. Whilst public opinion is often correct in terms of morals (those things which directly affect all of us), personal matters are often a question of taste or prejudice. But being offended by an opinion is no sign that another should not hold it, and such reactions are usually based only on subjective feelings.

Mill then goes on to give some examples. First, Muslims consider eating pork not only forbidden by God, but also highly disgusting. But this disgust should not have any force upon the behaviour of non-Muslims.

And yet, if a Muslim majority society were to enforce such an observance upon everyone in society, even non-Muslims, Mill argues that the only defence of the non-Muslim minority would be that it interfered with an individual's right for personal choice in such matters: our choice of diet is a self-regarding action. Non-Muslims could not appeal to religious freedom or complain of *religious* persecution – it is not part of any reli-gion that it's members *must* eat pork. The liberty of our self-regarding actions is the only basis for complaint.

Mill cites another example: Catholics consider it wrong for priests to marry. In a Catholic majority country such as Spain, it was there-fore frowned upon for *any* priest, of whatever denomination, to take a wife. However, the only complaint that Spanish non-Catholic clergy (e.g., Protestant) might have would be that marriage is a personal choice that does not affect the rights and interests of others. Once again, it is a self-regarding action.

Perhaps, Mill says, the reader might consider these examples inap-plicable because they are unlikely to occur in Britain or America. But consider, he says, the seventeeth-century Puritan intolerance against certain public and private amusements, such as the closure of theatres and banning of gambling under the rule of Oliver Cromwell. Since these were attitudes held by the middle classes, it is perfectly possible that such views could again gain a majority in parliament – and what defence would we have then, apart from that gambling and theatre-going are self-regarding actions?

Mill then looks to America, where he considered there to exist gen-eral public distaste for great shows of wealth. This attitude acted as a sort of unspoken curb on private extravagance, and there was a general disapproval of substantial property ownership and profits gained from non-manual work – basically, anything that highlighted those things that the working classes considered out of their reach. On occasion, within certain trades, many even banded together to veto higher rates of pay for more valued workers – why should you be paid better sim-ply because you possess higher skills or are more industrious? The effect of this form of misplaced solidarity seems completely illegitimate, and represents an abuse of public disapproval, but we may only oppose it if we consider that how much you earn or how you spend your money is your own concern.

Mill then turns to the topic of prohibition: the banning of the sale of alcohol. Prohibitionists often claim that the mere availability of alcohol affects *all* our rights and freedoms by making other members of society more likely to fail to act morally. So, for instance, even though *you* are a careful driver and a non-drinker, this won't save you from the dangers of the drunken driver. This may seem a fair point. However, Mill points out that accepting this principle would provide an excuse to infringe upon almost any personal choice with which we might disagree: 'there is no violation of liberty which it would not justify.' In other words, if we ban the sale of alcohol because some abuse it and go on to infringe the rights of others, we could extend this to other things. Let us say that you have no interest in computer games, that you think they rot children's brains, stop people getting exercise, and so on. Yet others get tremendous enjoyment from them, use them moderately, and even gain some educational benefit from them (or at least, improved hand-eye coordination). Just because the odd individual spends all night playing *Call of Duty 3* and forgets to show up for work, must we punish everyone for that? Illustrated in this way, the principle behind prohibition is revealed as an illegitimate infringement of personal liberty. Use of alcohol is no different, and is simply one of a vast number of things that most people use wisely and gain a positive benefit from, but which a minority abuse. Such is the price of free choice, and society and our lives would be much the poorer were it restricted in this way.

The same is true of those attempts to enforce the observance of Sunday as a day of rest. We may acknowledge, Mill says, that general trade must be suspended on Sundays, otherwise it would force others to do business also. For instance, to illustrate Mill's point, if you open your restaurant on a Sunday, then it may force other restaurants to open (so that they don't lose business), or for your restaurant's suppliers to work also so that you don't switch to a competing supplier. However, the attempt to stop private amusements, travel or other pastimes is an act of religious intolerance. Even if such things are an offence against deity (which is debatable), God is perfectly capable of sorting them out and it is not our job to persecute others. (Incidentally, that Sunday trading is now widely allowed simply suggests that commerce has become more important than strict religious observance.)

Mill's final example is Mormonism, which Victorian society commonly disapproved of for its perceived heresy and also its doctrine of polygamy. Whilst sharing this general dislike, Mill argues that we have no right to step in and, using force or other 'unfair means', try to 'civilise' the Mormons and wipe out the belief. By all means send missionaries, he concedes, or send help to those within the Mormon community who wish to oppose bad laws, but, he says, 'I am not aware that any community has a right to force another to be civilised' and we have no right to embark on a 'civilizade'.

Problems

We can see in this chapter that Mill explicitly rejects the social contract theory of ethics favoured by such as John Locke and Thomas Hobbes, and in modern times, by John Rawls. Social contract theory proposes that society should be guided by rules that rational people would recognise as in their own self-interest and mutual benefit. One reason why certain philosophers favour this theory is that it is seen as providing greater protection for individual rights, whereas utilitarianism must always follow the greater good, even if it occasionally contravenes those rights. As we've seen, Mill argues that respecting another's liberty and rights has a long-term benefit, and that we are not committed to maximising happiness as an act utilitarian might be, so we may argue that he avoids this problem. However, there is another issue. As outlined above, in order to allow and protect legitimate forms of individual freedom, Mill must distinguish between *self-regarding actions* (getting drunk at home) and *other-regarding actions* (being drunk on duty). But is this distinction always easy to make? If not, Mill is in trouble.

For instance, Mill would consider being overweight a self-regarding lifestyle choice. You might be offended by someone's obesity from an aesthetic perspective, but this is a subjective evaluation, and none of your business. However, as much as someone may be happy with their weight, it does have health related side-effects, such as diabetes and heart conditions. All of this requires medical treatment, which in a welfare state are provided by the state. We might argue that this puts an unnecessary burden on the health service, since people who are thinner do not have these problems. Recently, Japan, and certain states in America, have started imposing 'fat fines' on those who refuse to accept dietary advice. It seems that the distinction between self-regarding and other-regarding actions is not always so easy to define. Mill might concede the issue in terms of obesity, but it would seem to be a slippery slope. If we can establish a link between some tangible social harm (the state of the health service) and some self-regarding action, then it seems that – potentially – the state might claim involvement in anything. If you are depressed, might you find the state fining you if you refuse to take your psychiatrist's advice to stop reading Schopenhauer? This seems far fetched, but you can see where it's going.

Another interesting point here concerns the so-called *civilizade* – not a new brand of democratic soft drink, but Mill's term for the sort of 'civilisation crusade' that some of his contemporaries were partial to. Mill's target here was the sort of person who wanted to wade in and – by force, if necessary – stamp out the perceived evil of Mormonism. A modern parallel would be those sections of Western society that advocate military intervention in countries like Iran, North Korea, Iraq or Afghanistan, and who would sort everyone out according to their own ideal of how a society should be governed. However, Mill's position is complicated. He argues that we should respect another society or group's liberty and self-governance, whilst also lending aid if needed. Once again, this seems like a difficult line to draw. If a sovereign country suffers from insurgents, is it legitimate to invade in order to promote democracy and freedom by aiding the insurgency? The involvement of Western powers in foreign lands has often been justified on this basis. One problem is that there is always *some* element of a society that is dissatisfied and in need of support. The question is, how large an element would it have to be in order to justify interference? And should it depend on the values such an element espoused? How do we distinguish between a malign minority 'insurgency' and a popular, benign revolution? Unless we're very careful, Mill's guidelines might seem to justify what we would recognise as illegitimate interference. This may be harsh on Mill, but there is a real problem here. There is a fine line between rescuing an oppressed people and invading and imposing your own ideal, and distinguishing the two requires some fancy footwork.

This problem also arises in private life. We can interfere to prevent harm to individuals or their rights – but what if that 'harm' is consenting? Consider sado-masochism. If someone enjoys being beaten or mistreated, then on the one hand he is being harmed, and so there is an argument for stopping it; but on the other it is a self-regarding and consensual act, and he should be free to pursue it. Once again, it would seem that Mill's position implies certain standards of rationality and mental health. So, since Mill would forbid you from selling yourself into slavery, would he also forbid you from agreeing to being whipped? It seems that his only grounds for doing so would be to consider you mentally unwell. But is that the case? As argued by Michel Foucault (1926–1984), establishing standards of rationality and sanity are often a means whereby the authorities impose social values: application of the terms 'madness' or 'deviance' are means whereby the controlling interests within society exert influence and regulate behaviour. If we accept this point, the notions of harm and rationality that Mill relies upon are not perhaps as uncontroversially objective as he supposed.

V   Applications

In this final chapter, Mill offers various applications of his principles. To recap, these are: first, where a person's actions are self-regarding (concern only himself), he is not accountable to society, though we may criticise or give advice. Second, where a person's actions negatively affect the rights and interests of others, society may intervene – either legally, or by means of social disapproval.

Society may not intervene merely because its members' interests are damaged by the actions of an individual. Mill argues that certain damage is unavoidable – such as in the competitive environment of business – and we would not protect people whose business is damaged by a superior competitor, as long as this is done fairly, without fraud or force. Therefore, Mill backs the principle of free trade, but does so on different grounds to the principle of individual liberty. Governments shouldn't regulate prices or manufacture, but impose only minimal restraints in order to ensure fairness, because this is the best way to ensure general prosperity. Some issues concerning trade do have a moral aspect – prevention of fraud, enforcement of laws concerning health and safety – but even these should be mostly left to individuals and not regulated by law. So, even where products may potentially have a harmful effect – alcohol, opium, poisons – any restriction is an evil.

Mill concedes that there are occasions when government ought to intervene to prevent crime, and punish it upon discovery, but there is a danger of too much intervention. If poisons didn't have a useful purpose, then we would ban them, but since they do, restriction is problematic. Similarly, where danger is merely possible, we may warn but not forbid. Instead of limiting sale of poisons, we might therefore perhaps merely record their sale, making transactions traceable and emphasising to the buyer their responsible use.

However, the need for society to prevent crimes may in certain circumstances lead to interference in self-regarding actions. Mill argues that if a person has a track record of violence when drunk, then we would deal with his future crimes more harshly if drink were involved. Similarly, whilst idleness is not in itself a crime, failure to fulfil a contract or support one's family as a result of it would be. The subject of public decency is a similar case, where certain self-regarding actions that are only injurious to the agent, or not condemnable in themselves, become so when done publicly – literally, causing a public offence.

A more difficult question concerns the extent that individuals are free to persuade or facilitate others in carrying out actions which society disapproves of, but which are otherwise legal. For instance, Mill points out, having sex and gambling are not illegal, so is it OK to be a pimp or a bookmaker? (The laws to do with these two activities differ widely and subtly between countries and periods – we're just concerned with Mill's Victorian England here.) There are arguments on both sides. On the one hand, profiting from an act should not be illegal if the act which it promotes is itself legal. On the other hand, since we are dealing with actions which society may potentially disapprove of, then perhaps it's best to bar individuals from promoting them for private gain. This way, we're free to gamble or pay for sex privately, but not free to encourage others to do so. This would force such actions to take place privately (there being no advertising allowed), which, Mill suggests, is perhaps enough of a prohibition. In other words, whilst Mill agrees with the consensus that people should not gamble or pay for sex, he acknowledges that these cannot be legitimately proscribed, only perhaps frowned upon and otherwise discouraged. (We might compare this perhaps with the modern position on cigarette advertising.) It's debatable, he says, whether we ought to go further than this level of dissuasion – for instance, punishing the seller (the prostitute or bookmaker) but not the buyer (the client or the gambler), or to extend this principle to general buying and selling. Sellers must endeavour to make their wares sound appealing – it's part of business – and we should not place the fault with the seller for simply legitimately trying to encourage sales: for example, we shouldn't blame a brewer for describing his beer as 'delicious'. The fault therefore must lie with the buyer of the goods or services, who is ultimately responsible (for example) for contracting venereal disease, or losing his house at a game of cards. The ban against advertising prostitution or gambling should therefore represent an exception to the general principle of free trade.

Another issue concerns whether actions which are potentially harmful to the agent, but nonetheless legal – such as drinking – should be taxed more than other things. But, Mill argues, a tax is a degree of prohibition (putting people off by expense), and implies a form of disapproval, which – since once again the act itself isn't illegal – seems unfair. However, given that taxes must be raised, and that the state may occasionally need to raise additional revenue, inessential luxuries should be taxed more heavily than essential goods, especially concerning stimulants where immoderate use is likely to be harmful. So, Mill implies, you are free to drink, but drinking to excess will hit your wallet as well as your liver.

Regarding the places where alcohol is sold, Mill argues that it's legitimate to only allow access to respectable people, to limit opening hours and to close down disreputable places. He thought that restricting the number of pubs, however, would treat the working classes like children, which is not the way to develop responsibility. Having said that, in singling out the working classes here Mill himself appears somewhat patronising, and it is arguably a subjective call as to what we consider to be 'respectable' or 'disreputable'. However, Mill did think that the laws of the time were inconsistent in this respect – Britain was neither a true tyranny (where such forced moral education might work) nor a fully free society. This is the contradiction of 'paternal government' (what we might call 'the nanny state'): nanny knows best, but we're still free to ignore her advice.

Mill moves on now to contracts and agreements. Just as individuals are free to make decisions which affect only themselves, so groups are free to come to agreements. Such agreements and contracts between people should be enforced, except where they lead to a reduction in liberty. For instance, a person cannot sell themselves into slavery, for in so doing they would renounce the very principle that gives them freedom to do so in the first place. As Mill puts it, 'The principle of freedom cannot require that he should be free not to be free.' It is a self-contradiction. Other than that, whilst private contracts should be binding, they should be the sole business of the parties involved (as long as there are no third parties), and free to be dissolved by mutual agreement.

With this point in mind, Mill considers the marriage contract. Victorian marriage was a particularly one-sided affair, giving the male rights over the female, any children, and with no obligation to support either. Mill again cites Humboldt (with whom he largely agrees) that such marital agreements should require only the express will of either party to dissolve them. And yet, as Mill points out, there are issues of dependency and third-party support which Humboldt ignores. A man might not be legally bound to support his ex-wife or the children but there are moral obligations that spring up from long dependency. This is why we now have alimony payments and child support. A simple redress to this, he says, would be to accord the wife the same rights as the man.

But, Mill points out, there are further obligations, regarding the education of the child, which general consensus held to be a moral duty that falls upon the parent, but which in Mill's time was not legally enforced in any way. Mill recognises that the reason for this is the feeling that the state should not dictate what is taught, which would lead to state indoctrination. Visions of Soviet Russia swim before the eyes – or perhaps Plato's *Republic*. However, Mill suggests, if the state made education compulsory, leaving specific choices up to the individual and merely helping out with fees for the poor, and so on, then the situation would be remedied. The state could impose a fine, for instance, if a child was not able to read by a certain age, and periodic public exams, confined to educational basics and positive facts (*not* opinions), could ensure that standards are met without interfering with the free development of individuality. Study of other, higher subjects would be voluntary, but confer no authority other than granted by public opinion: a PhD would not give you any special privileges.

But the most fundamental obligation concerns the duty to provide a means of support to one's children. Mill controversially supports laws then current in certain European countries which forbade parents from conceiving children unless they possessed adequate means of support. These are not, he argues, an infringement of liberty; rather, they protect the *child's* liberty – that is, his *positive* freedom (ability to pursue ends that poverty might deny).

Finally, Mill briefly considers three main objections to government interference in matters where it does not infringe on liberty, and which are not really the subject of this essay. Mill is thinking here of such things as business and the affairs of local government.

First, Mill argues, most matters are best left to the individuals involved than to government or legislation, for example in business (see Mill's earlier comments regarding free trade). But this is strictly a matter for political economy, that is, economics, where Mill's ideas were also influential. Second, even if individuals don't always behave ideally, it is important that they learn by doing. So, we tolerate mistakes so that people in general improve in their ability to deal with matters. This applies to all manner of things – trial by jury, freedom of local institutions (for instance, councils), and so on. This is part of the general social education of the individual in learning what it means to act publicly and take public responsibility, to learn by experiment. Third, we shouldn't add unnecessarily to government's power. The larger the government, the less freedom we possess. If, for instance, the civil service were to attract the ablest minds, then people would be more tempted to leave important decisions to the authorities, which would become all powerful. This was the case in nineteenth-century Russia, he says, where the Tsar was practically powerless without the bureaucracy. In such cases, even revolutions only replace the titular head (the ruler); the civil service – the true power – remains unchanged. In contrast, he sees countries like France, and especially America, to have fostered an individual independence of spirit which is the essence of true political freedom. A powerful state will tend either to idleness or to ill-thought-out action, which is one good reason why ability and intelligence should not be concentrated in it, for to keep it healthy it must be capable of criticism and reform from outside, a role that Mill saw himself as fulfilling.

But striking the right balance between freedom and efficient organisation is tricky, he says. It is a question that requires attention to detail more than general rules. The one general principle we should aim for is 'the greatest dissemination of power consistent with efficiency; but the greatest possible centralisation of information, and diffusion of it from the centre.' In other words, let individuals run things as much as possible, but let government monitor and advise, concentrating on gathering and spreading information and good practice, and only compelling people to follow the agreed laws. Mill cites as an example here the Poor Law Board, which saw that local authorities obeyed the Poor Law of 1834, which was meant to guard against poverty. Thus, the ideal of government is one of minimal involvement. A government should focus on ensuring that agreed laws are abided by, and seek to monitor and advise, but should steer clear of the sort of over-involvement that dwarfs individualism – even in the name of some beneficent end. Such interference defeats its own purposes, since it leaves us with individuals who are incapable of fulfilling the roles which are necessary to keep society healthy. In Mill's own words: 'The worth of a state, in the long run, is in its individuals.'

Problems

The main target of this final chapter is paternalism, or the over-involvement of government in private affairs. Along with the economists Adam Smith (1723–1790) and David Ricardo (1772–1823), Mill is keen to see government keep its hands out of business matters, and to let free trade flourish. This is not because it would be an infringement of freedom, as such, but simply because that is the best way to encourage the production of wealth. However, as numerous commentators have pointed out (e.g., Sean Fitzpatrick in his book on Mill), neither Mill nor other classical economists truly advocated completely unregulated trade or complete libertarianism. The idea of simply encouraging the financial market to regulate itself, like some giant computer, is a naïve one, a realisation that is now perhaps finally dawning, in the light of the current economic climate.

As can be seen in his attitude to education, marriage and child support, Mill actually considered that the state should encourage people to fulfil their duties. The marriage contract was one-sided and sexist, hence it should be reformed so that both parties had equal rights and responsibilities. These responsibilities included providing their children with a minimum level of education – as noted, Mill suggested public exams at certain ages, and fines for the parents of those children who failed. Notice here also that he is concerned not that the state should decide the syllabus (he would have hated the National Curriculum, or any other state involvement in *what* should be taught), but that each individual met the minimum standard for participation in society.

It is this last point, actually, which highlights one of the problems with Mill's vision. It is, in a sense, a very idealistic one. Mill believed in social progress, and in the civilising force of education. The reason that he thought that government should resist interfering in private life was that, not only would it be counter-productive, since people need to grow and develop independently, but that we need the sort of rationally engaged and self-driven individuals that only liberty could produce. However, liberty doesn't always produce such people, and it is dubious whether the freedom to have a say will naturally lead to greater political involvement. In Western democracies, each person arguably has more education, freedom and potential influence today than ever before, but voter apathy is still high. The will to improve society, to engage with the important issues, may just be lacking. Perhaps we need a degree of paternalism after all.

Conclusion

Despite its possible flaws, *On Liberty* remains a substantial contribution to political and ethical philosophy. We have had limited space here to sketch out its ideas, but a detailed study will repay anyone interested in these issues, for Mill's insights still present a common focus for modern philosophers struggling with how to marry individual self-interest with a more general concern with the rights of others. As a man, Mill is also a fascinating and inspiring individual, also not without flaws, but whose life and work provide a context to *On Liberty* which reveals someone committed to high ideals. That these are ideals that many people today still broadly share perhaps accounts for the continued popularity and relevance of this work.

Summary

To what extent can government legitimately regulate our actions? Even democracies must guard against the **'tyranny of the majority'** – the suppression of minority interests through legislation or popular opinion. The appearance of consensus as to acceptable behaviour is an illusion, for people hide unpopular opinions. Common attitudes are also often irrational and unexamined. To protect both individual freedom and society, we should therefore employ a **principle of harm**: it is only legitimate to limit the freedom of the individual to protect others.

Authority should not limit **self-regarding actions** (concerning an individual's private interests) but may intervene in the affairs of minors, the mentally ill or 'backward societies' for their own good. This principle is not an abstract right, but a **utilitarian** principle, for it leads to the greatest happiness of both society and the individual. As long as they do no harm, people should be free to think, speak and act as they see fit.

Free speech should not be limited, for either what is suppressed is true, and society benefits, or false, and the truth is tested and reinforced. All opinions are **fallible**, and the closest we can get to certainty is for our opinions to survive criticism and doubt. No doctrine is so useful that it should be immune to examination. Intolerance and persecution are not a 'rite of passage' that every opinion must face, for they may extinguish truth. Intolerance forces unpopular views into hiding, leaving society robbed of the challenge of original and inquiring minds. This leaves false opinions unrevealed, stunts general mental growth and withholds the freedom necessary for great minds to develop.

Even where received opinion is true, every untested opinion is a 'dead dogma' – a mere prejudice or superstition. We must therefore seek out the strongest objections to our beliefs. Even expertise requires freedom of opinion in order to be thoroughly tested, and unchallenged, even true beliefs lose their meaning and can be misapplied. This need not lead to continuous dissent and uncertainty, but merely to keep an open mind and be prepared to revisit and question our assumptions.

Truth may also lie in between received opinion and unorthodox views. It's difficult to thoroughly test our own theories, so minority views provide a valuable and healthy challenge. Such openness would especially benefit nineteenth-century Christianity, for we must distinguish between Christ's teachings and the authoritarian structure of the Church.

An individual may pursue his own self-regarding interests at his own cost. Not everyone fits the mould of accepted behaviour, and freedom is necessary for unorthodox and creative types to develop. Freedom to question and make one's own mistakes is vital for self-development, for humans are not machines. Individuals with strong and original personalities are vital to the health of society, something which is lacking in nineteenth-century England, which is obsessed with conformity and produces a weakened form of individual. Eccentricity is a natural phenomenon, but most do not understand unusual people because such people are a minority. Increased uniformity is not a sign of progress but its opposite.

Society has rights over the moral actions of the individual, but not his private interests. This is not a **social contract**, but built on utility: by respecting this principle, both society and individual flourish. Individuals must respect others' freedom, and help protect society from outside aggressors, both things which are enforceable by law. Society protects the rights of the individual and allows him the freedom to pursue his own interests. However, behaviour is also regulated by public opinion. Here, we may express disapproval of private interests and a person's character, but we can only exert influence – in the end, it's up to the individual as to what he does with his life. If private pursuits have moral consequences (alcoholism), then we should censure the wrong not the interest. On no account should society seek to extend its formative control over the individual's personal life into adulthood.

The public is not fit to judge the acceptability of an individual's private choices since such opinions are usually subjective. As various examples show (the Muslim attitude to pork, the marriage of the clergy), we need respect for self-regarding actions to protect against the tyranny of the majority. The application of this principle may be complicated (prohibition, prostitution and gambling, Mormonism), but we should respect individual liberty, even where this leads the individual to self-chosen harm.

Society must not intervene merely because an individual's interests are damaged (e.g. legitimately, by business competitors). Government should not interfere in trade unless to prevent fraud, crime or malpractice. Government should generally not restrict commerce (sale of poisons, alcohol), but should content itself with lesser measures of regulation (accountability and traceability, restricted pub opening hours). However, society may occasionally intervene in self-regarding actions where there are moral and public consequences (violence stemming from alcoholism).

Actions of which society disapproves (gambling, prostitution), whilst not illegal (in nineteenth-century England), may be indirectly discouraged (e.g. a ban on advertising) whilst respecting private choice. Similarly, alcohol laws should encourage responsible drinking whilst not discouraging it through scarcity or cost. Government should be neither **paternalistic** nor completely *laissez-faire*.

Contracts between individuals should be a private matter, enforceable by law unless this infringes on personal liberty (one cannot sell oneself into slavery). The one-sidedness of nineteenth-century marriage laws, where divorce left wife and children potentially destitute, should be reformed accordingly. Legislation should ensure children's minimum fact-based level of education by public examination and fines for negligent parents. Other than that, education should be a private choice, but confer no privileges.

Regarding matters which are not strictly to do with individual liberty: individuals should be left to conduct their own business affairs; in local government, trial by jury, and similar matters, individuals should be granted autonomy to make their own mistakes; government should be as small as possible, and should avoid creating a powerful bureaucracy or civil service, contenting itself with monitoring, advising and ensuring general laws are followed without over-involvement at the local level.

Glossary

Act/rule utilitarianism   The two main forms of traditional utilitarianism, associated with Bentham and Mill respectively, that determine the right action in terms either of the consequences of a single action or a general rule.

Calvinism   A Puritan form of Protestant Christianity, stemming from theologian John Calvin, which professed determinism, the powerlessness of human will, and the need for divine grace.

Classical liberalism   The political view (held by both Mills) favouring individual liberty, free speech, limited government and free trade.

Creationism/intelligent design   The belief that the natural world reveals signs of design, and is not therefore the product of natural selection.

Cultural imperialism   The situation where one society seeks to impose its values upon another.

Dialectic   A process of argument which involves comparison and contradiction.

Ethical minimalism   Used to describe Mill's view that morality consists of a small number of primary concerns or principles which it is our duty to abide by, outside of which we are free to act as we wish.

Eudaimonia   Happiness, self-fulfilment or human flourishing (associated with Aristotles' concept of the 'good life').

Fallibilism   The general philosophical position that any of our views may prove mistaken in the light of fresh evidence (to be distinguished from scepticism).

Hedonistic utilitarianism   The view that pleasure is the ultimate good (associated primarily with Jeremy Bentham, later modified by Mill).

Laissez-faire   An attitude of non-involvement (often applied to business and trade).

Libertarianism   An extreme form of individualism and liberalism, opposed to any but the most minimal constraints on freedom.

Paternalism/nanny state   The over-involvement of government in private affairs.

Pragmatism   The philosophical position, often associated with US philosophers John Dewey, William James and C. S. Peirce, that held that absolute certainty was not achievable, and so we must adopt other working standards.

Principle of harm   Mill's contention that we are free to do or say what we want, so long as it does not harm another's interests.

Principle of utility   The basis of utilitarianism: actions are right in as much as they promote happiness or pleasure, and wrong if they promote the opposite.

Reformation   The Christian reform movement during which Protestantism broke away from the Catholic Church.

Self-regarding   Those actions and interests which are the personal concern of the individual and in which society may not legitimately intervene.

Social contract   A theory that proposes that society should be guided by rules that rational people would recognise as in their own self-interest and mutual benefit.

Tyranny of the majority   The situation where a majority may, by its actions or views, harm the interests of a minority (a common problem for certain types of utilitarianism).

Utilitarianism   The general view that moral actions should seek happiness for the greatest number (or, later, some other related quality, such as preference or welfare).

Further Reading

On Liberty and Other Essays, edited by John Gray (Oxford World's Classics). This also contains Mill's essays on *Utilitarianism* (the natural next thing to read) and his essays on *The Subjection of Women* and *Considerations on Representative Government*.

Starting with Mill, John R. Fitzpatrick (Continuum). An excellent and readable introduction to Mill's thought, which puts his ideas in detailed philosophical context.

John Stuart Mill, William Stafford (Palgrave Macmillan). A very well written account of Mill's views in relation to his life and times.

John Stuart Mill: Victorian Firebrand (Atlantic Books). A detailed but very readable recent biography.

5
Friedrich Nietzsche: *Beyond Good and Evil* (1886)

Background

To say that Nietzsche (1844–1900) was 'a man before his time' is now a cliché, but still an apt one. Born in a small town near Leipzig in 1844, his father and both grandfathers were Protestant ministers, and he might well have been expected to follow in their footsteps. Indeed, his first studies at university were theology and philosophy, but, ill at ease with the boorish behaviour of his fellow students at Bonn, and entertaining his first doubts about the religion of his forebears, he switched to Leipzig, in the process changing his studies to philology, the study of language in written, historical sources. It was as a philologist specialising in classical literature and language that he was to graduate, and in which role he would eventually obtain a professorship at the University of Basel, in Switzerland.

It is curious, then, that one of the great philosophers should in a sense be an outsider, having been trained in another field. And yet, this is what gives Nietzsche's philosophy its character, for he is not afraid – as someone more versed in tradition might be – of upsetting the applecart, or questioning the obvious. Ill health forced him to retire from academia at the mere age of 34, pushing him into the life of a wandering scholar – through Italy, France and Switzerland – as he chased a climate kinder to his physical frailties. However, as he took long walks and exchanged polite conversation with casual acquaintances in hotel restaurants, few who met him can have realised that the meticulous and well-mannered *Herr Professor* was – in his own mind – 'dynamite', a 'Superman', even an 'Anti-Christ', plotting the overthrow of everything they held dear.

At the time he died – fittingly, perhaps, at the the turn of the century he was to influence so profoundly – he was relatively unknown.

Following a mental breakdown in 1889, he spent the last 11 years of his life in a state of mental collapse, cared for by his sister and mother. The full impact of his ideas were only felt much later. Modern readers will find much that they can recognise in his worldview: he is broadly atheist, free-thinking, anti-nationalistic and life-affirming, valuing individuality and the life of the mind over moral conformity – all attitudes which would later influence Existentialism (see Chapter 6). He is a self-declared dispeller of delusion: a procession of sacred idols – democracy, Christianity, scientific rationalism, the idea of progress, the philosophies of Kant and Plato – are each subjected to the test of his hammer, and found to be hollow. His message isn't ultimately a negative one, as we shall see, but there is definitely a sense in which he thought European culture needed a fresh start. However, to do that, we must go beyond the world of tired old prejudices and accepted dogmas, beyond the old values, and ultimately, beyond 'good' and 'evil'.

The text

Written in 1886, the text may be seen as part of the destructive phase of Nietzsche's general plan to produce a profound philosophical and cultural revolution. *Beyond Good and Evil* (hereafter *BGE*) can be seen as concerned with pointing out the problems and shortcomings of contemporary philosophy and society, suggesting not only a new path, but a new type of person, which he calls variously the 'free spirit' or 'new philosopher', and what he elsewhere calls the *Übermensch* (variously translated as 'Overman' or 'Superman').

Unlike Descartes, or even Hume, Nietzsche is not a neat or systematic philosopher, so *BGE* is not organised according to an obvious plan. The text is split into nine parts, each one of which deals with different themes, but these overlap, and trains of thought seem to change abruptly or are taken up again at later points. Each part consists of numbered sections, which differ greatly in length, but are usually no more than a few paragraphs. Sometimes these sections are self-contained, and sometimes they link in with other sections. All of which, of course, makes *BGE* difficult to summarise, so bear in mind that our account necessarily misses out some of the twists and turns of Nietzsche's text, and just aims to present the most important ideas.

Another problem that we face in reading Nietzsche is the tone of his writing. Unlike many writers, he very rarely takes pains to make himself explicitly clear. Part of the reason for this is that he wants *you* to think, not just to swallow his ideas uncritically, and if you have to work for it, then you are more likely to do that. He is therefore a very *literary* philosopher, and uses many of the techniques that we would expect to find in fiction or even poetry – which is one reason for his broad appeal: as much as a philosopher, he is a *writer*. He adopts personas, employs metaphors and similes, uses puns (most of which are unfortunately lost in translation), is sarcastic and playful, and generally utilises all his wiles to disrupt the traditional picture of the philosopher as the serious-minded seeker of truth. Nietzsche is a joker, a heckler, disrupting the main act with inappropriate comments from the back row. This often makes for great entertainment, but is also the cause of much frustration and head-scratching for the reader.

Preface

The brief preface introduces one of the main themes of the book: an attack upon the traditional notion of truth. To date, Nietzsche argues, most philosophers have mistaken the real nature of truth; if truth were a woman, then they'd all be socially awkward, confirmed bachelors, for they don't know how to behave around her! Things are not as straightforward as they think, for truth is not some fixed thing that is 'out there', waiting to be discovered (as it was for Plato), but something much more subtle that we interact with, and that we must 'woo' in order to understand and get the most out of. This may already seem odd: why should we be concerned with 'getting the most out of' truth? Don't we just strive to find it and then accept it? But perhaps truth isn't like that. Perhaps it changes over time, or is different for each person, coloured by such things as personal history, culture, environment or even our own biological instincts. This view – known as *perspectivism* – therefore suggests that the idea that truth is objectively the same for everyone is a myth; we all necessarily possess different perspectives, no one of which is *the* truth. The belief that truth objectively exists – what he terms 'the will to truth' – is therefore one of a number of 'philosophical prejudices' that Nietzsche discusses in Part One, and it will be one of his main aims in *BGE* to show that most philosophers have been completely unaware of the existence of such prejudice, and the way that we shape truth by our own expectations and assumptions. This is not to say, of course, that Nietzsche was a complete *relativist* or *sceptic* concerning truth – arguably, he doesn't deny its existence, he merely questions what it consists of and how we may approach it.

Part One: On the Prejudices of Philosophers

The 'will to truth' – the desire (will) to seek a truth that we think objectively exists, for its own sake – is therefore the first prejudice. Is Nietzsche right here? Let's not pretend that it's a simple question to answer. Of course, philosophers have long disagreed as to what truth is: Plato thought that it consisted in the direct knowledge of a world of pure ideas; Descartes argued that it was something that it would be self-contradictory to deny; later empiricist philosophers and scientists concentrated more on things for which we might possess sensory evidence or proof. However, Nietzsche argues, each of these, in their different way, shape truth in their own image. We can show this, he argues, by pointing out how the 'truths' that such philosophers have relied on are not actually beyond question, but are merely prejudices or *dogmas* (unfounded beliefs). Let's briefly look at some of these.

One common prejudice that Nietzsche claims to identify is what he terms the 'faith in antithetical values', or, put more simply, a belief in the existence of opposites. Perhaps the best example is in ethics. To be 'good' (certain philosophers thought) true goodness must exist completely separately from 'bad' or 'evil'. If, by being 'good', we were serving selfish desires in some way, then it would be difficult to completely distinguish 'wrong' actions from 'right' ones. Helping an old lady across the road wouldn't be completely selfless, but selfish in a more *refined* way, making us feel or look good, perhaps. In order to avoid this, philosophers such as Kant and Plato have therefore traditionally seen 'good' acts as having a completely separate origin to 'bad' ones: for Plato, truly moral acts are driven by knowledge of 'the Good'; for Kant, they arise out of a recognition of rational duty, and nothing else. However, Nietzsche argues, isn't this just wishful thinking, a way of tricking people into believing that they must be 'good' because of the existence of something 'outside' of themselves – 'the Good', the moral law, or God, perhaps? Of course, Plato and Kant weren't deliberately trying to trick people – but were they tricking themselves?

There is also, in philosophy, a common tendency to distinguish between 'appearance' and 'reality'; between 'how things seem' and 'how things really are'. But, Nietzsche argues, how do we know that 'how things really are' isn't just another case of wish fulfilment? For instance, a particle physicist shows us the 'real' world at the sub-atomic level, but is this view any more 'real' than any other perspective? Isn't it just *different*? Philosophers and scientists also seem to assume that most things have a centre or point of origin (what Nietzsche calls *atomism*). However, this not only applies to physics, but also to psychology or theology: we possess an individual mind or soul which is the true centre of self. And yet, if – as modern physics has found out – the atom can be split, and contains more space than substance, might not the same thing be true of the self? For instance, modern experiments have suggested that brains may be 'split' and different centres of consciousness produced.

Another philosophical dogma involves thinking of things as having a set purpose or *teleology*: the heart's job is to pump blood; the bee's job to make honey and spread pollen – but aren't we just allotting purposes to things as we human beings see them, or as they relate to *us*? If God does not exist, then there is no creator or designer to give the things that exist a fixed purpose. Sartre would later pick up this idea and apply it to human nature, arguing that there isn't one, so we can be what we like (see the next chapter). Similarly, then, Nietzsche argues that perhaps there are no purposes in nature at all; we don't 'discover' something's function, we *create* it.

Philosophers often want to base knowledge on certainty – which is natural enough. This leads them to search for things that are beyond question, trust in which is immediate and absolute. Nietzsche cites Descartes's *cogito* argument as an example of this (see Chapter 2): I cannot doubt that I exist whilst I am actually thinking, for thinking involves existence. But is this the case? The 'I' that exists now might be a different one from the 'I' that existed a moment ago, or will exist in the future. So, there might be many 'I's, or no 'I' at all. If so, then the immediate mental certainty that Descartes relies on ('I think, therefore I am') is therefore perhaps only another form of self-delusion.

Some philosophers also seem to hold the belief that particular things may be self-caused. For example, faced with the famous chicken-and-egg problem (which came first?), it is tempting to put an end to the controversy by simply assuming that the first chicken (or egg) just existed. This sounds silly in relation to chickens, but is actually a standard view when applied to theology (the existence of God), the creation of the universe (which even some astrophysicists assume came from 'nowhere'), and human free will (free actions are not caused by anything else, but originate in our own free choice). But, once again, all this seems to be based on a *desire* to believe rather than proof or likelihood. We'd *like* to think that our choices are free, or that the universe had a first cause (God), but what is the evidence for this? It seems to be an article of faith.

Another prejudice concerns the way in which philosophers and scientists often give in to the temptation to treat events as if they were 'things'. For example, we see something happen, and we think of it as 'the cause', or 'the result', but these are just ways of speaking. For example, we can say 'the crowd surged down Stanley Terrace', but, strictly speaking, there is no such thing as 'the crowd' – it is just a way of describing a loose collection of individuals. So, perhaps, we should not confuse useful ways of speaking with a fundamental picture of reality. We can apply this observation to any number of things: perhaps, like the crowd, an individual is just a collection of biological and mental processes that it is merely convenient to describe as 'Tracy' or 'Dave'. But perhaps there is no 'Tracy' or 'Dave'. They are just convenient labels for certain properties and events.

We have passed quite quickly over these various prejudices, but they will reoccur throughout *BGE*, for they are central to Nietzsche's thinking, and so underlie the general approach of the book. However, their main point is simply this: philosophers tend to think in ways that reflect their own desire to see the world in a particular way. This desire in based on mostly *unconscious* influences – Nietzsche, like the father of psychoanalysis Sigmund Freud (1856–1939), thought that the conscious, rational aspect of the mind was only a small part. The unconscious influences – or *drives*, as Nietzsche calls them – are therefore chiefly responsible for shaping our ideas and forming these prejudices. Even the greatest minds are guilty of this – in fact, especially so, for they have greater ambition to change the world and how people see it.

Problems

The most obvious objection to Nietzsche's approach is that it undermines the very basis of philosophy. How can we even assess whether Nietzsche's arguments are 'true' if truth is just a matter of 'perspective'? This is a problem for any philosophical position that admits that truth isn't absolute, so Nietzsche isn't alone here. But, as already stated, Nietzsche isn't denying the existence of truth; he wants us to understand the role that human values play in the search for truth, and how an understanding of this will deepen our appreciation of the central problems of philosophy. Also, we might ultimately find that, even though truth is 'relative' to our own perspective, that perspective itself is driven by values that we do not want to deny. We want to survive, to be happy, and the like, so even if it is true that these concerns colour our appreciation of truth, they may be too fundamental a part of our own being – of *human* being – to turn our backs on. In this way, rather than denying truth, Nietzsche *redefines* it.

Another problem lies with Nietzsche's criticism of the alleged prejudices of other philosophers. In this and the following parts, he criticises many of the greats – Plato, Descartes, Kant, Spinoza – but his points are often quite personal, what are called *ad hominem* arguments. So, for instance, he argues that the way that Spinoza sets out his arguments in a rigorous mathematical system betrays a hidden weakness: he wanted to make his system *invulnerable*, because he himself was *vulnerable*. So, in a sense, Nietzsche is *psychoanalysing* these philosophers. But such interpretations are difficult to prove – and even if we could, what has that got to do with the truth of their philosophy? Perhaps we could also apply that form of analysis to Nietzsche himself?

There is a serious point to be made here about Nietzsche's general approach to philosophy. On the one hand, we might point out that his arguments aren't rigorous or systematic enough; on the other, we must recognise that the traditional, rigorous and systematic approach to philosophy is one of the very things that he is attacking. This occasionally leaves us in a tricky position: it's not that Nietzsche *never* presents arguments in a more traditional manner, but some of his more profound insights – the nature of truth, the existence of moral and philosophical prejudices – seem closer in spirit to a form of psychology, in that he is more concerned with the role of the subject in thought and knowledge. Historically, this question has come to mark a divide between more traditional *Anglo-American* philosophy and its *Continental* counterpart, which has taken on and built upon the more radical aspects of Nietzsche's approach.

Part Two: The Free Spirit

Having begun to show what is wrong with past and contemporary philosophy, Nietzsche proceeds to outline how his own approach will be different. In this part, he talks of his hopes for a 'new philosopher' or 'free spirit' who will adopt his approach to philosophy and begin to question the hidden values upon which the ideologies of the past were based. Nietzsche draws various links here between language, culture, thought and personality, and argues that the new philosopher must be aware of how all these things colour and shape rational thought, and be prepared to evaluate such influences with a view to evolving the most life-affirming philosophy possible.

In doing this, since there is no 'will to truth', the new philosopher must ask a strange question: what is the value of *untruth*? Why, in some cases, do we prefer falsehood to fact? Might untruth actually be *more useful* than truth under certain circumstances? To understand what Nietzsche means here, we need only consider our day-to-day lives. For instance, people say unkind things about one another all the time, but perhaps we would rather not know what is said about us: we recognise that we can't be liked by everyone, and that we all think mean things about one another on occasion that often don't reflect our considered opinion. Is it therefore a lie to assume that this or that person is our friend, or that we are generally liked and popular? Possibly, but we prefer untruth or not knowing to the potentially damaging truth. Is there an innate human tendency to shy away from such unwelcome truths? If so, then our search for 'truth' is in fact driven by our own unconscious needs and desires.

The 'will to ignorance', as Nietzsche calls it, is therefore an important part of life, and also plays a fundamental role in all our attempts to secure knowledge: we concentrate on certain 'facts' and 'truths' because it is more beneficial to do so. We might make Nietzsche's point in evolutionary terms: our senses have developed to filter out less useful information, and to focus on things that can aid our survival. An example of this would be the way the mind 'wakes up' to an unusual sound, or a baby crying; such selective alertness has proved of evolutionary benefit.

But we might also apply Nietzsche's principle within a scientific setting. Scientific knowledge is closely linked to technology and social progress. It might happen that a certain experiment proves some important principle, which then allows us to develop some tremendously useful new technology. However, extremely infrequently, the experiment also throws up an anomaly – something which suggests that things are not exactly as our original findings suggested. But this happens so infrequently that we might put it down to a fault with the experimental apparatus – a glitch. Or is it? The decision to treat it as such – it could be argued – is driven more by a concern for the usefulness of the discovery than for 'objective' truth, for its own sake. Whether we like it or not, it seems many of our decisions as to what is 'the truth' are influenced by pragmatism: if a view or theory works, and serves our purposes, then we'll ignore the small possibility that it might not be 100 per cent accurate or true. For instance, there may be health scares to do with mobile phones or genetically modified crops, but are these things just too useful to do without? This is not to suggest that those conducting safety studies on such things are deliberately lax or even dishonest, but merely that 'the truth' in such situations is often under pressure from other concerns – perhaps not all of which we are, or even *can be*, aware.

Another important idea in Part Two is Nietzsche's account of the various stages of morality. Since, for Nietzsche, 'right' and 'wrong' are not God-given absolutes, or external standards that we act in accordance with, it is possible to trace the development of morality through history. Originally, he argues, in what he calls the 'pre-moral' stage of human society, 'right' simply described the consequences of an action, and morality was primarily a matter of what was useful, pleasurable or desirable. So, an axe is 'good' for chopping wood, a certain fruit 'good' to eat, or an attitude of respect towards equals or superiors 'good' for social harmony (it is always wise to respect those who might be equal or more powerful). There is an obvious connection, then, between what we think of as 'good' and the thing so described: a blunt axe, a poisonous fruit or a disrespectful attitude are therefore *demonstrably* 'bad', because they are ineffective or harmful.

As we move into more sophisticated modern societies (the 'moral stage', in which Nietzsche thought we then existed), moral values begin to be ascribed to the origin of the motive to act: from possession of moral knowledge (Plato's idea of 'the Good'), a recognition of moral duty (Kant), or from obedience to God (Christianity). The upshot of this is that certain actions become good or bad *in themselves*. In turn, morality becomes fixed in relation to a hierarchy of values, which often reflects and justifies the social one. For instance, to illustrate Nietzsche's point, in Plato's ideal society in *Republic*, kings and rulers should be fit to govern by virtue of their possession of wisdom and moral goodness (see Chapter 1).

In contrast to these two stages, Nietzsche proposes a third stage: the *extra-moral*. This comes about as the social and philosophical systems which shape the old values begin to come apart, and we are forced to re-evaluate them, leading to the construction of new values, and a new attitude to morality. This is the specific job of the new philosopher, who will understand moral history, and use that to critically evaluate the accepted standards of 'good' and 'evil' – and go *beyond*. It is probably fair to say that Nietzsche was at least partly right in thinking that European society was on the threshold of this stage. Morality and culture have always contained diverse elements, but perhaps – to us – never more so than now, and combined with a growing tendency – and *permission* – to question the basis of our moral and philosophical systems, we might agree that Nietzsche was quite prophetic here.

This concept of the new philosopher – which is, of course, a picture of Nietzsche himself – is therefore central to *BGE*, and Nietzsche spends some time outlining the type of person he must be and the qualities he must possess. First, he stands apart from the ordinary person, because he must take a critical and sceptical view of the things that most people simply accept. In this sense, others may view him with suspicion, because he is forced to develop qualities which they may consider 'bad': cunning, distrust, aloofness, and so on. In consequence, he is often forced to hide these qualities beneath a socially acceptable 'mask' (e.g. 'the philosopher' or 'the scholar'). However, whilst he is critical of prejudice and dogma, he is not a 'free thinker' in the normal sense – he is not concerned with liberating anyone from social injustice, or in promoting freedoms. Nietzsche's freethinking is not political, and there is no movement of social reform that he would necessarily back. The new philosopher might go on to shape a new society – as a Napoleon or an Alexander – but his main concern is to establish a new set of *values*. Nietzsche's view is therefore elitist: not everyone is 'equal', and not everyone can be a philosopher.

Problems

Perhaps the first of Nietzsche's views that we may question here is the so-called 'will to ignorance'. Nietzsche's principal point is that human beings are perhaps not as interested in truth for truth's sake as philosophers have supposed. Findings in psychology and neuroscience would back this up: the way our brains filter out the information from our sensory apparatus suggests that, in terms of information, sometimes less is more; in such cases, the 'truth' (the complete unfiltered information) is unhelpful to us, and we must concentrate on a particular part of it in order to function. As suggested above, through evolution, we have therefore learned to 'lie' in certain useful ways. However, Nietzsche's point extends to concepts also – a more radical point, but still an interesting and plausible one: we believe that 'every effect has a cause', for instance, because thinking in this way somehow serves our purposes (evolutionary, cultural, and so on).

The exact nature of his views here is debated. Some want to interpret him as proposing the radical position that there is no such thing as truth – or, rather, truth is 'in the eye of the beholder'. However, there may be a difference between saying 'truth is relative' (to being human) or partial (in filtering out certain aspects of experience in favour of others), and saying that truth doesn't in fact exist, and that it's *all* a matter of individual perspectives, none of which can be shown to be wrong. The first position preserves the idea that some opinions are truer than others, that there is something that holds together these differing perspectives, whilst the latter makes everything a free-for-all – and where would that leave philosophy? In support of the former position, it does seem that he is primarily concerned with rejecting the idea that we are naturally inclined – and constitutionally able – to seek truth for its own sake. So, there may not be one, absolute, objective point of view *which can be divorced from our own self interests*. However, this is not to deny truth, but merely to propose that our concepts and metaphysical views are influenced by unconscious attitudes, biological drives, and so on. All views are therefore, in a sense, subjectively motivated and fallible, open to falsification. But this does not mean that we cannot get closer to truth. Indeed, if Nietzsche did not believe in truth at all, why would he have asserted that the ultimate test of the courage of a philosopher lies in how much truth he can endure? It is difficult to make sense of this if we merely interpret Nietzsche as arguing that truth is relative and ultimately non-existent. Rather, it seems to support the view that he sees truth as perpetually obscured by our own instinctual drives – as governed by our 'will to power' (we'll investigate this concept shortly).

Many philosophers, however, see him as suggesting that the notion of any sort of 'truth' is a completely baseless ideal. This interpretation would seem to undermine the quest for knowledge itself, thus resulting in scepticism, a criticism to which those who adopt this approach – including post-modern and deconstructionist thinkers – would seem to leave themselves open, often happily.

Regarding Nietzsche's contention that morality should be understood in terms of historical stages, the most obvious objection is that Nietzsche presents little direct evidence for this. Of course, this is typical of Nietzsche's philosophy in general, for as has already been noted, he seems to dismiss the traditional approach to scholarship whereby certain positions are presented and defended in a systematic fashion. This does not mean that his account is false – he was, after all, a professor of classical culture, and so perhaps well placed to draw such conclusions – but there is scant evidence presented here. We find it (or at least, more of it) in his subsequent book, *On the Genealogy of Morals*, where the transition from the pre-moral to the moral stage more or less corresponds to (or contributes toward) what he calls the 'slave revolt in morals'. We'll deal with this a little later, but suffice to say that his arguments for the historical characterisation of the different stages of morality rest on the more detailed arguments presented there. We don't have room to fully outline them here, but, in brief, they rest on the contention that traditional moral terms have their origin in the values of aristocratic elites. 'Good' and 'bad' therefore originally indicated what was valued and despised, respectively, by the ruling classes. The 'slave revolt in morals' therefore represents a hijacking of these terms by the 'slaves' (the oppressed classes), and a revolution in moral meaning: the valuations 'good/bad' are replaced by the *metaphysical* notions, 'good/evil'; the former are an expression of aristocratic value, the latter a *justification* and support for the disempowered view of the 'slaves'. By redefining good so that it becomes an attribute of the weak and powerless, the disadvantaged were able to accept their plight rather than have to struggle against it or admit they were indeed life's losers. This, at least, seems a testable hypothesis, and Nietzsche's general theory of morality seems to rest on it. So, is he right?

This is an etymological and historical question, in part, which specialists will undoubtedly be better placed to answer, but there does at least seem to be a plausibility in Nietzsche's account. First, it is true that many terms have their origins in natural descriptions – a point noted by Ralph Waldo Emerson in his famous essay, 'Nature':

> Every word which is used to express a moral or intellectual fact, if traced to its root, is found to be borrowed from some natural appearance. *Right* means *straight*; *wrong* means *twisted*. *Spirit* primarily means *wind*; *transgression*, the crossing of a *line*; *supercilious*, the *raising of the eyebrow*.

(Emerson was actually an influence upon Nietzsche, so it's not unlikely that he found the idea – or at least support for it – here.) Nietzsche's logic is straightforward: early moral terms have simple natural correlates. 'Right' is synonymous not only with 'straight', but with 'strong', 'healthy', 'natural'; 'wrong', with 'crooked', but also with 'weak', 'unhealthy' – and so on. It seems obvious, then, that, as morality evolved, those who possessed 'goodness' in this natural sense – health, strength, power – should help to define the meaning of these terms – in fact, to embody them.

The more controversial aspect of Nietzsche's argument, however, concerns the so-called 'slave revolt in morals'. Since the inferior aspects in society were not themselves strong, wealthy or powerful, they must reinvent these terms to paint themselves in a better light. Thus, the terms take on a different meaning: 'good' and 'evil' get their sense not from natural qualities, but from their relation to a system of *otherworldly justification*. This is why Nietzsche terms Christianity 'Platonism for the people', because these moral and spiritual ideals exist *beyond* the natural world (just as Plato took the Forms to exist – see Chapter 1). Such a metaphysical world is therefore needed to compensate for this one – where the 'slaves' lack 'goodness' in its traditional sense.

Where we might challenge Nietzsche here is on this interpretation of modern moral values – democracy, equality, compassion. Are these merely the product of the 'slave' mentality, the 'herd'? An alternative interpretation would argue that, actually, the sort of denial of our bestial urges that Christianity promotes is in fact a necessary part of moral development. Yes, 'good' might have originally meant 'strong', et cetera, but, in order to evolve a fuller sense of goodness, we must realise that respect for others, compassion, and so on, represent *higher* ideals.

These arguments are still controversial, and we have only outlined the general debate here, but they do represent Nietzsche's most sustained attempt at backing up this aspect of his philosophy. Furthermore, this approach has in turn influenced later philosophers, most notably French post-structuralist Michel Foucault (1926–1984), who attempted to apply a similar 'genealogical' method to such subjects as sexuality, criminality and madness. Nietzsche's views here are therefore not to be dismissed out of hand, and those interested are encouraged to read the *Genealogy*, which is one of his clearest and most accessible works.

Part Three: The Religious Nature

As with morality, Nietzsche wants to know *why* people develop and hold certain religious attitudes and beliefs. In other words, he wants to interpret religion from a psychological and historical perspective, tracing its development through, for instance, the influences of culture, temperament, race, environment, and all sorts of factors which have traditionally been ignored when considering religious questions.

It is here that he introduces a number of key concepts. First of all, he argues that Christianity is the expression of the previously discussed 'slave revolt in morals'. Nietzsche's views here are easily misinterpreted – and were, notoriously so, by Hitler and Nazism in general. The basic contention is that all morality is a form of 'will to power'. Everything that lives wishes to impose itself and its values on other forms of life. However, this does not mean that everyone seeks a sort of thuggish dominion over others, that 'might is right' and we must live by the law of the jungle, but merely that, whatever form of life we are concerned with, its basic drive is to perpetuate its type. This is as true of plankton as it is of pacifism, of lions as it is of libertarianism. So, whether we are talking of an idea, attitude or social movement, a type of behaviour or a physical organism, there is something, some goal, that drives it on: this is its 'will to power'. As such, then, Nietzsche argues, traditional pagan cultures – the ancient Greeks and Romans, the Vikings and 'barbarian' tribes – were concerned with perpetuating a certain ideal of strength, vitality, courage and honour. The word 'virtue', from the Latin *virtus*, originally meant 'strength', and 'aristocracy' literally meant 'rulership by the best' (Greek, *aristos*). The worldview which is associated with such peoples is therefore what Nietzsche terms the 'master morality', since it is a moral code which embodies the ideals of the conquering rulers.

In contrast to this, as already discussed, the 'slave morality' of the subjected and the conquered – the 'slaves' – is quite different. Since they are powerless, their choice is either to accept the values that their masters prescribe for them, and thus see themselves negatively, or else to *invert* those values, and thereby set up ideals in opposition to those held by their rulers. And this, Nietzsche argues, is what they did: 'strength' becomes 'tyranny', 'self-worth' becomes 'pride' or 'arrogance', and so on. Also, the 'bad' qualities take on positive meanings: 'poor self-esteem' becomes 'humility', 'timidity' becomes 'meekness'. We can see here how Christianity springs from such a 'revolt' or inversion in values. The downtrodden have no earthly power, but they will receive their rewards after death, in 'Heaven'; accordingly, those who now have earthly power will ultimately receive just and eternal damnation.

The chief motive behind this whole process is one that Nietzsche christens *ressentiment*, a French word which carries more than the English equivalent of 'resentment'. The 'slaves' not only 'resent', their masters, but are driven by envy and desire for psychological compensation. Their 'will to power' – their need to express themselves and seek their own form of dominance – therefore expresses itself as a subtle form of humility, compassion, a spirit of equality and gentleness – the very opposite of those ideals that their 'masters' embody. In social and historical terms, this results in a revolution: politically, democracy overthrows monarchy, ensuring that everyone is equal (or equally powerless); religiously, Christianity overthrows paganism, instating the idea that everyone is equal in the eyes of God; even in terms of morality, such philosophers as Plato and Kant enshrine the idea that 'the Good' is somehow an ideal that is forced upon us from outside, a duty or constraint upon our behaviour, keeping unruly desires in check (whereas the old pagan culture saw religion and morality as embodying their own highest qualities – wealth, power, privilege, honour).

Nietzsche therefore argues that in democracy, Christianity and Judaism, and the hugely influential philosophies of Kant and Plato, the 'slave morality' had supplanted the 'master morality'. However, Nietzsche argues, the result is ultimately a harmful one for human development in general. Whilst the Master morality might at times appear brutish or egoistic, it nonetheless promoted healthy values – strength, courage, and so on. However, in opposing this morality, the Slave mentality ultimately celebrates *unhealthy* values. Aggression, pride, et cetera, are not *in themselves* bad, but depend upon their application. But in rejecting such values – in replacing them with self-effacement, gentleness, and so on – Nietzsche argues that we risk opposing the very principles of the life force itself.

His primary illustration of this is what he calls 'the religious neurosis'. Because the 'slave' mistrusts and turns away from all that was previously associated with the 'master' morality, this attitude becomes a sort of psychological disease: a revolt against tyranny becomes a revolt against *all* forms of rulership; a distrust of strength and dominance becomes a distrust of basic bodily health and well-being. This in fact supplies the ascetic or 'Saint' (as Nietzsche calls him) with a certain mystique and power: opposing one's own natural desires is itself a form of 'will to power'. Eventually, however, the runaway logic of this leads to a philosophy of *life-denial*, or *pessimism*. Life is worthless, there is no meaning or God, no order or joy in nature, no point in living at all. Ironically, then, this 'disease' – the religious neurosis – ends up in *nihilism* (belief in nothing) and atheism. Nietzsche sees this process as a 'ladder of sacrifice', where gradually the believer feels compelled to give up more and more of his central ideals.

Against this, Nietzsche asks, how can we promote a positive attitude to life without either falsifying it (creating, as previous philosophers have done, a comforting view out of our own desires and prejudices) or giving way to pessimism and nihilism? His solution is what has become known as the doctrine of the 'eternal return'. Its clearest expression is in *The Gay Science*, section 341: if someone were to offer you immortality, with the condition that you must live your life over again and again, for all eternity, exact in every detail – not only the pleasures and joys, but the boredom, the pain and disappointment – would you take it? Nietzsche argues that only the most positive, life-affirming person could say yes. What better attitude, then, to adopt to our day-to-day life; to say 'yes' to everything, and thus embody an unconditional love for one's fate (*amor fati*). This is not to lay down and accept everything, or not to struggle against adversity, but rather, whilst striving for our highest ideal, to accept – to *love* – the setbacks and the disasters as much as the triumphs.

Problems

There is a lot that is controversial in this section. Firstly, defenders of Christianity have argued that Nietzsche mischaracterises it (of course, it is not only Christianity that he attacks, but also Judaism and Buddhism – but let it speak for the others for now). As suggested in the comments to the previous section, such apologists argue that it is not *ressentiment* that drives Christian virtues, but a desire to overcome ego and worldly obstacles to true goodness, and thereby get closer to God. However, Nietzsche is not alone in identifying a petty and vengeful side to Christianity. In his classic account, the *History of the Decline and Fall of the Roman Empire* (which Nietzsche was probably aware of), historian Edward Gibbon had noted that the early Church Fathers were not *entirely* free of a seemingly un-Christian desire for revenge. Gibbon's favourite example was the second-century Church Father Tertullian: faced with the earthly injustices which the Roman authorities directed against Christians, Tertullian gleefully anticipates the eternal torment of his earthly rulers come Judgment Day:

> How shall I admire, how laugh, how rejoice, how exult, when I behold so many proud monarchs, so many fancied gods, groaning in the lowest abyss of darkness; so many magistrates, who persecuted the name of the Lord, liquefying in fiercer flames than they ever kindled against the Christians.
>
> (Gibbon, Vol. 1, Ch.14)

The question therefore perhaps isn't whether certain Christians were driven by *ressentiment* (judging by Tertullian, some arguably were), but whether Christianity in general sprang from it. Answering this question is more difficult, and leads us into discussion of Nietzsche's notion of 'will to power', for we must decide whether a philosophical outlook which does *not* propose the egoistic and inegalitarian values that pagan religion and morality did, can still be positive and life-affirming. Are Christian virtues – humility, temperance, compassion – ultimately unhealthy and 'anti-life'? Not necessarily, and Nietzsche arguably recognised this, for his portrait of Jesus in a later work, *The Anti-Christ*, draws a distinction between Jesus the man (whom he respected), and Christianity as a whole (which he was highly critical of). Jesus was a man of high ideals, but not (for Nietzsche) the *highest* ideals, for his ideology, like the Buddha's, still involved turning one's back on life – on the world, on sensual enjoyment and bodily satisfaction. Nietzsche's ideal is therefore presented as a higher alternative which recognises the role of sensuality, pride, anger, et cetera, in the higher forms of self-fulfilment.

Another controversial issue involves Nietzsche's notion of 'will to power', which some see as a root cause – or prefiguring of – Nazism and Hitler's anti-Semitism. However, whilst on the surface there would seem to be a resemblance between Nietzsche's 'master morality' and Hitler's 'master race', Nietzsche was not trying to return to a mythical age of Aryan purity, or rid the German people of Semitic qualities, but rather seeking to reassess the course that Western culture had taken. In adopting Christian and democratic values, it had turned its back on a pagan culture than embodied – in his opinion – attitudes essential to psychological and social health. So, his ideal was not barbarism or thuggishness, but a call to recognise the essential good contained *within* such barbarism which Christianity had disavowed. But the point was not to *return*, but to *move on*. It is true that Nietzsche thought the inter-mixture of race and culture was largely responsible for pessimism and other undesirable social and cultural effects. However, the goal of the new philosopher was to reinvent both himself and culture, and create something *new* – or rather, a new synthesis out of the ruins of the old.

If we need more conclusive proof of Nietzsche's abhorrence of anti-Semitism, there is no shortage of unambiguous material we could quote from. Perhaps the most telling is from a letter to his own sister, Elisabeth, whose recent marriage to a confirmed and active anti-Semite Nietzsche described in a letter of 1887 as

> One of the greatest stupidities you have committed – for yourself and for me! Your association with an anti-Semitic chief expresses a foreignness to *my* whole way of life which fills me ever again with ire or melancholy.... It is a matter of honour to me to be absolutely clean and unequivocal regarding anti-Semitism, namely opposed, as I am in my writings.

Elizabeth took over care of Nietzsche after his breakdown and became responsible for his literary estate, lending her support (and by exten-sion, Nietzsche's) for the Nazi regime in return for funding for the Nietzsche archive. Hitler even attended her funeral. As for Hitler him-self, it is clear that he must have read Nietzsche selectively, and then with a jaundiced eye.

As for Christianity, whilst ultimately pessimistic in its outlook, Nietzsche considered that it had nonetheless unwittingly provided a further tool in the armoury of cultural development: it was *useful* to the sort of free spirit or new philosopher that Nietzsche envisaged to be able to call upon the sort of ascetic discipline that Christianity espoused *if necessary* – but in the service of a higher, life-affirming ideal and not, as he argued Christianity had, in *denial* of life.

In discussion of the 'will to power', we should note that it may be interpreted in two ways. Firstly, it may merely be taken purely *descriptively*, as a sort of psychological or moral principle, something that might explain human action and motivation; or it may be applied *prescriptively* as a justification of moral action (such as the utilitarian *principle of utility*, perhaps – see Chapter 4 on Mill). Nietzsche did employ the concept in this way, but influenced by contemporary writers on biology such as Wilhelm Roux (1850–1924) and William Rolph (1847–1883), he seems to have considered that 'will to power' was actually also a biological principle, an explanation of the nature of life itself. Thus, in *BGE*, his comments on Darwin's competing theory – which criticise its mechanicalness – can perhaps best be made sense of in light of this attitude.

Viewed biologically, we could question whether a fundamental principle which drives all life actually exists. Darwin considered that there was no 'vital force' or *élan vital* (as French philosopher Henri Bergson later christened his own similar concept). Evolution is not driven by any desire or goal-seeking force but is merely the inevitable effect of organic beings with differing traits living together with limited resources, meaning that only those most able to survive will pass on their genes. Modern evolutionary science seems to support Darwin. So does that mean that the 'will to power' is – in this biological sense, at least – a non-starter? Though informed, interested and well-read, Nietzsche was not a scientist, so conducted no experiments or studies. This does not rule out the possibility that he was right, but any challenge to Darwin's authority would need to show that his theory of evolution by natural selection did not succeed in fully accounting for evolution. And here, the consensus of evolutionary biology would seem to be against Nietzsche, for whilst Darwin's theory is not without its critics, the overwhelming majority of scientists and evolutionary biologists would seem to reject the notion of *vitalism* (that life is driven by the will of some vital force) in favour of *mechanism* (the view that evolution can be explained purely in terms of mechanical cause and effect). So, unless the tide turns, 'will to power' would seem somewhat out of favour in its biological guise.

What, then, if we interpret 'will to power' in a psychological sense? If so, we must ask whether it is in fact a correct description of actual motivation. Are people in fact driven – albeit unawares – by a desire to dominate, promulgating a worldview which empowers them and provides legitimacy for their actions and attitudes? This is at least plausible. If Nietzsche is right about the various philosophical prejudices, and that we adopt them to suit our own unconscious needs, then the will to power might suggest a reason for this. The fact that there are different and more subtle forms of 'domination' also seems fair, so that *ressentiment* also seems at least occasionally valid as a psychological explanation of certain attitudes and values. But whether this succeeds as a more general explanation of psychological motivation is harder to say. The problem here is how we might prove this view. As with psychological hedonism – the view that we are always motivated by pleasure – there is difficulty in proving that every action is in fact motivated in this way. The fact that an explanation *can* be explained in these terms is not enough: I give to charity – a seemingly selfless act which causes me a degree of deprivation (pain); but this does not disprove psychological hedonism, for someone might argue that there is a *secret* or *subtle* pleasure which is being served. It is the same, then, with 'will to power'. A Christian who adopts a selfless attitude might still be serving his own subtle ends, and thinking 'I'm better than you by being selfless'. But if every act can be explained by the principle, it seems impossible to disprove it. So, Nietzsche may be right, but it appears difficult to know it.

Lastly, even if 'will to power' remains out of favour as a biological principle and unproven (unprovable?) as a psychological one, might it not still succeed as a *normative* principle of how we *should* act? In other words, by seeking to express our most life-affirming values, do we achieve some sort of ethically valuable goal? But this too has its problems. Some critics argue that following our 'will to power' would lead to actions which we cannot ethically defend. If it is Nietzsche's intention to go *beyond* traditional values – beyond 'good' and 'evil' – then this is perhaps not a problem. But do we want to follow him? The critic argues that applying the will to power as an ethical principle leads to such atrocious and inhuman doctrines as so-called 'Social Darwinism' – that we should simply let society's weakest elements die out (be 'deselected') – a view which Nietzsche is often thought to be in favour of. It is certainly true that Nietzsche criticises Christianity's emphasis on pity, and its tendency to preserve what is weak in society, whereas pagan culture would have simply let it die out. Is Nietzsche therefore anti compassion? In one sense, yes: he does not value compassion and pity *at all costs*, for he argues that our values should reflect health and excellence, whilst he sees Christianity as almost *celebrating* weakness. However, this is only a partial picture of his views, for he also argues that compassion *can* be a positive value when it comes from an overflowing of positive qualities – such as the generosity of the rich and powerful man. To give from an abundance of health, wealth and power is therefore genuine compassion. Arguably, then, 'will to power' still has legs as an ethical theory, both in its descriptive and normative senses.

Part Four: Maxims and Interludes

Nietzsche loves the *aphorism* – short, pithy observations, often only a sentence or so, that are not always clear at first reading, but perplex the reader and encourage us to meditate on their meaning, making connections that might otherwise not be made. Part Four collects together 125 of these, which deal with a wide range of subjects, and draw together the main themes of the book (and are therefore topics with which we deal critically elsewhere). Some of these are difficult to categorise, but there are four clearly identifiable topics.

The first grouping of aphorisms underpins and expands upon the theme of the first chapter, and highlights the prevalence of prejudice and dogma in philosophy and moral systems. The second, expanding on Part Two, concerns the free spirit or new philosopher, and shows his relation to – and difference from – the aristocratic or 'master' type. The third are on religious topics, and continue the themes of Part Three: the religious neurosis, the concept of God within Christianity and monotheism, et cetera. The other main grouping concerns the sexes, especially the role of women, and reflects Nietzsche's attitude to the democratisation of gender roles – which Nietzsche seems to have disapproved of. This latter attitude has proven understandably controversial, and has led many commentators to accuse him of sexism and bigotry. In his defence, we might perhaps point out that arguing that the sexes have inherent differences is not necessarily 'sexist' if those differences can be shown to have a biological basis. Evolutionary psychology might argue something similar: men and women are set up to think and act differently by evolution. However, Nietzsche's opinions are somewhat more provocative: woman's nature does not befit her to be a true scholar (144); she is closer to nature than man, more 'like a cat' (131); she has a secondary role, and is concerned with surface fineries (145). In attempting to characterise the female in this way, Nietzsche therefore invites – and perhaps deserves – the charge of misogyny. A more sympathetic reading is perhaps possible if we bear in mind his own misfortunes in love, and his general lack of romantic experience with women. However, such views cannot really be excused, and we'll investigate whether there is anything salvageable about them later on when we look in more detail at Nietzsche's views on gender.

Part Five: On the Natural History of Morals

As the title suggests, one of Nietzsche's themes in this section is the study of morality – or, rather, the lack of it, since most approaches to what he calls the 'history of morals' have to date been naïve. What is needed, he argues, is the ability to stand back from questions of 'right' and 'wrong' and view moral values as an expression of biological, environmental or historical causes. This is a theme that he has already raised in relation to religion, but he explores it further here, drawing links between specific *rational* moral opinions and their *non-rational* causes. As Freud would later argue, the instincts influence how and what we think unconsciously. To understand moral values, we therefore need to investigate the role these instincts play and how they have developed.

An interesting notion here is the idea that morality can be a form of arbitrary discipline. As suggested in the Preface, and again in Part Two, moral or philosophical belief systems can often have unforeseen effects. For instance, a puritanical attitude that constrains the instincts (such as desire for pleasure and sensuality) develops and trains the will. The stated goal of such a code (for instance purging oneself of 'sin') is therefore not necessarily the same as its potential *usefulness* when viewed from a broader perspective: Nietzsche doesn't agree with such a restrictive moral outlook, but he can recognise that such 'training' has other benefits. It is in this way, therefore, that we must view morality; not as a search for the 'correct' values, but as a means of shaping and training – of 'breeding' – a particular type of human being.

In this light, Nietzsche asks what type of individual contemporary morality is designed to produce. His answer is that it is a 'morality of timidity', which aims at producing the 'perfect herd animal'. It is a code based on fear, and seeks to control and regulate the behaviour of society's members so that each is protected from the other. The need for this is obvious: the aggressive elements within society must be kept in check for the sake of social harmony. But the danger of taking this too far – the democratic and Christian ideal, where everyone is equal – is that society breeds a herd of sheep, who all play very nicely together, but lack any outstanding qualities (interestingly, this is a view which Mill also shared – see Chapter 4). Even the political doctrine of anarchy, which seeks to do without leaders, is an extension of the democratic ideal, where no one is *above* anyone else. Is this, then, the highest ideal of human development? Nietzsche obviously thinks not. In order to create a higher type of person, there must be (as he later puts it in Part Nine) a 'pathos of distance', whereby the 'higher' can look down upon the 'lower' – that is, producing a class structure of ruler and ruled.

Another interesting notion here is the idea of 'self-overcoming'. Since cultural and hereditary factors shape individuals, and democracy has increasingly mixed these influences, this occasionally produces 'men of diversified descent' – that is, in whom 'master' and 'slave' moralities mix. Such persons are fascinating, because they represent the very dilemma in which society increasingly finds itself: how to resolve the fundamental difference in these attitudes. In some cases, it results in internal conflict and a general weakening of the overall character (Nietzsche cites St Augustine as an example here). However, it sometimes gives rise to an individual who 'overcomes' himself, and forges a new character out of the conflict. Such men – such as Julius Caesar, Leonardo da Vinci – point the way for the new philosopher or *Übermensch*. Nietzsche's comments here on Jewish culture should also be read in this light. Like Christianity, Judaism is an expression of 'herd morality'. However, as he later argues (section 251), the future of Europe lies not in the eradication of Semitic influence, but in a *blending* of its good qualities with those of classical pagan culture.

Problems

Nietzsche's comments here on culture and morality are quite fascinating, though obviously controversial. The idea that the apparent purpose of morality is not its true one is particularly interesting, as it suggests that in order to truly understand the nature of morality we need to study the relation of moral codes to such things as culture, history, instinct and environment – which is, in fact, exactly what Nietzsche proposes. What is 'good' or 'bad' should therefore be seen in terms of the true purpose behind forbidding or encouraging particular things (the underlying 'will to power'). For instance, to return again to the idea of *ressentiment*, we can argue that the true goal of the Christian attitude of turning one's back on worldly things was to develop a superior will than those in possession of more traditional 'goods' – strength, health, wealth – in other words, to develop a different sort of 'strength' (as possessed by the 'Saint' mentioned earlier). What 'good' means, for this worldview, should therefore be interpreted in light of how these attitudes developed (their cultural context and history). This was an approach which Nietzsche considered had been totally neglected.

And in this sense, at least, he is right – though this is certainly no longer the case. As already noted, Michel Foucault especially has carried the Nietzschean approach into various fields, and shown how it can cast a remarkable new light on human culture, revealing the competing power interests within society which underlie and explain various social attitudes and philosophies. But this approach is in stark contrast to the Anglo-American or *Analytic* attitude to the study of ethics, which continues to view moral philosophy very much in terms set out by Kant, Plato and Mill. As a critic of this tradition, Nietzsche marks a turning point in philosophy, or a fork in the road: if we accept his approach, we are in a better position to understand subsequent *Continental* philosophy; if we reject it, then we assume that his criticisms are not substantial – that, for instance, Kant or Plato were not driven by secret instincts, or perhaps that it is simply better to criticise their positions in more traditional terms.

However, there are some attempts to create a dialogue between these two approaches, and it is not clear that Nietzsche's call for a new philosophy of morals need present a choice between two roads. After all, we find great philosophers in the analytic tradition, such as Bernard Williams, drawing on Nietzsche. Perhaps, then, he is simply too original and unique a philosopher to be claimed entirely for either tradition.

Part Six: We Scholars

In this section, Nietzsche surveys his contemporary philosophical and scholarly landscape. The main thing he notes is the advance of so-called objective science, which is primarily concerned with the collection of 'facts' (what is termed *positivism*). The influence of this attitude has spread more generally to all academic disciplines, even philosophy, with the result now that philosophers are increasingly mere 'labourers' on behalf of science. Nietzsche sees in this the influence of democracy, and the 'herd' mentality, which wants to bring everything down to the same level. Thus, the scientific debunking of superstition and religious dogma are just a part of a more general scheme to reduce everything to the evidence of the senses.

However, in doing this, Nietzsche argues, much of importance is lost. Our attitude to life shouldn't just be dictated by what can be proven, or what we have evidence for, and ultimately what we gain in certainty we lose in meaning and the richness of experience. Ironically, then, whilst on the surface the scientific spirit seems to *oppose* the subjective evaluation of life associated with certain religious attitudes, it is ultimately an expression of *the same* 'religious neurosis' (as he terms it), that wants to sacrifice everything 'noble'.

Nietzsche then proceeds to disentangle the genuine scientific spirit – which he is fully in support of, incidentally – from the *positivistic* need to reduce everything to its most basic elements. Objectivity is possible (to a limited extent), in as much as we can *step away* or *back* from our own perspectives (yet more support for the idea that Nietzsche was not ultimately sceptical about truth). We can never reach an *absolutely* objective position, but we can use this 'stepping back' in order to gain a less subjective perspective on life. The new philosopher is therefore someone who will employ many of the same tools as the scientist, but for the purpose of arriving at an attitude to life that best serves our interests. In other words, to serve the true philosopher's 'will to power', not some illusory 'will to truth'.

Problems

Nietzsche's provocative take on certain prevalent scientific attitudes may come as a surprise to those who see in him only a champion of atheism and freedom of thought. Nietzsche's philosophy is almost always more subtle and insightful than the general caricature of him would lead us to expect. His point is that philosophical prejudices express themselves not only in religious or moral dogma, but in any system of thought that assumes what it cannot prove. This is as much true of science as it is of religion.

In support of Nietzsche's point, we may consider certain problems with the philosophical trend known as *logical positivism*. Associated with such philosophers as A. J. Ayer (1910–1989), logical positivism attempted to reduce all meaningful statements to those which were either logically true, or else ultimately supportable by some form of sensory evidence. This allowed them to ditch whole swathes of philosophy on the grounds that it was 'metaphysical nonsense'. The influence of the scientific attitude here is obvious, and it illustrates just the sort of switch of status between philosophy and science that Nietzsche is complaining of (the former having traditionally been considered the deeper and more fundamental discipline). However, on what basis can we assume that statements that are not adequately based on sense evidence are 'meaningless'? What, ultimately, is the proof of *this* principle? As Karl Popper later pointed out – and Nietzsche would have agreed – it is *dogmatic*, and simply assumes itself to be true.

This debate rumbles on in what has become known as the 'science wars'. Influenced by such thinkers as Nietzsche, some post-modern philosophers argue that science is no more than another 'perspective', and therefore not an ultimate arbiter of truth. In reaction, of course, the scientific community merely points to the fact that scientific knowledge has provided the basis for space travel, nuclear power and other extraordinary technological advances: if it were 'just another perspective', how would these things have been possible?

Without getting too far into this debate, we can picture Nietzsche as occupying a sort of middle ground: since all human knowledge is coloured by specifically *human* concerns (which would be different from Martian or Kryptonian ones), we must not only give up the notion that absolute objectivity is possible, but be aware that scientific methods are merely tools in the service of ultimately *non-rational* drives. To take up a point raised earlier, this isn't to say that truth doesn't exist, merely that we must see truth in a different way. In fact, against those who interpret Nietzsche as a radical sceptic, we may quote this passage from one of his late works, *The Anti-Christ* (section 50):

> At every step one has to wrestle for truth; one has had to surrender for it almost everything to which the heart, to which our love, our trust in life, cling otherwise. That requires greatness of soul: the service of truth is the hardest service.

Does this sound like a man who has given up on science, or for whom truth was merely a matter of personal whim?

Part Seven: Our Virtues

As with the previous part, the title of this section questions the status of what is being considered: are these things which we are to consider really 'virtues'? The chapter draws together many of the themes already raised, but the main focus is modern man and contemporary society, and their relationship to the philosopher. As already argued, Nietzsche sees modern society as shaped by the 'herd' or 'slave' mentality, and more precisely as a mixture of both 'master' and 'slave' outlooks. Underlying this situation is the problem of how the new philosopher is to respond to this: he finds himself in a world which values equality, even mediocrity, and which is antagonistic to any form of difference or privilege. But is this healthy? As should be obvious by now, Nietzsche thinks it is not, and uses this chapter to explore what the new philosopher can do about it: what are *his* virtues, and how do they differ from contemporary ones?

Nietzsche sees the philosopher as traditionally at odds with society. He stands on the fringes, his nature forcing him to withdraw from the concerns of the everyday person in order to gain a better perspective on the meaning of life. This drawing back is a form of self-discipline, or *cruelty* against oneself, for he does it half reluctantly (there's an envious part of him that would love to fit in and be 'normal'). This is an important idea for Nietzsche, because it highlights one key difference between the 'virtues' of modern society and the common person, and his own: to evolve, to progress and develop – whether as a culture or society, or in matters of character or personality – it is necessary to critically analyse the values involved. However, to do this, we must turn away from what is natural or seemingly 'good', and question whether it is in fact what we want. For example, an athlete puts himself through the rigours of training and diet in order to achieve a higher goal (excellence in competition); or, at a more mundane level, we might go to the gym or take up a sporting hobby (to lose weight or get in shape). Such things are not (or not always) pleasant in themselves, but are a means to a more pleasurable end (winning, being fit, looking attractive). Such 'cruelty' against oneself is therefore a vital component of development. Similarly, all cultural and social advance, all true artistic creativity, is based on some form of cruelty.

The same is true for the philosopher, who must develop 'negative' character traits – mistrustfulness, cynicism, scepticism and hardness of heart – in order to question the value of traditional attitudes. Such analysis is therefore a form of 'cruelty', and places the philosopher outside and against the normal range of human experience and thought. As such, the philosopher is the 'bad conscience' of his age, pointing out its flaws and deficiencies.

Among the deficiencies which Nietzsche identifies is the general trend toward sexual equality. As mentioned earlier, Nietzsche's views here are somewhat old-fashioned, and represent a general opposition toward the uniformity of gender. His main argument seems to be that, just as the removal of class distinctions leads to the production of a mediocre individual, so the abolition of sexual differences results in a loss of what is good about each of the sexes: traditional manliness and womanliness.

Problems

Nietzsche has often been accused of misogyny, and not without cause. To put this in context, we may perhaps compare his views to those of someone like Arthur Schopenhauer (1788–1860), who was a great influence upon Nietzsche's early thought. Schopenhauer saw woman as 'a kind of intermediate stage between the child and the man', and as a generally inferior creature (see his essay, 'On Women'). Nietzsche's views are nowhere near as bad as this, but they are still pretty awful. However, if there is anything to rescue from them, we must first give him a fair hearing.

We may sum up his attitude in the following sentence: it is not that woman *cannot* be man's 'equal', but rather that so-called 'sexual equality' is a false goal. Nietzsche's point is therefore that, like man, a woman's strengths lie in a particular direction dictated by nature. To take issue with Nietzsche here we would therefore need to challenge two assumptions: first, that there are genetic differences between the sexes that go beyond physical characteristics; and second, that, given such differences, it is woman's duty to develop only those qualities given to her by nature.

Regarding the first point, even if there are clear differences, it is far from obvious that these are strictly rooted in biology. Most social scientists will agree that culture plays at least some part, and that gender roles are not strictly determined. For instance, anthropological studies have revealed cultures where women play a more equal part in traditionally 'male' roles such as hunting (such as the Agta in the Philippines), or even where traditional roles are frequently reversed or interchangeable, and the men stay home to cook and to raise children (such as the Aka, in Africa). How we should interpret such studies is still debated, but it seems to be clear that the sort of clear-cut gender differences that Nietzsche envisages are simply neither necessary nor universal. Furthermore, given Nietzsche's own concept of 'self-overcoming' – that we may transcend our own biological urges or cultural indoctrination – there seems no good reason for him to hold that such roles are unalterable. And of course, if they were determined, then there would be no need to argue against female emancipation, for such differences would persist anyway!

This leads us to the second assumption: that somehow it is 'better' for women to adopt traditional roles – to play to their strengths, Nietzsche suggests. First, it should be acknowledged that to strive for 'sexual equality' may in fact backfire, as there is a danger either of an unhealthy masculinisation or feminisation of culture, or the creation of a uniform gender. What's more, if, as Nietzsche also implies, the social movement for sexual equality has ulterior motives, such as the creation of an easily manipulated social herd-cum-workforce, then there are good reasons to be wary. As G. K. Chesterton famously and humorously put it, 'Ten thousand women marched through the streets of London saying: "We will not be dictated to", and then went off to become stenographers.' Liberation which results in equality of drudgery is no liberation at all.

However, this is really as far as we can take our sympathies, for Nietzsche's attitudes seem otherwise outdated, and on occasion simply offensive. It's fair enough to warn against false equality, but a return to traditional roles is not the only alternative. Of course, if a woman wants to pursue a traditional path – marriage, motherhood, domesticity – then she is free to do so. But to say that it is 'better' for her to do so needs a much bigger justification than simply 'it's her natural role'. Uncharacteristically, Nietzsche's thinking seems quite shallow here. Curiously, one of the few women we know him to have had romantic inclinations toward, Lou Andreas-Salomé (1861–1937), was quite indomitable. Aside from Nietzsche (whose proposal of marriage she turned down), she formed intellectual friendships with the composer Wagner and the poet Rilke, was an author, was analysed by Freud and herself became the first woman psychoanalyst. Nietzsche's traditional view of woman seems therefore somewhat at odds with the object of his own admiration – unless it is in fact a reaction against her rejection.

Part Eight: Peoples and Fatherlands

As the title suggests, this chapter is about nationhood, particularly that of Germany. Contrary once again to the common misconceptions (and as those who associate Nietzsche with Nazism might expect), Nietzsche positions himself in opposition to all forms of patriotism, political aggression, racism and anti-Semitism. His vision is of a pan-European culture, which draws on the best of the national qualities of its constituent countries, and presents an ideal of 'the good European', a non-nationalistic and cosmopolitan individual, such as Nietzsche saw himself to be.

Nietzsche here is highly critical of the German character. Once again, one of his central themes is the mixture of classes and cultures that we find in the Germany of his time. What is holding the development of German culture back, he suggests, is a failure to 'digest' these different cultural aspects, and to progress toward a new synthesis. Accordingly, he criticises anti-Semitism as a failure to recognise that simply because a culture is 'mixed' does not mean that the required step is some sort of purification or 'ethnic cleansing' (Hitler obviously skipped this part). The future success of Germany – and of all nations – therefore lies in the degree to which they can assimilate these diverse elements in a new and positive way.

Problems

Once again, it can be seen from this section how little weight the charge of proto-Nazism has against Nietzsche. He goes out of his way to advocate a form of 'interbreeding' with, and assimilation of, Jewish culture, and criticises anti-Semites for their shortsighted intolerance. However, modern readers may still find in his characterisation of various cultures and nationalities a tinge of racism: the Jewish are shrewd and good with money, the Germans are boorish, the English are unimaginative, and so on. Is there, then, a sense in which, as with his views on women, Nietzsche is simply employing stereotypes and crude caricatures?

To begin with, we may observe that generalisations are not in themselves offensive. To say that Muslims do not drink alcohol, or that vegans do not wear leather, are largely accurate and useful characterisations. Also, historically, generalisation can be quite acceptable: we may still talk of the ancient Greeks' toleration of homosexuality, or the Elizabethans fondness for bear baiting, without implying that every Greek was tolerant or every Elizabethan bloodthirsty. However, the problem arises when we start to characterise whole cultures in terms of attitudes or personality traits – and, worse, to provide these differences with a biological basis. To say that the Germans are boorish, or the French arrogant, is bad enough; worse, to imply that it is in their blood.

So, are Nietzsche's characterisations fair or not? We may distinguish here between casting unwarranted slurs and making generalised observations. From our modern perspective, we are understandably sensitive to culture and race, and accordingly eager to be respectful of such differences, but also mindful not to be influenced by prejudice or common associations. In fact, we might argue that the long list of atrocities perpetrated in the name of racism and ethnically-based patriotism has made us wary of any form of cultural generalisation or characterisation. However, some of Nietzsche's generalisations might simply be considered as general cultural observations – regarding philosophy, literature or music.

For instance, his characterisation of the English as dry and unimaginative is based on a reading of their prominent empiricist philosophers – Bacon, Locke, Bentham, Mill. But his purpose is surely just to identify a cultural perspective, an influential trend of thought, which he labels 'English', rather than to stigmatise a whole people for all eternity with the label 'boring'. The test of Nietzsche's alleged prejudice would be to see how he treats *individuals*: does he *prejudge* the qualities of this or that writer or thinker based on national stereotypes? He does interpret thought and outlook in terms of culture and background, it's true; but he is also sensitive to how individuals stand apart from common cultural attitudes – Goethe, for instance, he sees as not typically 'German'.

However, other generalisations seem less allowable, and Nietzsche seems to see cultural development in biological terms – 'interbreeding' – mixing the qualities of this and that race for a perfect European blend. Arguably, it is a sign of progression that we now see social and political problems less in terms of race and culture (for example, 'the Jewish Problem'), but more in terms of ensuring individual rights and that the basic human needs are met, regardless of culture or race. Nietzsche's nationalist and racist characterisations, then, even if defensible, seem a somewhat outdated way of approaching such problems.

Part Nine: What is Noble?

The final chapter concentrates on the notion of nobility or aristocracy, which is seen as the flower of society – in fact, the very reason why society exists. This, perhaps, is the idea that most sticks in the throat of modern readers: shouldn't society exist for the good of everyone? Nietzsche argues that the class system is what originally gave rise to the feeling of superiority of feeling – what he terms 'pathos of distance' – that allowed early humans to develop and improve themselves in relation to that which was 'below' them. Thus, through a sense of social superiority, we develop a sense of self-betterment, of there being a potential ladder of qualities that we can aspire to.

However, the 'slave' morality, which embodies what he terms 'the cult of suffering', nullifies this process by doing away with this ladder of qualities (for a succinct overview of the difference between master and slave moralities, see sections 260–1). Christianity and pessimistic philosophy – such as that of Schopenhauer – view all life as suffering and hardship, but the 'higher' man, like Jesus, suffers in a different way, and is rather ennobled or set apart by it. (There are obvious links here with Nietzsche's comments on self-cruelty and its role in self-development in Part Seven.) Finally, Nietzsche considers once again the qualities of the philosopher in relation to traditionally noble and aristocratic ideals, finding similarity between the two, and suggesting that, perhaps, all culture really aims at the production of the true philosopher as its highest expression.

Problems

Nietzsche's views here are an expression of extreme individualism. It is a commonplace of ethical and political theory to see the individual in terms of his usefulness to society in general – 'the needs of the many, outweigh the needs of the few' as Mr Spock puts it, *Star Trek II: The Wrath of Khan* – though the thought is older, being the central principle of *utilitarianism*. However, in reversing this, Nietzsche is valuing quality over quantity: the sacrifice of the majority for a single goal – not 'the common good' but 'the highest'. Can this be justified? Not in utilitarian terms: no matter how wonderful such an achievement might be – the production of a small minority of highly evolved individuals – the needs of the mass of humanity will always seem to outweigh it.

However, the utilitarian perspective is not the only one. For instance, think of the first moon landing. If we weigh this up in terms of person-hours, resources, other beneficial ways in which the money and time might have been more widely and wisely spent, then we can see that it just doesn't make sense as a purely utilitarian calculation. However, there is a case for saying it had value as an expression of the highest achievements that humanity is capable of – which is not, incidentally, a selfish ideal, done merely to please a small group of people. Similarly, then, Nietzsche saw the purpose of society as to breed select individuals and send them into *philosophical* orbit. Is that the highest expression of 'will to power'?

From High Mountains: *Epode*

The final section is a form of lyric poem (*epode*), which anticipates the coming of these 'new philosophers', calling for them to join him in the metaphorical 'high mountains'. However, those who arrive are merely 'old friends', who no longer understand him, leaving the narrator still awaiting his 'new friends'.

The symbolism here is not hard to decipher. Nietzsche was increasingly isolated, having become estranged from his mother and sister, his only remaining family, and maintaining only a few friends. He also recognises that his philosophical opinions are somewhat unique, and – as yet – there are few who understand his message.

Conclusion

Beyond Good and Evil was a battle cry for a new philosophy. It was controversial, antagonistic and iconoclastic, and can still be guaranteed to ruffle feathers. As such, it is one of the key expressions of Nietzsche's philosophy, and a text that will greatly repay closer study.

What you take from the text partly depends on your familiarity with the targets that Nietzsche attacks. His criticisms of many of philosophy's greats – Kant, Plato, Descartes, Spinoza – and his broadsides against Christianity and religion in general, are often insightful and subtle, but can only be fully appreciated in the light of a knowledge of what exactly is being attacked. So, getting the most out of *BGE* will lead you to a greater awareness of philosophy and religion in general – and, who knows, to disagreement with Nietzsche himself. But even this is a journey worth taking, for the value of the great philosophers lies not so much in agreeing with them, but in the stimulus they provide for you to think for yourself.

Summary

Philosophers to date have assumed that we possess some sort of dispassionate '**will to truth**'. However, in this they are naïve, for most philosophies are the result of personal, hidden prejudices. These **philosophical prejudices** can take many forms – belief in an uncaused cause, a hidden reality behind appearances, **atomism**, and so on – but all serve the interests of the philosopher, who wants to paint the world in his own image, and is unknowingly influenced by non-rational factors rooted in history, environment and biology. The central urge that drives his philosophy is what is termed his '**will to power**', a fundamental force that governs each organism as it seeks to express itself to its fullest potential.

In contrast to the traditional model, Nietzsche proposes a new philosopher, or '**free spirit**', who will critically analyse the prejudices that drive philosophy (and philosophers), and attempt to establish a life-affirming outlook, seeking to identify and express the highest positive 'will to power'. This philosopher will recognise that there is no 'will to truth', but rather that truth is a matter of '**perspective**', driven perhaps more by what is useful or beneficial to the organism (perhaps a '**will to ignorance**') than what is 'true'.

Morality should be studied historically. In the 'pre-moral' stage, 'good' and 'bad' simply reflected whether something was valued or not; later, in the 'moral' stage, the ideas reflected the origins of an action (e.g., rational = good, non-rational = bad). However, in the last 'extra-moral' stage – which Nietzsche proposes we are entering now – values will be assessed in terms of their life-affirming qualities and usefulness to human evolution.

The task of this new philosopher is hampered by a prevalent form of **pessimism**, which is particularly found in Christianity. Such a view is life-negating, and is almost a psychological disease – a **'religious neurosis'** – which even infects (ironically) the scientific attitude, and atheism itself, which attempts to reduce life to 'facts' and sense experience (**positivism**). In contrast, Nietzsche proposes that even if life were to reoccur in every detail forever in an **'eternal return'**, the most positive possible attitude to life is *amor fati*, or 'love of fate', which affirms all of life, no matter what happens.

While morality should be viewed historically and scientifically, there have been few real thinkers who are prepared to do that. What needs to be assessed is the role that moral codes play in the development of the human being. The history of morality so far is best understood as a conflict between **'master'** and **'slave'** moralities, the latter of which has overturned the former (the 'slave revolt in morals'), and recast morality in terms of the powerless and dispossessed (hence the Christian virtues of humility and meekness). However, this will not allow for the development of a strong and noble type of man, but only a 'herd animal'. Since all societies are now a mixture of these moralities, what is needed is a deliberate **'self-overcoming'**, allowing certain individuals to critically generate a new set of values out of the old.

Even philosophy and science is infected by the pessimistic and 'herd' mentality, and 'objectivity' and positivism are signs of this. The new philosopher must employ scientific methods, scepticism, and so on, but with a critical eye, building a new system of values, not 'truth for truth's sake'. Philosophy must reassert its dominance over science, which has taken its place.

The new philosopher must not be afraid to be at odds with popular opinion, and even to employ 'bad' qualities in the service of the hunt for a higher truth. All cultural and personal development has been a form of 'cruelty' or self-discipline, without which nothing could ever be created. Progressive social movements – democracy, sexual equality – will bring about a weakening of vital instincts, and are a backward step in social evolution.

Europe is a mixture of master and slave moralities, dominated by the latter. The mixture of cultures and classes has brought about a loss of social cohesion. However, the way forward is not national and racial intolerance, but selective interbreeding and cultural synthesis.

Society should be fundamentally aristocratic, aiming to produce a small number of highly evolved individuals, who then act as rulers and law givers (and philosophers) to the rest.

Glossary

Ad hominem   A type of illegitimate argument directed irrelevantly against the qualities of the person holding the argument, not the argument itself.

Amor fati   'Love of fate' (*see eternal return*).

Atomism   The philosophical prejudice that there is a fixed centre to things (the physical atom, the self).

Causa Sui   The idea that something can be its own cause.

Eternal return   The idea of living the same life again and again, forever. To embrace this is to embrace *amor fati* ('love of fate') and so have an ultimately positive attitude to life.

Ladder of sacrifice   The stages whereby the religious neurosis gradually 'sacrifices' or gives up what it holds dear (ultimately, God).

Master morality   The original morality that defines 'good' in terms of power, health, strength, et cetera, and 'bad' simply in terms of the lack of these.

Nihilism   Belief in nothing, or the view that life is meaningless.

Pathos of distance   The sense of superior difference that 'noble' or 'higher' persons feel in relation to those below them, which is the origin of self-development.

Perspectivism   The idea that there is no objective and absolute truth, but merely different possible perspectives that are informed by individual 'wills to power'.

Pessimism   The philosophical attitude that life has a negative value, or is primarily suffering and pain (as held by Schopenhauer, for instance).

Philosophical prejudice/dogma   Ideas current in philosophy that appear to have no basis or proof but simply reflect the unconscious prejudices of the philosopher concerned.

Positivism   The general view, often underpinning scientific practice, that things should be understood solely in terms of facts and evidence.

Ressentiment   The hidden motive of resentment, envy and revenge that drives the 'slave' morality.

Religious neurosis   The attitude of self-denial and sacrifice that characterises Christianity and other 'slave' moralities.

Self-overcoming   Nietzsche's doctrine that the true philosopher must 'overcome' himself by critically evaluating his values and attitudes, in order to free himself from inner conflict and prejudice.

Slave/herd morality   The moral code that developed from slaves or conquered peoples that inverts the values of the masters that rule over them (the 'slave revolt in morals').

Social Darwinism   A view (which Nietzsche is often accused of holding), influenced by Darwin's theory of natural selection, that suggests that the weakest in society should be left to die out.

Teleology   The purpose or use that something naturally possesses (identified by Nietzsche as a prejudice).

Übermensch/overman/superman/free spirit/new philosopher   Nietzsche's concept of the new man/philosopher who will go beyond 'good and evil' and establish a new attitude to life and knowledge.

Will to ignorance   The unconscious tendency of human beings to simplify and 'falsify' reality for their own benefit.

Will to power   The fundamental, non-rational drive that all organisms possess to express themselves; a vital force which seeks to express itself to the fullest extent.

Will to truth   The naïve philosophical belief that we seek 'objective' truth for its own sake.

Further reading

Beyond Good and Evil, translated by R. J. Hollingdale, is published by Penguin Classics. Hollingdale also provides a very readable biography and general survey of Nietzsche's thought, *Nietzsche: The Man and His Thought* (Cambridge University Press).

A Beginner's Guide to Nietzsche's Beyond Good and Evil, by Gareth Southwell, provides a detailed summary, commentary and analysis of the text, and is published by Wiley-Blackwell.

What Nietzsche Really Said, by Robert Solomon and Kathleen Higgins, is an excellent and readable overview of Nietzsche's thought and dispels many of the common myths and misconceptions (Schocken Books).

Regarding Nietzsche's other works, *On the Genealogy of Morals* expands in more detail upon many of the central themes of *BGE* (particularly the origin of the 'master' and 'slave' moralities), and is probably a good place to carry on. *Twilight of the Idols* covers Nietzsche's attitude to many of the philosophical greats, and *The Anti-Christ* presents his attitude to Christianity.

6

Jean-Paul Sartre: *Existentialism and Humanism* (1947)

Background

Jean-Paul Sartre (1905–1980) is one of the most famous philosophers of the twentieth century. In addition to being a major writer of philosophy, he was also a novelist, playwright and an important social and political commentator, both in his native France and internationally.

His reputation today, however, is mixed. He has fallen somewhat out of fashion in France, where once he was an idol. In Britain and America, his public fame is not always matched by his reputation among academics. In part this is because of the cultural divide between so-called Anglo-American 'analytic' philosophy and 'Continental' philosophy. How deep the differences between the two traditions run is a matter of dispute. But its effect has been to keep Sartre off the syllabuses of many university philosophy courses.

Sartre is usually described as an existentialist philosopher. What it means to be an existentialist is one of the questions Sartre raises in Existentialism and Humanism. One of the most striking features of existentialism is the wide variety of opinions held by its figureheads. Søren Kierkegaard (1813–55) is usually considered to be the father of existentialism, and he was a devout Christian. Martin Heidegger (1889–1976) was an existentialist who supported the Nazi regime in Germany. Sartre, on the other hand, was a left-wing atheist. This wide disagreement may seem odd, but it is perhaps an inevitable consequence of existentialism's defining feature.

All existentialists stress human freedom to choose. We find ourselves in the world confronted by big questions. Why are we here? Is there a creator? What should my life's objective be? What are my moral values? Throughout history, people have argued that these questions can be settled for good. Through recourse either to religious faith, authority, or the power of reason, these are questions which have answers which, once understood, are there just for us to accept.

What the existentialists stress is that nothing can settle these questions other than human free will. Whatever the evidence, it is always inconclusive and we are left having to decide for ourselves. For example, Kierkegaard tells of the story of Abraham, who was asked by God to sacrifice his only son. God's will could be seen as providing an objective moral law. On this view, Abraham wouldn't need to choose what is right, he would just have to obey God. But Kierkegaard argued Abraham did have to make his own choices. How did Abraham know this was God speaking to him? How did he decide he ought to obey God, even though he was being commanded to do something which by all moral standards was wrong? The evidence couldn't settle these questions one way or another. Abraham had to choose for himself. This placed a lot of power and responsibility on his own free will. Abraham's case is extreme, but Kierkegaard's point is that we too have to rely on our own free will – what we must do is not set out clearly for us.

The problem is particularly acute when it comes to moral values. You can't prove that, for example, murder is wrong, in the same way you can prove $1 + 1 = 2$, or that water is H_2O. Values have to be chosen. This is again a great responsibility for human freedom.

So what unites existentialists is their view that we have to choose and that our choices cannot be seen as inevitable, or determined by the facts. That is why different existentialists could have chosen different values and still all been existentialists.

The text

Existentialism and Humanism must be read carefully for several reasons. First, it is in fact a public speech Sartre gave rather than a detailed philosophical work. It is designed to put over some key points in an accessible way to a wide audience. For that reason, it is perhaps unfair to scrutinise it as if it were a complete argument.

Nevertheless, when reading any philosophical text, one has to examine the arguments as they are set out. *Existentialism and Humanism* is no exception. But we should be careful not to generalise from this one work to making judgements about Sartre's philosophy as a whole. Indeed, Sartre himself was said to have disowned the work later in life, dissatisfied with what it said.

A second reason for caution is that the book is in part an outline of a project Sartre never completed. Critics of existentialism complained that it had no place for moral values, or ethics. Sartre wanted to construct a coherent existentialist ethic and *Existentialism and Humanism* is in part a sketch of how he thought that ethic might look. The sketch was never turned into a finished picture, which again gives us reason not to judge the book as a completed work of philosophy.

The book remains of great interest, however, because it is Sartre's clearest and most accessible writing on his own philosophy. His magnum opus, *Being and Nothingness*, is a huge and difficult work. *Existentialism and Humanism* is, in contrast, short and easy to read, but still direct from the pen of one of philosophy's finest.

The attack on existentialism

Existentialism and Humanism begins with an outline of its purpose. It is clear that one of the main aims of the book is to defend existentialism against its critics. The first criticism he cites is that existentialism leads to quietism, the belief that one should do nothing because nothing one can do can change anything. On this view, existentialism is a philosophy of despair which can provide no hope for life. As Sartre's comments make clear, this criticism was particularly made by the communists. They believed that human action was necessary to end the subjugation of the working classes by the bourgeoisie. Inaction, which they thought followed from existentialism, is therefore reactionary, a means only of sustaining the current, unjust *status quo*.

The second accusation is that existentialism debases humanity. This is because existentialism emphasises the individual. Your choice and your free will are of central importance. You can only see the world from your point of view and you cannot rely on other people to give your life value or meaning. This, it was claimed, led to solipsism – the view that each person is essentially alone, and that the world only exists from their viewpoint. In Descartes's famous phrase, a person is essentially a 'cogito' – an 'I think' – and is thus in essence a private mind, separated from others by her subjectivity.

A third accusation is that existentialism leads to a lack of values, where everything is permitted and no-one can be condemned. After all, if values have to be chosen by each individual, how can they really be moral values at all? Isn't it the point of moral values that they apply to everyone, not that they are things we just choose for ourselves?

Whether or not you judge *Existentialism and Humanism* to be a successful work of philosophy depends to a large part on whether you think it
successfully answers these criticisms.

Humanism

Sartre now moves on to discuss the second word in his lecture's title:
humanism. Traditionally, humanism is the view that 'man is the measure of all things', and that humanity is in control of its own destiny.
Humanists claim that all humans are part of one brotherhood and that
without God's help, we can achieve progress.

It is perhaps because humanism is optimistic and existentialism is perceived as pessimistic that the combination of the two seems surprising.
But it is clear there is a large overlap between them. Both put people at the centre of their own destinies and both can do without God
(although, as we have seen, there are religious existentialists). However,
where Sartre believes they part is that existentialism leaves the individual with responsibility for her own actions and destiny, denying that
she can rely on other people to help her, whereas the humanist believes
in human solidarity almost as a given. What the humanist takes on
faith – progress and the family of man – the existentialist warns cannot
be taken for granted.

Sartre tries to overturn the preconception that existentialism is pessimistic and humanism optimistic. People believe existentialism is pessimistic (and hence anti-humanist) because it denies a universal human
nature and it is our common human nature that provides hope for
shared values and enterprises. But, in fact, how often is human nature
attributed as the cause of all kinds of wrongdoing? Conservative belief is
that human nature is base and self-seeking and that only the constraints
of a civilised society can keep it in check. How, Sartre asks, can existentialism, which denies this inherent evil and claims we have the freedom
to choose our own destinies, be considered pessimistic compared to this?

The unstated conclusion of this part of the book is that existentialism is humanist because it puts humanity at centre stage, master of
itself, even though each human is taken as an autonomous individual,
as compared to the homogeneous 'humanity' of traditional humanism.

Existentialism

Having considered humanism, in a key section Sartre then defines and
explains what existentialism is. As Sartre defines existentialism, the

central point is that, for human beings, '*existence* comes before *essence*, or if you will, that we must begin with the subjective'. Sartre chooses, perhaps misleadingly, to discuss essence in terms of an artefact and its creator. An artefact, such as a paper-knife, is created with specific functions in mind. What is more, the knife itself obviously cannot alter that function. The essence of the knife is thus its purpose and function, what it was made for. This essence came before its existence, as it was created *for* a particular purpose. If God existed, humans too would be like this. God would have created humanity with a specific essence. We would possess a human nature which God himself had put there. This nature would comprise our essence, and so our essence would precede our existence.

But Sartre denies that God exists. If God does not exist, humanity has no creator, and if it has no creator it has no predetermined essence. Rather, humanity first exists, and then as its self-awareness increases, the individual confronts herself, and is able to choose, to will for herself her own nature, purposes and values. In this way, humanity's existence precedes essence. 'There is no human nature, because there is no God to have a conception of it.'

We should be careful not to assume that what Sartre says of his own existentialism is true of all existentialists. If we take Sartre's definition as applying to all existentialism, it comes up against some serious objections. First, one can be an existentialist and believe in God. As we have seen, it was Kierkegaard who really founded existentialism, and he believed in God. So what made him an existentialist? He believed that reason could never provide answers to ultimate questions of meaning and purpose in human life, which meant that we have to choose for ourselves, in an act of faith, what to believe in. Hence, it is the impotence of reason and the importance of subjective choice which are crucial to his being an existentialist. So whereas Sartre starts from God's non-existence and ends up with man's abandonment, Kierkegaard *begins* with man's abandonment, seeing this as part of the human condition whether God exists or not. This shows how the non-existence of God is not vital to the key existentialist belief that we must choose for ourselves.

A second objection is more specifically directed at how Sartre constructs his argument about essence. It seems clear that something can have an essence which it can't choose, even if there is no God. If God does not exist, that means nobody created trees and prawns, for example. Does that mean their existence precedes their essences? That would be absurd. Essence seems to be connected with purpose or a creator only in the case of artefacts. In natural objects, such as animals and plants, essence is just the essential properties of a thing. What makes humanity different is our ability to choose for ourselves. It is for this reason that man's existence precedes his essence, not because there is no God.

Sartre makes much of the idea that there is no human nature. As we have seen, even without God, things can have a nature, so why not humans? Certainly, we have something like freedom of choice, but there may be certain features of humans as a species like any other which are just there, whether we like them or not. Anthropologists would probably support the view that there are some characteristics which all humans share, which could fairly be called human nature. Bear this in mind in later arguments where the non-existence of human nature is assumed.

Subjectivity

The unimportance of God is perhaps supported by Sartre's claims about the importance of subjectivity in existentialism. Our subjectivity is the way in which we perceive the world from a particular point of view. My thoughts, feelings and perceptions are all located 'in' me, which gives me a set of private 'inner' states – the subjective – which is separate from the public, 'outer' world of objects.

It is the fact that humans possess a subjective life which marks them out from other things and places on them responsibility for what they are. A tin can cannot be responsible because it has no view of the world. It just *is*. We, however, can think and feel and this enables us to decide what we want to do and who we want to be. This places responsibility on us for those choices and freedoms.

But our responsibility extends beyond our own being. Sartre argues that when we choose for ourselves, we also choose for all others. The reasons for this are deceptively simple: when we choose how we want to be, we are fashioning an image of mankind as we believe it ought to be. To choose one way is to affirm the value of what is chosen.

The idea is simply that by doing something we are condoning it, and we cannot consistently condone it for ourselves but not for all others as well. For example, if I don't pay my bus fare, I am effectively saying it's okay for anyone in a similar situation not to pay bus fares. My choice for me contains within it an implied recommendation or endorsement of the action for others. Hence, to choose for all humanity is not to impose one's will upon it, but merely to choose how one would want other people to be.

Although what Sartre says seems to make sense, it perhaps contradicts one of his basic tenets, namely that there is no universal human nature.

If all people are alike, then when I choose for myself it follows that, to be consistent, I am choosing what I think would be best for anyone. But if there is no human nature, then all people are not alike and free to choose whatever they want. In that case, I can consistently argue that what I choose for myself is irrelevant for others, as I see that each person makes their own essence. If someone chooses as I do, I should be neither approving nor reproachful, because he is different to me in different circumstances, so it is impossible for me to say whether he chose wisely or not. Hence, it does seem possible to fashion oneself whilst in no way condoning anything for other people.

A further criticism is that even if we accept that by choosing for myself I assert that my action is permissible, it by no means follows that I am actively seeking to fashion how others should be. It is like the difference between enjoying music and claiming that everyone should enjoy music. Thus, even if Sartre is right, our responsibility is perhaps not so great as he would have us believe. So long as we do nothing which we think should never be done, what we choose only adds to the list of permissible actions, not to what should be done. There is a gap between 'may' and 'ought'. Just because I think something *may* be done, it doesn't mean I think it *ought* to be done.

Anguish

What follows from our responsibility for our actions is anguish. Anguish is what a person feels when she is confronted with a choice, fully realising that when she chooses, she chooses for all, like a legislator for humankind. Anguish is thus the sense of 'profound responsibility' felt. Sartre asserts that everyone either feels anguish, disguises it or is in flight from it, but that no-one can escape it altogether.

Sartre echoes Kierkegaard by illustrating anguish with the story of Abraham, who is told by an angel to sacrifice his own son. The problem Abraham faces is that only he can decide whether it really is an angel, whether he really is delivering God's will and so on. Could it not be a malicious demon? Think of all the serial killers propelled by commanding voices. However Abraham decides, he will be asserting his choice for others (particularly his son!). How does he deal with such responsibility? Sartre also gives the example of military leaders, whose decisions will affect the fates of thousands.

This anguish is not a call to quietism, to do nothing. It is rather a condition of action. It is only because we do have choices that we can act at all. Without choices, our actions are merely mechanical. But with choice comes anguish. Of course, if we don't really choose for all humanity, then Sartre's anguish is avoidable in all but the cases where our actions have a direct result on others (see previous section). It is no coincidence that Sartre's examples of Abraham and generals are of this sort, because in such cases the anguish seems so hard to avoid. We would be less convinced by an example of a person deciding whether or not to obey a 'do not walk on the grass' sign.

Sartre's claim that we all feel, flee or deny our anguish is a very dubious one for two main reasons. How do we assess Sartre's claim that everyone falls into one of these three categories? Certainly, Sartre's idea would explain why so many people don't show this anguish, but then, unless he has good reasons for backing up his claim, his thesis is empty.

We can see what is dubious in his claim by considering an exact analogy. What if I were to claim that everyone loves toffee, disguises their love for toffee or is in flight from their love for it? Of course, if anyone denied they loved toffee, my theory would explain that denial. But unless I have good reasons to suppose my theory is true, it is empty. No evidence would either support or refute it. Furthermore, because anguish is an emotional reaction, the only way to show all people felt it would surely be through empirical psychology. It is clear, however, that the only psychology in Sartre is purely speculative. Throughout *Existentialism and Humanism*, there are a number of claims which are of this armchair psychology variety. This means assessing them is very difficult. If, from our armchairs, people's minds appear as they do to Sartre, we are likely to agree with him; if not, then we won't. But this kind of judgement is philosophically unsatisfactory. Since Sartre claims there is no human nature, generalising from our limited experience to that of all people seems particularly unreasonable.

This leads into the second reason why Sartre's account of anguish is dubious: it claims a kind of reaction is universal to everyone when there is no universal human nature. Perhaps we need to read Sartre more carefully. Sartre claims here that human nature cannot be ascribed *a priori*. If something follows *a priori*, it means that you do not need to appeal to experience to demonstrate its truth. In this context, it means that human nature is not a given, handed down from above or something which exists by necessity. Could human nature therefore be ascribed *a posteriori*? In other words, is it possible to ascribe certain universal human characteristics based on experience and observation of human behaviour?

There are two problems for this. The first is that this would severely water down what Sartre seems usually to be saying, namely that there is no human nature, full stop – *a priori* or *a posteriori*. Second, Sartre provides no evidence from experience for his claim that everyone fits into the three categories of feeling, fleeing or denying their anguish. The claim thus seems baseless – he simply offers it up to us to accept or reject, based on our own experience. This is, perhaps, fully within the spirit of existentialism, which denies the power of reason to provide objective answers to the important questions in life, but it also demonstrates how hard it is to assess existentialism's claims.

Abandonment

Sartre sees 'abandonment as no more than drawing out the logical consequences of God's non-existence'. This is where Sartre's existentialism differs from traditional humanism. The humanists claimed that, though God did not exist, or is not worth believing in, there could still be *a priori* moral values which society could follow. Removing God would thus leave our moral framework more or less intact. Sartre, on the contrary, believes that without God there cannot be any *a priori* values. For where would these values come from? There is no human nature to derive them from, as our existence precedes our essence. Nor is there any world other than our own, where objective moral rules are set out in metaphorical tablets of stone. Without moral rules either inscribed in human nature or in the natural fabric of the universe, we are truly abandoned, 'condemned to be free'. The odd conjunction of the ideas of condemnation and freedom is a product of the fact that we are born without any say in the matter (hence condemned), but thereafter free to choose our own destiny.

There is one other way in which we could deny our freedom, namely through determinism. Determinism is the thesis that human free will is an illusion. When we decide, for example, to choose a cup of tea instead of a coffee, we feel that our choice is a free one. That is to say, we feel sure that we could have chosen otherwise. However, the determinist argues that this feeling deceives us. In fact, the choice we made is somehow inevitable. How is this so?

In nature, we are familiar with the idea that nothing happens without a cause. If a tree falls down, we suppose it is because there was a strong wind, or because its roots had decayed, or something else which would explain it. The wind or the decayed roots would itself have a cause and so on. In short, we suppose that every event is the consequence of a complex chain of prior causes.

Are humans any different? We too are part of nature. We are organic beings. What we see and do comprises physical events, such as talking or moving an arm. Some argue that these physical events are caused by events in the brain. These events too must be caused by something else and so on. Such reasoning can lead us to conclude that human actions, just like events in the physical world, are the consequence of prior causes. It may seem to us that a decision to choose tea is a free action, but that choice is as much part of the causal chain of nature as a tree falling over.

If all our actions are determined, it is hard to see how we can truly choose or be responsible. But Sartre rejects determinism, using passion as an example. Many people claim that they could not help what they did, because they were swept away by passion of one sort or another. This is one way of saying that their actions were not freely chosen, but part of some causal chain over which they had no control. Sartre claims this is little more than an excuse. He follows a line of reasoning which echoes Aristotle, who claimed that we are doubly responsible for actions committed when drunk: we are to blame for putting ourselves into a drunken state and for the subsequent action. The same could be said for passion. By the time we have been swept away by passion, we have effectively already made our choice. Our choices put us in a situation where passion would take effect, but as we chose to put ourselves in that position, we cannot avoid responsibility.

Sartre's psychology is compelling here. We all recognise the phenomenon of falling into temptation because we allow ourselves to be tempted. The problem Sartre has here is that he gives no argument against the deeper claims of determinism: he simply flatly denies it is true. Determinists would say that the fact that we feel free when making cool choices and don't feel free when swept away by a passion is beside the point. In neither case are we really free at all. Sartre seems to be simply saying that determinists are making excuses. This doesn't address their deeper philosophical concerns about the nature of causation and human action.

Of course, there is much that could be said about this issue. Consider Hume's compatibilism, for example, which claims that it can be true both that all our actions are the inevitable consequence of past causes and that we are in an important sense still free (see Chapter 3 on the *Enquiry*). There is also the belief that it is psychologically impossible to believe in determinism, and thus that we have to live as though it were not true. But as Sartre doesn't address these issues at all, we have to conduct the debate for ourselves – and it is a long debate.

Returning to abandonment, Sartre's example concerns a young man who goes to him for advice during the war: does he stay and look after his mother, to whom he is everything, or go to fight in the resistance, which has a nobler aim but a less certain outcome? Sartre's helpful advice is, 'you choose!' The point is that choosing is unavoidable. If we seek advice, we have to decide whether to act upon it. If we choose someone to choose for us, we have already chosen, for when we choose an advisor, we already have an idea of what that person will advise. If we choose an ethical system (religious, Kantian, utilitarian, et cetera), we are responsible for that choice. And we also still have choices within that system. For example, if I choose a morality that says I must love my neighbour, do I best love my neighbour by looking after him or fighting for his country?

Sartre perhaps overstates the extent to which choices are always in the balance. Certainly, there are many choices which for the Christian, Kantian or utilitarian are very clear-cut. The point is surely more fundamental. We choose the system we follow, and therefore even if the system sets out clearly what we have to do, we have still made our choice.

A nagging concern about Sartre's account of freedom is whether or not he has really hit upon some deep truth or expressed a mere tautology. A tautology is a statement which appears to be informative, but in fact adds nothing to our understanding. For example, if we know what the word 'bachelor' means, the statement 'all bachelors are unmarried men' is a tautology. It appears to be telling us something about bachelors, but in fact it only says in other words what is already contained in the meaning of 'bachelor'. Is the fact that we have to choose ourselves a tautology? Anything I do, I do *myself*. The addition of the word 'myself' adds nothing to the meaning of 'I do'. This would be true even if God did exist. Abandonment is surely not just an expression of this tautology, but a statement of the extent to which we are alone. But are we as alone as Sartre says? If we count the advice of others, the help we get from ethical systems and so on, it becomes less clear that we are totally abandoned. Once we see the tautology involved in the statement 'man *himself* chooses', it becomes imperative to say what makes abandonment more than just this tautology.

Sartre also talks about the importance of action. It is only by doing something that I can really be said to believe in doing that thing. How do I know if I really want to do something? Only if I do it. If I don't do it, it shows it wasn't that important to me. For example, if I really want to write a novel, I will. If I don't, it shows that I didn't really want to do it at all. Thus, we only know our true feelings when we act. This means our actions reveal, to ourselves and others, our feelings. In this sense, actions come first, and thus we cannot consult our feelings to decide whether to act one way or another.

Sartre seems to be downplaying conflicts of feeling here. If the young man, for example, chooses to join the resistance, that doesn't show he doesn't want to help his mother, merely that he feels helping the resistance is more important. But as Sartre puts it, neither he, nor we, can ever know how much he felt for his mother if he chooses not to look after her. This seems to be a form of extreme behaviourism, the view that statements about our inner lives – our feelings, beliefs and so on – are no more than products of our outer actions. This seems implausible. Though it may be true that the way we act shows the hierarchy of our emotions – that is to say, which ones are stronger – that doesn't mean that the emotions we don't act on are not real and capable of being felt and consulted prior to action. Hence Sartre could be charged with overstating the importance of action over emotion.

Despair

Despite his assertions that existentialism is an optimistic philosophy, Sartre claims that we should act without hope. Contrary to appearances, there is no contradiction here. We should act without hope in the sense that we cannot rely on others, or an inevitable tide of history, to achieve what we desire. 'Hope' here means hope that things will come to pass without our making them so. It is this which cannot be relied upon, for there is no determinism and no human nature, according to Sartre. One must limit oneself to what one can be sure of. But how can one strive for justice and so on if one has no faith in others, as what one can personally achieve is always limited? Sartre responds, 'one need not hope in order to undertake one's work.' Thus the despair of not being able to rely too much on others should not lead one to inaction.

On Sartre's view, one cannot blame circumstances for what one hasn't done. It is pointless to say, 'I could have done better in my exams if I had worked harder', as the fact is that one didn't work harder. Why attribute to someone the ability to do precisely what she hasn't done? To talk of the exams, for example, is to assume the person could have worked harder. But seeing as they didn't, what justifies this claim? Because 'you are nothing else but what you live', it is only by action that we make ourselves what we are. Hence, we have to act, despite the despair of not being able to count on others.

We can now understand what Sartre means by 'the sternness of our optimism.' We can be whatever we choose to be. We are not born heroes or cowards, which is a cause for optimism. But as each person is forced to choose their own destiny, this optimism is stern, as it forces each of us to act with despair, abandonment and anguish.

Once more, Sartre may be overstating the extent of our freedom. In what sense, for example, is the arachnophobe free to touch spiders? It is perhaps true that humans are freer than they believe themselves to be, but until they are made to realise this, they are truly constrained. For example, the psychiatrist can show to the arachnophobe that they are free to touch spiders, but until this is shown to them, they really are not free to do so. We often have to rely on others beyond our control to make us realise the true extent of our freedom, which means that we are not free to fully realise our own capacity for freedom.

The *cogito*

The French philosopher René Descartes is most famous for his declaration *'cogito ergo sum'* – 'I think therefore I am'. Descartes casts a long shadow over all modern philosophy. The *cogito* argument is taken as establishing several things. One is that the essence of a person is to be a thinking thing (see Chapter 2 on the *Meditations*). That is to say, we are by nature creatures which have a private, inner mental life and a unique perspective on the world. There is something it feels like to be me, sitting here, whereas there is nothing it feels like for my pen to sit on the table.

The problem with this view is that it seems to erect a barrier between my private inner life and the outer world. As Sartre says: 'Outside of the Cartesian *cogito*, all objects are no more than probable.' As all you can be sure of, for example, is that you can see this book, you cannot be sure that the book actually exists outside your perceptions. It could be a figment of your imagination or perhaps you are dreaming. Even more worrying is that you cannot be sure other people have minds. When you talk to someone, all you are aware of are the words they say, the facial expressions they make and their bodily movements. How do you know that behind that, inside, they are genuinely thinking and feeling like you?

Sartre takes up some consequences of Descartes's *cogito* argument. Sartre believes it contains an elevating aspect: the *cogito* establishes that humanity uniquely is subject rather than mere object. This establishes us as separate from the material world. Where Sartre differs from Descartes, however, is that he claims: 'when we say "I Think" ... we are just as certain of others as we are of ourselves.' We live in a world of 'intersubjectivity', where one's own subjective existence is dependent in some way on interacting with the subjective existence of others. Far from trapping us inside our own private subjectivity, the *cogito* opens us up to the subjectivity of others. As Sartre does not justify this radical amendment to Descartes, it is up to us to try and make sense of it.

One key idea is that of the 'intentionality' of mental states. This means that mental states are always *about* something, they always contain a reference to something other than themselves. Hence, to perceive a colour is to have the mental state – in this case an awareness – and what that awareness is *of*. There is always such an 'of-ness' to mental states. Thus, it could be argued that the very having of a mental state presupposes something other than the subject of the mental state: there is also what the awareness or perception is of. Perhaps Sartre is suggesting that a perception of another person is a perception of another mind. However, there is no reason why the thing the mental state is about or of may not itself be mental and private to the subject of thought. Hence, awareness of green, for example, may be awareness of a certain sense experience which is mental and private to the individual.

A further explanation may be that Sartre takes the existence of others to be a deep assumption or basic belief, that is to say, though not *a priori* necessary, it is so integral a part of our thinking that it cannot be dispensed with. Compare this to Hume's view of cause and effect, being the idea that though cause and effect cannot be shown rationally to exist, it is so fundamental to our thinking that we cannot do without it (see Chapter 3 on his *Enquiry*). The existence of others could equally well be presupposed in virtually every thought we have.

Perhaps the most persuasive explanation comes from Sartre's writing in other work, where he talks about something he calls 'the look'. Imagine you are alone in a room. Suddenly, you realise that someone is looking at you through a keyhole. Your experience changes. You are suddenly aware of the look of another subject. This is not something you have to think about or justify through reason. You are aware of the other person as another being with a subjective perspective on the world. In this way, the existence of other minds is something that is justified, not through reason, but phenomenologically. That is to say, we experience other people *as* subjects of experience like ourselves. This makes some sense of Sartre saying: 'When we say "I Think" … we are just as certain of others as we are of ourselves.' This certainty comes from the way in which we experience others, not in our reasoning about them. Whether or not this provides genuine certainty or not is, of course, highly debatable.

The human condition

The existence of others leads Sartre to talk about the human condition, as opposed to human nature. The human condition is the set of limitations placed upon humanity. This is very important, because it sounds as though Sartre is contradicting himself. There is no *a priori* human nature and humans are absolutely free, and yet the human condition places limits on humans which are partly *a priori*, in that all humans are born to work and die, and partly historical, in that we may be born slaves or kings, for example. But the contradiction, if it is there at all, is not so obvious. Human nature is determined by the individual, and as this is internal, is wholly within their control. The human condition is external, and thus not wholly within the individual's control. Any philosophy which doesn't acknowledge this would be doomed to absurdity. I cannot, for example, choose to be nine feet tall, as my height is beyond my control.

Sartre talks about what is objective and subjective in the human condition. The human condition is objective because it applies to everyone. This is because we all have to live within limits of what is humanly possible and because we share many limits, we can understand others and the purposes they make for their lives. The human condition is also subjective, because, as individual beings with a subjective viewpoint on the world, we each have to live within these limits in our own ways and determine our own proposes.

His account of the human condition can thus be summarised as follows:

Objective	Subjective
Limits apply to all people	Limits have to be lived within by individual subjective beings
These objective limits enable us to understand others' purposes	Our purposes are determined wholly by ourselves

Is this a case of Sartre trying to have it both ways? Sartre's philosophy hinges upon subjectivism and individual choice, and yet he wants to defend existentialism against the charge of solipsism. The human condition is a way of grasping hold of an objective framework within which we can understand the subjective lives of other individuals. But there is a two-pronged dilemma here. If the human condition is only a matter of external limitations, how can this help us to understand others that well? After all, rats face many of the same external limitations as us, but we cannot relate to their purposes very well. If, on the other hand, the human condition is also about internal similarities (which Sartre says it is not), then hasn't the divide between the human condition and human nature been breached? The point is that this last possibility seems to accord most with our intuitive view. Surely the reason why we can understand the purposes of others from different times and places is not because they face the same external limitations (they often do not), but because we believe ourselves to be like them, which is to believe in a human nature.

Does it matter what you do?

Sartre goes on to consider three more charges against existentialism, all of which are somehow based in its subjectivity. The first is that, as human choice is rooted in the subjective, with no absolute values, what one chooses is unimportant. Sartre's response is that as humans are fully responsible for their own actions, they cannot act solely out of caprice or fancy. All actions have consequences for which the agent is responsible, so there can be no *acte gratuit* or act without cost, as André Gide put it. For this reason, it matters very much how we choose. Add to this the idea that when one chooses one chooses for all humanity, and our choices matter even more.

Sartre compares moral choice to artistic creation. In both one is free to do what one wants, as there are no *a priori* values determining the outcome. However, this analogy rather plays into the hands of Sartre's critics. He says: 'we never speak of a work of art as irresponsible.' But if his analogy is good, then nor should we talk of moral choice as irresponsible, which seems to imply that it doesn't matter how we choose. Though it may matter to *me* if I paint well or badly, or how I choose, that is not very much of a reply to critics who say Sartre's view makes moral choices unimportant.

Can you judge others?

If we are free to choose, then how can we ever judge others for how they choose? How can we condemn the Nazis or rapists, for example? Sartre's reply is that we cannot judge the substance of their decisions, but we can judge the basis on which they were made. Judgements should be made on the plane of free commitment, in good faith. To act in good faith is to act in full awareness of one's freedom to choose and awareness of how one's choice is also a choice for all humanity. If one does not choose on this basis, one is in self-deception, and one's choice will thus be founded on an error. Hence, one can make a logical, if not a value, judgement, on a person whose choices are made in bad faith, in other words, in denial of their freedom and responsibility. If someone chooses to deceive themselves, then that too can be criticised for being an act of self-deception.

But on top of this, there is also a moral judgement that can be made. To act in good faith is to assert the value of freedom not just for oneself, but also for all humanity. Therefore, all those who deny their freedom are denying the value of freedom and should be judged accordingly, as 'cowards' or 'scum'. This seems to be a claim which flies in the face of all Sartre has said. He notes, 'although the content of morality is variable, a certain form of this morality is universal'. This is the distinction between substantive ethics which concerns which actions are right or wrong (non-universal, according to Sartre) and non-substantive ethics (which Sartre says is universal) which concerns the nature of moral judgements, rather than their actual content. The universal form is acting freely, whereas the substantive content of our choices varies. But saying that he can judge others for denying their freedom is to claim that there is at least one substantive moral value that is universal and *a priori*, namely the value of acting freely. This is to make an exception to his own rule that no moral values are *a priori*, which he reasserts only the page before. Therefore, to be consistent, Sartre can only criticise the person of bad faith for their logical error, not their error of values.

All this fails to answer the key objection. The worry is that, for existentialists, all is permitted. Sartre has basically agreed with this, adding that we can criticise the way in which we choose. But unless he can show that choosing genocide, rape, torture and so on are logically incompatible with acting in good faith, the charge against existentialism will stick. And even if he can do this, surely we must insist that the torturer is not just making a logical error, but a moral one too. In this section, Sartre certainly does little to address these worries.

Sartre's examples of Maggie Tulliver in *The Mill on the Floss* and Stendhal's character, La Sanseverina, are supposed to show how two people in identical situations can make different choices and yet both be acting in good faith. He also shows how two people could make the same choices, but in bad faith. This is interesting, as it shows that actions alone do not determine values, which seems to contradict what Sartre says earlier (see the section on abandonment.) In this section, Sartre is basically saying that it is the spirit in which we undertake actions rather than the actions themselves which is important, whereas previously he said that 'the deeds that one does are of central importance, not the feelings that inform them.' It seems Sartre is treating values differently from reasons without a clear justification. Our private *reasons* are felt to be crucial for deciding whether we act in good faith or not, and yet private *emotions* can only be gauged through behaviour. This is not a formal contradiction, since there could be one rule for reasons and another for emotions. But without some justification for this distinction, it seems Sartre is inconsistent in what he counts as important.

A case of give and take

Sartre addresses the criticism that the existentialist takes what they give. In other words, since we choose our own values, they cannot really be values. The whole point about moral values is that they are there, whether you choose to act on them or not. If you say values are chosen, you essentially stop them being values.

Sartre replies: 'I am very sorry that it should be so.' Without God, it cannot be any other way. Values have to be chosen because no God can choose them for us. In a sense, there is a stark choice. Either values are chosen by us or there are no values. Which you believe to be true will depend on whether you accept that values can be chosen and still be genuine values. There is little in this text to help us decide the matter.

Humanism again

Sartre goes on to distinguish between good and bad humanism. Bad humanism sees value in humanity as a species. We can take pride in humanity's achievements as we also are humans. Sartre thinks this absurd for, as each person creates their own nature, I cannot take pride in what others have chosen independently of me. Good humanism is the view that humanity is 'self-surpassing', which simply means that as a person creates her own nature, she is always making more of herself than the being she was born as. A cow is a cow is a cow, but a person can choose for herself and thus transcend the being she once was. This is existential humanism, which puts humanity in control of itself, but as individuals, not as a species. With this point Sartre echoes his opening thoughts.

Conclusion

The book began with three complaints against existentialism, that it implies quietism, solipsism, and ethical relativism. Has Sartre successfully seen these off? As to the first, Sartre seems to have done a good job. Existentialism does not lead to inaction. In fact, it demands action of us, and shows us that even when we think we're just going with the flow, we have actually and actively chosen.

As to the second, Sartre's claim that the *cogito* implies intersubjectivity is not very well supported. But then we could question how important the *cogito* is to existentialism. After all, we are still condemned to be free, no matter where we stand on the debate over the *cogito* and certainty. In this sense, the best response to critics is not to refute the charge of solipsism, but to say that solipsism is a general philosophical problem, not an especial one for existentialism.

As to charges of relativism, Sartre's replies seem very weak. Unless there is at least one universal moral value, then no moral judgement can be universal. Instead, we would just have a battle of wills – what one person thinks is right versus what another thinks is right. Maybe Sartre should have just bitten that particular bullet (as Nietzsche did) and tried to move on from there, instead of desperately trying to find something objective with which to defend himself. Sartre wanted to sketch out his existentialist ethics in this lecture, but the resulting picture does not escape the problem that for existentialists, how one chooses is more important than what one chooses.

Summary

The charges against existentialism are that it leads to **quietism, solipsism** and extreme moral **relativism**. One aim of *Existentialism and Humanism* is to rebut these charges. Existentialism and **humanism** both put humanity at the centre of our world-view, but existentialism does not have humanism's faith in the inevitable progress of humanity.

Existentialism can be summarised in the slogan: 'existence precedes **essence**'. We have no creator and therefore we have no preordained purpose or function. Rather, it is up to us to carve our own destinies. In this way, Sartre's brand of existentialism is based on the non-existence of God.

The emphasis on the individual gives **subjectivity** an important role in existentialist thought. But this does not lead to solipsism because Sartre argues that when we choose for ourselves, we choose for everyone.

When we realise that we are fully responsible for our own choices, we feel **anguish**: This is inevitable, even though some flee from it or disguise it. This anguish is a result of our feeling of **abandonment**, the fact that we are alone in the universe, with no God, no universal values and no determinism; just ourselves, our consciences and our freedom to choose.

This means we must feel a particular kind of **despair**, since we cannot rest our hopes on the actions of others, or even that our own projects will succeed. We must forge our own values and it is in our acts rather than our words that we reveal our true feelings.

There are some ways in which we are linked to others. In some way, being conscious ourselves, we are directly aware of others as conscious beings too. We also share with our fellow humans the **human condition**: the objective limits on what humans can do. This contrasts with **human nature**, which is undetermined and free.

Sartre is thus able to repel some accusations levelled at existentialism. It is not true that it doesn't matter what we do, because with freedom comes complete responsibility. We can judge others because if they act in **bad faith**, they are denying their own freedom and the freedom of humankind. And existentialist values are real values because we can only have values if they are freely chosen.

Glossary

Abandonment The state humans find themselves in when they realise that there is no God, no universal values or any other higher reality or truth to guide them.

Anguish The fear or *angst* that grips us when we realise that we are entirely responsible for our lives and the moral values we choose.

Bad faith When someone denies their own freedom and pretends that their actions are determined or constrained by external forces or higher values.

Despair The feeling one gets when one realises that one cannot rely on others, humanity or any other inevitability that what we value will prevail.

Essence The essential, fixed nature of a thing as determined by its creator. Sartre denies humans have an essence.

The human condition Those features of human existence which we share with others and which provide objective limits to our actions, such as the need to eat.

Human nature Humanity's fixed essence, which Sartre denies we have.

Humanism The optimistic belief in the potential for humanity to progress without God.

Quietism The belief that there is no point in doing anything since nothing we can do can change anything.

Relativism The view that there is no universal standard for truth (epistemological relativism) or morality (moral relativism).

Solipsism   The view that the only certain reality is my own existence and that the existence of everything else is no more than probable.

Subjectivity   The way in which the world appears from the point of view of a particular, conscious being.

Further reading

Existentialism and Humanism, translated by Philip Mairet, is published by Methuen.

A good route into Sartre's other works is *Jean-Paul Sartre: Basic Writings* by Stephen Priest (Routledge). If you want to get serious about your Sartre, you'll have to tackle *Being and Nothingess* (Routledge).

Iris Murdoch's book *Sartre* (Vintage) is still considered to be a classic introduction to his thought, while *Existentialism* by David E. Cooper (Blackwell) puts Sartre in the context of the wider existentialist movement.

Glossary

A glossary for each text is found at the end of each chapter. Here are a few more general philosophical terms that are found throughout the text.

A posteriori   Reasoned from experience.

A priori   Reasoned from first principles, the truth of which are not established by the evidence of experience.

Deduction   A form of reasoning where, if the premises are true, the conclusion must also be true.

Empiricism   The style or school of philosophy which takes as the starting point of knowledge the data of experience.

Epistemology   The branch of philosophy concerned with questions of knowledge and its foundations.

Existentialism   The style or school of philosophy which takes as its starting point the idea of the necessity for humans to choose their own values.

Induction   A form of reasoning that uses the experiences of the past or future as evidence for truths about the past, present or future that cannot be established by more direct means.

Metaphysics   Philosophy concerning the fundamental structure and nature of reality.

Ontology   An account or theory of being.

Premises   The starting points of arguments, from which conclusions are derived.

Rationalism   The style or school of philosophy which believes the most important and fundamental truths can be established by the correct operation of reason, without reference to experience.

Relativism   The general view that there are no universal truths, facts or moral standards.

Scepticism   The view that knowledge or certainty is impossible, or even that truth does not exist.

Sound   An argument which is both valid and the premises of which are true.

Valid   A successful deductive argument where the truth of the conclusion does follow necessarily from the truth of the premises.

Further Reading

Suggestions for further reading are provided at the end of each chapter. Here are a few more general recommendations.

The companion volume to this book is *Philosophy: Key Themes* (Palgrave Macmillan). As you might guess, it adopts a similar approach but looks at the themes of knowledge, moral philosophy, philosophy of mind, philosophy of religion, political philosophy and aesthetics.

The Philosophers' Magazine, which Julian co-founded, is a quarterly aimed at general readers as well as professionals. Its website is www.philosophers net.com

The best single-volume reference book on the subject is the *Oxford Companion to Philosophy*, edited by Ted Honderich (Oxford University Press).

For more ways into classic texts, Nigel Warburton's *Philosophy: Basic Readings* (Routledge) is an excellent anthology.

The Philosopher's Toolkit, by Julian Baggini and Peter S. Fosl (Blackwell) is a comprehensive guide to the techniques of philosophical thinking and argument.

Index

a priori, 69, 77, 82, 84, 93, 184–5,
190–3
a posteriori, 184
abandonment, 181, 185–7, 196
abduction, 7–8
acte gratuit, 192
action, 92–3, 118, 187–8, 194
acts and omissions, 109
ad hominem arguments, 148
afterlife, *see* immortality
amor fati, 156, 174
analytic vs. continental philosophy,
11, 148, 164, 177
anguish, 183–5, 196
animals, 93–4, 102
aporia, 37
appearance and reality, 145
Aquinas, Thomas, 69
argument from design, 96–8
argument to the best explanation, *see*
abduction
arguments, 3–10, 49–50, 52–3, 56–8,
61–4, 69–73, 80, 85–6, 89, 100,
148
aristocracy, 39, 42
Aristotle, 13, 62, 124
atheism, 113, 116, 118
atomism, 145, 173
Ayer, A. J., 165

Bacon, Francis, 171
bad faith, 193, 196
behaviourism, 188
Bentham, Jeremy, 104–5, 122–3, 171
Bergson, Henri, 159
Berkeley, George, 99

Calvinism, 120
Cartesian circle, 70
category mistake, 58
causal reality principle, 62–4, 75

cause and effect, 83–4, 86–93, 97,
100–1, 185–6, 190
certainty and doubt, 51–6, 58–9, 61,
67, 70–2, 74–5, 83, 86, 97, 111,
146
character, 126
children, 27–8, 119, 135
choice, 178–9, 181–3, 186–7, 189,
191–4
Christianity, 112, 116, 120, 138,
153–6, 157–63, 171, 173–4, 187
clear and distinct perception, 55, 58,
60–1, 65–8, 70–2, 75
cogito, 56, 146, 189–90, 195
cognitivism, 41
compatibilism, 92, 102, 186
Comte, Auguste, 110
conclusion (of an argument), 4–9, 49,
61, 85
constant conjunction, 86, 88–91
creationism, 117–18

Darwin, Charles, 117, 159
deceiving demon, *see* evil demon
deduction, 4–5, 8, 32, 49
democracy, 25, 30, 39, 42, 46, 106,
110, 121–2, 131, 162–4
Descartes, René, 6, 8–9, 11, 31–3, 35,
37, **49–76**, 77, 80–1, 98, 143,
145–6, 148, 173, 179, 189–90
  Discourse on Method, 56
  Meditations, 6 , 8–9, 11, 37,
  49–76, 98
despair, 188, 196
determinism, 92, 185–6
dialectic, 33, 36, 37–8, 46
dianoia, 32, 37, 46
dogmatism, 100
doubt, *see* certainty and doubt
doxa, 32, 46
  see also opinion
dreaming argument, 53, 73–4

education, 20–4, 30, 34, 36, 119, 121, 135, 137, 140
eikasia, 32, 46–7
elenchus, 14, 37, 46
  see also Socratic method
Emerson, Ralph Waldo, 153
empiricism, 32, 35, 77–8, 82–3, 112, 145, 171
Epicurus, 96
error, 64–6, 73, 87
essence, 58, 67–8, 71–2, 74, 181, 183, 195
  existence precedes, 181, 195
eternal return, doctrine of, 156, 174
ethical minimalism, 110
eudaimonia, 124
eugenics, 25, 29
evil demon, 53–4, 72, 74
evolution, 117, 149, 159
evolutionary psychology, 161
existentialism, 143, 177–82, 185, 188, 191–6
experience, 6–8, 35, 77, 81–6, 90–1, 93–6, 100, 112

fallibilism, 117, 138
first principles, 37
  see also self-evident truths
flourishing, 124
Foucault, Michel, 131, 154, 164
foundationalism, 54, 56, 74, 79–81, 85
free speech, 111, 113–17
free spirit, 143, 148, 159, 173
free trade, 136
free will, 66, 92, 102, 106, 120, 146, 178–9, 185
freedom, 40, 42, 91–2, 105–11, 113–14, 116, 118–25, 129–39, 177, 180, 182, 185–6, 189, 191–3, 195–6
Freud, Sigmund, 27, 147, 162, 169

gender roles, 29, 161, 168–9
Gibbon, Edward, *History of the Decline and Fall of the Roman Empire*, 157
Gide, André, 192
gnōsis, 32, 46

God, 50, 53, 61–70, 75, 82, 89, 93, 95–100, 129, 145–6, 150, 155–7, 161, 178, 180–2, 185, 194, 196
  essence, 67–8
  existence, 50, 62–4, 67–70, 74
  perfections, 67–9
good and evil, 145, 150, 152–3, 163
good faith, 192
goodness, 30–1, 34, 41, 43, 116, 123, 126, 130, 145, 150, 153–5
Gorgias, 41
Gray, John, 124

happiness, 46, 105, 109, 119, 123–4
hedonism, 36, 105, 160
Heidegger, Martin, 177
herd, 17, 154, 162–4, 166, 174
  see also slave morality
higher and lower pleasures, 123
Hobbes, Thomas, 125, 130
human condition, 191–2, 196
human nature, 79, 180–4, 191–2, 196
humanism, 180, 185, 194–5
Humboldt, Wilhelm von, 119, 122, 134
Hume, David, 6, 11, 49, 56, 69, 77–103, 143, 186, 190
  Enquiry Concerning Human Understanding, 6, 11, 49, 77–103
  My Own Life, 78
  Treatise of Human Nature, 56, 78
Hume's Fork, 83, 88, 100
Huxley, Aldous, *Brave New World*, 25, 29

ideas and impressions, 81–3, 88–91, 101
illusion, 32, 34, 43, 46–7, 53, 55
immortality, 43–4
individual, 179–80
individual and society, 26–7, 39–40, 105–6, 108, 112, 118–27, 131–9
induction, 6–8, 86, 101
inferences, 6–8
intentionality of mental states, 190

justice and injustice, 16–19, 25–7, 35, 37–40, 45, 105, 107, 123
Juvenal, 25

Kant, Immanuel, 27, 35, 68, 108, 145, 148, 150, 155, 164, 173
Kennedy, J. B., 36
Kierkegaard, Søren, 177–8, 181, 183
knowledge, 32–5, 37, 41–3, 46, 51, 54, 59, 65–6, 70, 74, 77, 79–81, 84, 99, 101, 112, 115, 149, 152

laissez-faire, 126, 140
liberalism, 104, 122, 124, 136
liberty, *see* freedom
life-denial, *see* pessimism
Locke, John, 35, 77, 79, 81, 88, 99, 125, 130, 171
logical positivism, 165
Luther, Martin, 113

Marcus Aurelius, 112
Marx, Karl and Engels, Friedrich, *The German Ideology* 20
master morality, 155–6, 163, 166, 174
matters of fact, *see* relations of ideas vs. matters of fact
mental substance, 56–8
method of doubt, 51, 70, 74
Mill, John Stuart, 11, **104–41**, 159, 162, 164, 171
  On Liberty, 11, **104–41**
mind and body, 58, 71, 73, 75, 89
miracles, 94–6, 102
misogyny, 161, 168
Moore, G. E., 35
moral realism, 41
moral values, 154–6, 162, 177–9, 194–6
morality, 150, 152–3, 155, 162, 174
  stages of, 150, 152, 174

necessary connection, 88–93, 101
Nietzsche, Friedrich, 11, 17–18, 27, 122, **142–76**
  The Anti-Christ, 157, 166
  Beyond Good and Evil, 11, **142–76**
  The Gay Science, 156
  On the Genealogy of Morals, 152, 154
nihilism, 156
noēsis, 33, 37, 46

occasionalism, 89
oligarchy, 39, 42, 46
ontological argument, 67–70, 75
open question argument, 35
opinion, 32–4, 43
optimism, 180, 188–9
Orwell, George, *1984*, 29

paternalism, 118, 134, 136, 140
perceptual errors, 55, 98
perspectivism, 144, 147, 151, 154, 166, 173
pessimism, 156, 158, 174, 180
Phaedo, 44
Phaedrus, 26
philosophical dogmas, *see* philosophical prejudices
philosophical prejudices, 144–8, 151, 173
pistis, 32–3, 46
Plato, 11, **13–48**, 69, 115, 135, 144–5, 148, 150, 153, 155, 164, 173
  art, 20–1, 42–3, 47
  charioteer analogy, 26
  Divided Line analogy, 31–3, 37, 42–3, 46
  Guardians, 19–23, 25–9, 36, 39, 45
  Myth of Er, 43–4, 47
  Noble Myth, 23–5, 45
  Republic, 11, **13–48**, 135, 150
  Ring of Gyges myth, 18, 43, 45
  sex, 21
  ship analogy, 30
  Simile of the Cave, 31, 33
  Sun Simile, 31–2, 46
  social classes, 19–20, 23–6, 39, 45
  theory of the Forms, 31, 34–8, 41–2, 46, 69
pleasure, 31, 35–6, 40, 46, 105, 123–4
Popper, Karl, 22, 165
  The Open Society and Its Enemies, 22
positivism, 110, 164–5, 174
pragmatism, 100, 117, 149
premises, 4–9, 49, 61, 73, 85
principle of charity, 10–11
principle of harm, 108–9, 123, 131–3, 138

probability, 88, 101
problem of evil, 64
Pythagoras, 36

quietism, 195
Quine, W. V. O., 80

rationalism, 31, 35, 49–50, 77
Rawls, John, 130
reading philosophy, 2–3, 10
relations of ideas vs. matters of fact, 83–4, 100–1
relativism, 112, 144, 147, 151–2, 195
religion, 154, 156, 164–5, 174
res cogitans, 59
responsibility, 178, 183, 186–7, 1993
ressentiment, 155, 157, 160, 163, 165
Ricardo, David, 136
rights and duties, 108, 110, 122–3, 125–6, 129, 135, 137, 145, 150
Rolph, William, 159
Rousseau, Jean-Jacques, 115, 125
Roux, Wilhelm, 159
Russell, Bertrand, 7–8, 82
   The Problems of Philosophy, 7
Ryle, Gilbert, 58

St Augustine, 163
Sartre, Jean-Paul, 6, 11, 146, **177–99**
   Being and Nothingness, 179
   Existentialism and Humanism, 6, 11, **177–99**
scepticism, 55, 83, 85–7, 90, 98–100, 102, 112, 116–17, 144, 152, 174
Schopenhauer, Arthur, 168, 171
science, 33, 112, 117, 149, 164–6, 174
self-deception, *see* bad faith
self-evident truths, 49, 64, 71
self-overcoming, 163, 168, 174
self- and other-regarding actions, 108, 119, 127–8, 130–2, 138–9
self-regarding virtues and faults, 126
sense perception, 32–3, 51–2, 55, 59–61, 72, 74, 86, 94, 99
slave morality, 152–6, 163, 166, 171, 174
   see also master morality

Smith, Adam, 136
social contract, 125, 130, 139
social Darwinism, 160
Socrates, 14–19, 21–2, 24–31, 33–42, 112
Socratic method, 16–17, 37, 46
solipsism, 179, 191, 195
sophists, 17–18, 30, 46
soul, 26, 35, 43–4, 51, 57
sound and unsound arguments, 4–5, 52, 61
Spinoza, Benedictus, 148, 173
Stephanus pages, 15
subjectivity, 181–2, 190–2, 195
Superman, 142–3
syllogism, 3–5

tabula rasa, 35, 77
tautology, 187
teleological argument, *see* argument from design
teleology, 146
Tertullian, 157
Thaeatetus, 32
theodicy, 64
thumos, 26
timarchy, 39, 46
timocracy, *see* timarchy
truth, 38, 53–5, 111–13, 115–17, 138, 144–5, 147–9, 151–2, 166, 173
tyranny, 40, 46
   of the majority, 107, 138

Übermensch, 143, 163
   see also free spirit
   see also Superman
unconscious, 147, 149, 162
utilitarianism, 35, 104–6, 109, 123–4, 130, 138, 143, 163, 172
   act utilitarianism, 123
   indirect utilitarianism, 124
utility, 125
   principle of, 109, 159

validity, 4–5, 61, 73, 85–6
virtues, 25, 45, 155, 157, 166–7
vitalism vs. mechanism, 159

wax, piece of, 59–60
will, 75, 92
will to ignorance, 149, 151, 173
will to power, 18, 27, 152, 154–5,
    157–61, 163, 165, 172–3

will to truth, 144–5, 148,
    165, 173
Williams, Bernard, 164

Zeno's paradoxes, 99